Microsoft® SQL Server 7 For Dummies®

Cheat Sheet

Microsoft SQL Server 7.0 Datatypes

Datatype	Description	Storage size (in bytes)
binary	Fixed-length binary data	≤ 8,000
bit	Integer data, holding a boolean value of either 0 or 1	1 for 8 bits
char	Fixed-length non-Unicode character data	≤ 8,000
datetime	Date and time data from January 1, 1753, to December 31, 9999, with a 3/100 second accuracy	8
decimal	Fixed precision and scale numeric data for up to 38 digits	5, 9, 13, or 17, depending on precision
float	Floating precision number data for up to 15 digits	4 or 8, depending on precision
image	Variable-length binary data	≤ 2,147,483,647
int	Integer (whole number) data from -2,147,483,648 to +2,147,483,647	4
money	Monetary data values from -922,337,203,685,477.5808 to +922,337,203,685,477.5807, with a 4 decimal place accuracy	8
nchar	Fixed-length Unicode data	≤ 4,000
ntext	Variable-length Unicode data	≤ 1,073,741,823
nvarchar	Variable-length Unicode data	≤ 4,000
real	Floating precision number for up to 7 digits	4
smalldatetime	Date and time data from January 1, 1900, through June 6, 2079, with a 1 minute accuracy	4
smallint	Integer data from -32,768 to +32,767	2
smallmoney	Monetary data values from -214,748.3648 to +214,748.3647, with a 4 decimal place accuracy	4
text	Variable-length non-Unicode data	≤ 2,147,483,647
tinyint	Integer data from 0 to 255	1
varbinary	Variable-length binary data	≤ 8,000
varchar	Variable-length non-Unicode data	≤ 8,000

...For Dummies: Bestselling Book Series for Beginners

BESTSELLING
BOOK SERIES
FROM IDG

Microsoft® SQL Server 7 For Dummies®

Microsoft SQL Server 7.0 Enterprise Manager

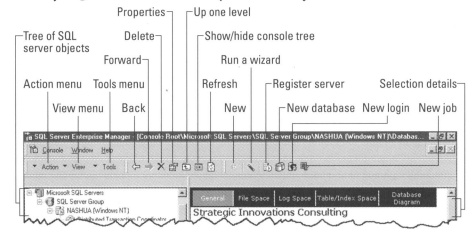

Properties ┐   ┌ Up one level
Tree of SQL
server objects
Delete ┐   Show/hide console tree
Forward   Run a wizard
Action menu   Tools menu   Refresh   Register server   Selection details
View menu   Back   New   New database   New login   New job

Microsoft SQL Server 7.0 Query Analyzer

Clear query
window   ┌ Query options
Save
query/
result   ┌ Execute query
┌ Execute query into grid
Load
SQL
script   ┌ Display SQL execution plan
┌ Perform index analysis   Results pane
New
query   ┌ Cancel executing query   Query pane
┌ Hide results pane   Database

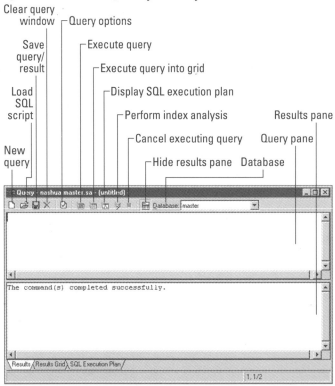

MICROSOFT®
SQL SERVER 7
FOR
DUMMIES®

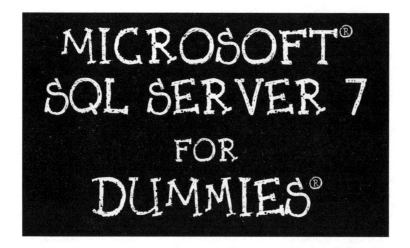

MICROSOFT® SQL SERVER 7 FOR DUMMIES®

by Anthony T. Mann

IDG Books Worldwide, Inc.
An International Data Group Company

Foster City, CA ♦ Chicago, IL ♦ Indianapolis, IN ♦ New York, NY

Microsoft® SQL Server 7 For Dummies®

Published by
IDG Books Worldwide, Inc.
An International Data Group Company
919 E. Hillsdale Blvd.
Suite 400
Foster City, CA 94404
`www.idgbooks.com` (IDG Books Worldwide Web site)
`www.dummies.com` (Dummies Press Web site)

Library of Congress Catalog Card No.: 98-86185

ISBN: 0-7645-0416-9

Printed in the United States of America

10 9 8 7 6 5 4 3 2 1

1O/RS/RQ/ZY/IN

Distributed in the United States by IDG Books Worldwide, Inc.

Distributed by Macmillan Canada for Canada; by Transworld Publishers Limited in the United Kingdom; by IDG Norge Books for Norway; by IDG Sweden Books for Sweden; by Woodslane Pty. Ltd. for Australia; by Woodslane (NZ) Ltd. for New Zealand; by Addison Wesley Longman Singapore Pte Ltd. for Singapore, Malaysia, Thailand, Indonesia and Korea; by Norma Comunicaciones S.A. for Colombia; by Intersoft for South Africa; by International Thomson Publishing for Germany, Austria and Switzerland; by Toppan Company Ltd. for Japan; by Distribuidora Cuspide for Argentina; by Livraria Cultura for Brazil; by Ediciencia S.A. for Ecuador; by Ediciones ZETA S.C.R. Ltda. for Peru; by WS Computer Publishing Corporation, Inc., for the Philippines; by Unalis Corporation for Taiwan; by Contemporanea de Ediciones for Venezuela; by Computer Book & Magazine Store for Puerto Rico; by Express Computer Distributors for the Caribbean and West Indies. Authorized Sales Agent: Anthony Rudkin Associates for the Middle East and North Africa.

For general information on IDG Books Worldwide's books in the U.S., please call our Consumer Customer Service department at 800-762-2974. For reseller information, including discounts and premium sales, please call our Reseller Customer Service department at 800-434-3422.

For information on where to purchase IDG Books Worldwide's books outside the U.S., please contact our International Sales department at 650-655-3200 or fax 650-655-3297.

For information on foreign language translations, please contact our Foreign & Subsidiary Rights department at 650-655-3021 or fax 650-655-3281.

For sales inquiries and special prices for bulk quantities, please contact our Sales department at 650-655-3200 or write to the address above.

For information on using IDG Books Worldwide's books in the classroom or for ordering examination copies, please contact our Educational Sales department at 800-434-2086 or fax 317-596-5499.

For press review copies, author interviews, or other publicity information, please contact our Public Relations department at 650-655-3000 or fax 650-655-3299.

For authorization to photocopy items for corporate, personal, or educational use, please contact Copyright Clearance Center, 222 Rosewood Drive, Danvers, MA 01923, or fax 978-750-4470.

is a trademark under exclusive license to IDG Books Worldwide, Inc., from International Data Group, Inc.

About the Author

Anthony T. Mann has been developing and instructing in the field of Client/Server architecture and technology for many years. He holds the Microsoft Certified Solution Developer (MCSD) credential and is working on achieving the Microsoft Certified Systems Engineer (MCSE) credential.

Anthony is Senior Vice-President/CTO of Strategic Innovations Consulting, Inc. (SIC). SIC is headquartered in Denver, Colorado, with an office in the Boston area and coming soon to a city near you (Houston, Atlanta, New York City, and San Jose). SIC specializes in client/server computing solutions via LAN or Web. SIC offers full outsourcing services, as well as on-site complete solutions including design, development, integration, testing, training, documentation, and more. For more information about SIC, please visit www.strategic-innovations.com.

Anthony is a veteran author of many Visual Basic books, published by SAMS, including *Real-World Programming with Visual Basic, Visual Basic 4 Developer's Guide, Real-World Programming with Visual Basic 4, Visual Basic 5 Developer's Guide,* and *Visual Basic 5 Development Unleashed.* This is his first (hopefully of many) *...For Dummies* book. He can be e-mailed at tmann@vbasic.com. He lives in southeastern New Hampshire with his wife and two shelties.

ABOUT IDG BOOKS WORLDWIDE

Welcome to the world of IDG Books Worldwide.

IDG Books Worldwide, Inc., is a subsidiary of International Data Group, the world's largest publisher of computer-related information and the leading global provider of information services on information technology. IDG was founded more than 25 years ago and now employs more than 8,500 people worldwide. IDG publishes more than 275 computer publications in over 75 countries (see listing below). More than 90 million people read one or more IDG publications each month.

Launched in 1990, IDG Books Worldwide is today the #1 publisher of best-selling computer books in the United States. We are proud to have received eight awards from the Computer Press Association in recognition of editorial excellence and three from *Computer Currents'* First Annual Readers' Choice Awards. Our best-selling ...*For Dummies*® series has more than 50 million copies in print with translations in 38 languages. IDG Books Worldwide, through a joint venture with IDG's Hi-Tech Beijing, became the first U.S. publisher to publish a computer book in the People's Republic of China. In record time, IDG Books Worldwide has become the first choice for millions of readers around the world who want to learn how to better manage their businesses.

Our mission is simple: Every one of our books is designed to bring extra value and skill-building instructions to the reader. Our books are written by experts who understand and care about our readers. The knowledge base of our editorial staff comes from years of experience in publishing, education, and journalism — experience we use to produce books for the '90s. In short, we care about books, so we attract the best people. We devote special attention to details such as audience, interior design, use of icons, and illustrations. And because we use an efficient process of authoring, editing, and desktop publishing our books electronically, we can spend more time ensuring superior content and spend less time on the technicalities of making books.

You can count on our commitment to deliver high-quality books at competitive prices on topics you want to read about. At IDG Books Worldwide, we continue in the IDG tradition of delivering quality for more than 25 years. You'll find no better book on a subject than one from IDG Books Worldwide.

John Kilcullen
CEO
IDG Books Worldwide, Inc.

Steven Berkowitz
President and Publisher
IDG Books Worldwide, Inc.

Eighth Annual Computer Press Awards ≥1992

Ninth Annual Computer Press Awards ≥1993

Tenth Annual Computer Press Awards ≥1994

Eleventh Annual Computer Press Awards ≥1995

IDG Books Worldwide, Inc., is a subsidiary of International Data Group, the world's largest publisher of computer-related information and the leading global provider of information services on information technology. International Data Group publishes over 275 computer publications in over 75 countries. More than 90 million people read one or more International Data Group's publications each month. International Data Group's publications include: **ARGENTINA:** Buyer's Guide, Computerworld Argentina, PC World Argentina; **AUSTRALIA:** Australian Macworld, Australian PC World, Australian Reseller News, Computerworld, IT Casebook, Network World, Publish, Webmaster; **AUSTRIA:** Computerwelt Osterreich, Networks Austria, PC Tip Austria; **BANGLADESH:** PC World Bangladesh; **BELARUS:** PC World Belarus; **BELGIUM:** Data News; **BRAZIL:** Annuario de Informática, Computerworld, Connections, Macworld, PC Player, PC World, Publish, Reseller News, Supergamepower; **BULGARIA:** Computerworld Bulgaria, Network World Bulgaria, PC & MacWorld Bulgaria; **CANADA:** CIO Canada, Client/Server World, ComputerWorld Canada, InfoWorld Canada, NetworkWorld Canada, WebWorld; **CHILE:** Computerworld Chile, PC World Chile; **COLOMBIA:** Computerworld Colombia, PC World Colombia; **COSTA RICA:** PC World Centro America; **THE CZECH AND SLOVAK REPUBLICS:** Computerworld Czechoslovakia, Macworld Czech Republic, PC World Czechoslovakia; **DENMARK:** Communications World Danmark, Computerworld Danmark, Macworld Danmark, PC World Danmark, Techworld Denmark; **DOMINICAN REPUBLIC:** PC World Republica Dominicana; **ECUADOR:** PC World Ecuador; **EGYPT:** Computerworld Middle East, PC World Middle East; **EL SALVADOR:** PC World Centro America; **FINLAND:** MikroPC, Tietoverkko, Tietoviikko; **FRANCE:** Distributique, Hebdo, Info PC, Le Monde Informatique, Macworld, Reseaux & Telecoms, WebMaster France; **GERMANY:** Computer Partner, Computerwoche, Computerwoche Extra, Computerwoche FOCUS, Global Online, Macwelt, PC Welt; **GREECE:** Amiga Computing, GamePro Greece, Multimedia World; **GUATEMALA:** PC World Centro America; **HONDURAS:** PC World Centro America; **HONG KONG:** Computerworld Hong Kong, PC World Hong Kong, Publish in Asia; **HUNGARY:** ABCD CD-ROM, Computerworld Szamitastechnika, Internetto online Magazine, PC World Hungary, PC-X Magazin Hungary; **ICELAND:** Tolvuheimur PC World Island; **INDIA:** Information Communications World, Information Systems Computerworld, PC World India, Publish in Asia; **INDONESIA:** InfoKomputer PC World, Komputek Computerworld, Publish in Asia; **IRELAND:** ComputerScope, PC Live!; **ISRAEL:** Macworld Israel, People & Computers/Computerworld; **ITALY:** Computerworld Italia, Macworld Italia, Networking Italia, PC World Italia; **JAPAN:** DTP World, Macworld Japan, Nikkei Personal Computing, OS/2 World Japan, SunWorld Japan, Windows NT World, Windows World Japan; **KENYA:** PC World East African; **KOREA:** Hi-Tech Information, Macworld Korea, PC World Korea; **MACEDONIA:** PC World Macedonia; **MALAYSIA:** Computerworld Malaysia, PC World Malaysia, Publish in Asia; **MALTA:** PC World Malta; **MEXICO:** Computerworld Mexico, PC World Mexico; **MYANMAR:** PC World Myanmar; **NETHERLANDS:** Computer! Totaal, LAN Internetworking Magazine, LAN World Buyers Guide, Macworld Netherlands, Net, WebWereld; **NEW ZEALAND:** Absolute Beginners Guide and Plain & Simple Series, Computer Buyer, Computer Industry Directory, Computerworld New Zealand, MTB, Network World, PC World New Zealand; **NICARAGUA:** PC World Centro America; **NORWAY:** Computerworld Norge, CW Rapport, Datamagasinet, Financial Rapport, Kursguide Norge, Macworld Norge, Multimediaworld Norge, PC World Ekspress Norge, PC World Nettverk, PC World Norge, PC World ProduktGuide Norge; **PAKISTAN:** Computerworld Pakistan; **PANAMA:** PC World Panama; **PEOPLE'S REPUBLIC OF CHINA:** China Computer Users, China Computerworld, China InfoWorld, China Telecom World Weekly, Computer & Communication, Electronic Design China, Electronics Today, Electronics Weekly, Game Software, PC World China, Popular Computer Week, Software Weekly, Software World, Telecom World; **PERU:** Computerworld Peru, PC World Profesional Peru, PC World SoHo Peru; **PHILIPPINES:** Click!, Computerworld Philippines, PC World Philippines, Publish in Asia; **POLAND:** Computerworld Poland, Computerworld Special Report Poland, Cyber, Macworld Poland, Networld Poland, PC World Komputer; **PORTUGAL:** Cerebro/PC World, Computerworld/Correio Informático, Dealer World Portugal, Mac*In/PC*In Portugal, Multimedia World; **PUERTO RICO:** PC World Puerto Rico; **ROMANIA:** Computerworld Romania, PC World Romania, Telecom Romania; **RUSSIA:** Computerworld Russia, Mir PK, Publish, Seti; **SINGAPORE:** Computerworld Singapore, PC World Singapore, Publish in Asia; **SLOVENIA:** Monitor; **SOUTH AFRICA:** Computing SA, Network World SA, Software World SA; **SPAIN:** Communicaciones World España, Computerworld España, Dealer World España, Macworld España, PC World España; **SRI LANKA:** Infolink PC World; **SWEDEN:** CAP&Design, Computer Sweden, Corporate Computing Sweden, Internetworld Sweden, it.branschen, Macworld Sweden, MaxiData Sweden, MikroDatorn, Natverk & Kommunikation, PC World Sweden, PCaktiv, Windows World Sweden; **SWITZERLAND:** Computerworld Schweiz, Macworld Schweiz, PCtip; **TAIWAN:** Computerworld Taiwan, Macworld Taiwan, NEW ViSiON/Publish, PC World Taiwan, Windows World Taiwan; **THAILAND:** Publish in Asia, Thai Computerworld; **TURKEY:** Computerworld Turkiye, Macworld Turkiye, Network World Turkiye, PC World Turkiye; **UKRAINE:** Computerworld Kiev, Multimedia World Ukraine, PC World Ukraine; **UNITED KINGDOM:** Acorn User UK, Amiga Action UK, Amiga Computing UK, Apple Talk UK, Computing, Macworld, Parents and Computers UK, PC Advisor, PC Home, PSX Pro, The WEB; **UNITED STATES:** Cable in the Classroom, CIO Magazine, Computerworld, DOS World, Federal Computer Week, GamePro Magazine, InfoWorld, I-Way, Macworld, Network World, PC Games, PC World, Publish, Video Event, THE WEB Magazine, and WebMaster; online webzines: JavaWorld, NetscapeWorld, and SunWorld Online; **URUGUAY:** InfoWorld Uruguay; **VENEZUELA:** Computerworld Venezuela, PC World Venezuela; and **VIETNAM:** PC World Vietnam.   5/7/98

Dedication

To the love of my life, companion, and best friend — my wife, Alison. She, once again, has given me the support I need to tackle anything. . . .

Author's Acknowledgments

There are so many people I want to thank and acknowledge for efforts in putting this book together. Putting one of these things together requires so much effort by me (of course), everyone at IDG Books Worldwide, Inc., and all the people who put up with me during the process.

On the home front . . . I wish to thank Alan Ruth (President), and Dr. Daniel Price (Director of Business Development), both with Strategic Innovations Consulting. As the three of us work very closely to run our business, they have put up with my crankiness (this could be stronger, but it is, after all, a family book) and irritability over the past six months.

At IDG, I wish to extend an extra special thanks to Jill Pisoni (Senior Acquisitions Editor), Bill Helling (Project Editor), Rowena Rappaport (Copy Editor), Linda Stark (Copy Editor), Christy Beck (Senior Copy Editor), Phil Worthington (Copy Editor), Michael Watterud (Technical Editor), and the rest . . . (from Gilligan's Island). The very close interaction with all these people is critical to the success of the book.

Publisher's Acknowledgments

We're proud of this book; please register your comments through our IDG Books Worldwide Online Registration Form located at http://my2cents.dummies.com.

Some of the people who helped bring this book to market include the following:

Acquisitions, Editorial, and Media Development

Project Editor: Bill Helling

Acquisitions Editor: Jill Pisoni

Copy Editors: Rowena Rappaport, Linda S. Stark, Christine Meloy Beck, Phil Worthington

Technical Editor: Michael Watterud

Media Development Editor: Marita Ellixson

Associate Technical Editor: Joell Smith

Associate Permissions Editor: Carmen Krikorian

Editorial Manager: Kelly Ewing

Media Development Manager: Heather Heath Dismore

Editorial Assistant: Paul E. Kuzmic

Production

Associate Project Coordinator: Tom Missler

Layout and Graphics: Lou Boudreau, Linda M. Boyer, J. Tyler Connor, Angela F. Hunckler, Brent Savage, Janet Seib

Proofreaders: Christine Berman, Kelli Botta, Betty Kish, Nancy Price, Rebecca Senninger, Janet M. Withers

Indexer: C^2 Editorial Service

General and Administrative

IDG Books Worldwide, Inc.: John Kilcullen, CEO; Steven Berkowitz, President and Publisher

IDG Books Technology Publishing: Brenda McLaughlin, Senior Vice President and Group Publisher

Dummies Technology Press and Dummies Editorial: Diane Graves Steele, Vice President and Associate Publisher; Mary Bednarek, Director of Acquisitions and Product Development; Kristin A. Cocks, Editorial Director

Dummies Trade Press: Kathleen A. Welton, Vice President and Publisher; Kevin Thornton, Acquisitions Manager

IDG Books Production for Dummies Press: Michael R. Britton, Vice President of Production and Creative Services; Cindy L. Phipps, Manager of Project Coordination, Production Proofreading, and Indexing; Kathie S. Schutte, Supervisor of Page Layout; Shelley Lea, Supervisor of Graphics and Design; Debbie J. Gates, Production Systems Specialist; Robert Springer, Supervisor of Proofreading; Debbie Stailey, Special Projects Coordinator; Tony Augsburger, Supervisor of Reprints and Bluelines

Dummies Packaging and Book Design: Robin Seaman, Creative Director; Jocelyn Kelaita, Product Packaging Coordinator; Kavish + Kavish, Cover Design

♦

The publisher would like to give special thanks to Patrick J. McGovern, without whom this book would not have been possible.

♦

Contents at a Glance

Cartoons at a Glance

By Rich Tennant

"We sort of have our own way of preparing our people to become database administrators."

page 277

"For further thoughts on that subject, I'm going to run a query on Leviticus and then perform an inner join on the Job tables. The result reads...".

page 121

"One of the first things you want to do before installing SQL Server is fog the users to keep them calm during the procedure."

page 7

"Okay, young man, it's time to wash your hands, brush your teeth and back up your date."

page 197

"OK, make sure this is right.'Looking for caring companion who likes old movies, nature walks and quiet evenings at home. Knowledge of creating SQL Server objects and manipulating stored procedures, a plus.'"

page 45

"Hey—who died to make you database administrator? I'm doing the best I can!"

page 297

Fax: 978-546-7747 • E-mail: the5wave@tiac.net

Table of Contents

Introduction

....

Welcome to the wonderful world of Microsoft SQL Server 7.0. This latest version of the very popular relational database management system (RDBMS) is extremely exciting. Microsoft has spent much time and effort (not to mention money) in improving the prior version, 6.5.

If you are new to Microsoft SQL Server, you will find that creating and administering databases is extremely easy. If you are an old hand with Microsoft SQL Server or any other RDBMS, you'll find the improvements to be second to none. Microsoft has established itself (once again) as the industry leader.

About This Book

I've spent much time writing this book so that you can benefit from my years of experience. I present the material in an easy-to-read format that will have you up and running in no time.

I've done my best to make sure everything in the book, from text to screen shots, is accurate. However, please know that to get the book into your hot little hands in a timely fashion, I used a beta version of Microsoft SQL Server 7.0. It was a later beta version (beta 3), but nevertheless, a beta version. Therefore, the screens and text may vary slightly from the actual product — but it is unlikely.

I wrote this book to be equally useful to beginners and intermediate users alike. I don't cover many advanced topics, such as complex database design issues and considerations — I just don't have the space in this book. With this book, however, I do show you how to:

- Use many of the built-in wizards
- Find out about data modeling
- Create database objects

> ✔ Discover stored procedures
>
> ✔ Build a data warehouse
>
> ✔ Secure your data

And much more! With this in mind, I hope you enjoy reading the book as much as I enjoyed writing it.

Conventions Used in This Book

I use some terms throughout the book that you should know about:

Select — You highlight an item by clicking it. This usually affects an item in a list box or grid.

Click — This describes an action where you use the left-mouse button to press and release while the mouse is positioned over an area of the screen. For example, if I say, "Click the OK button," I mean that you must press and release the left-mouse button, positioned anywhere over the OK button.

Double-click — You must click the left-mouse button twice in rapid succession. This action either selects an item and closes a dialog box, or expands an item in a hierarchical tree (see Chapter 1 about expanding trees).

Right-click — This means the same as a "click action," except that you use the right mouse button to click instead of the left mouse button.

Who Should Read This Book?

The answer is simple — everyone interested in SQL Server 7.0. You don't need to be a Database Administrator (DBA) or even a programmer to use Microsoft SQL Server 7.0. Microsoft has incorporated many wizards to help you do numerous everyday tasks in a very fast and efficient manner. At one time, you needed to be a database genius to perform even the simplest tasks. With the new wizards, virtually anyone can use SQL Server. If I've piqued your interest, you've picked up the right book.

Organization Is the Key to Life

If you are thumbing through this book in the bookstore, you'll want to know how the book is organized before you take the financial plunge. If you already bought it, you can use this section as a quick reference.

Part I: An Introduction to Microsoft SQL Server 7

Here I give you an overview of Microsoft SQL Server 7. I give you an introduction to the tools available to you, such as Enterprise Manager, Query Analyzer, and others. Because I know many of you aren't new to Microsoft SQL Server, I also show you what's new in the latest and greatest version of Microsoft's flagship database product.

Because Microsoft also has a database product called Access, I compare and contrast Access with SQL Server. This overview helps you to determine which product to buy.

Part II: Database Design

This is what it's all about! The difference between a good database and a poor database is its design. A well-designed database is fast and efficient. If you design your databases well, you'll also get the approval of your peers (something everybody needs).

In this part, I show you what the relational data model is all about and how it works. I tell you all about primary and foreign keys and how to use database objects. In addition, I show you how to create all sorts of database objects such as tables, indexes, rules, defaults, and triggers.

If all of that doesn't get you going, I discuss stored procedures and extended procedures.

Part III: Interface Design

Interface design is the term I use to describe what you do with Microsoft SQL Server after you've created all the objects and designed your database. After all, what's a database if you can't use it?

In this part, I show you how to use Structured Query Language (or SQL). SQL is an inevitable part of using any relational database. If that isn't enough, I show you how to use the Query Analyzer in detail, as well as cursors.

Part IV: Enterprise Issues

Well, well, well. This is a particularly interesting section (if I do say so myself). I show you about security and views. I also include how to back up in case the worst happens (losing your data), as well as restoring backups.

Now the topics you've all been waiting for . . . Microsoft SQL Server 7 and its support for data warehousing and publishing data to the Web.

Part V: The Part of Tens

As with all _...For Dummies_ books, this book contains Part of Tens chapters. This section contains valuable information about the best top-ten resources for use with Microsoft SQL Server. In addition, you can find here ten ways to give SQL Server 7 more pizzazz with add-ons and other programs. Some of the add-on tools listed in this section contain demos on the CD-ROM. I'll bet you can't wait!

Part VI: Appendixes

Here I show you what's on the CD, a glossary of all new terms discussed in the book, and flowcharts of how many of the wizards work.

What About All Those Icons?

To help you identify key pieces of text, I put these icons in the margins throughout the book:

This icon indicates a tip that I give you, based on my experience. Paying attention to this icon can save you lots of time.

You don't want to miss any of these. This icon indicates that you need to look out for something. Generally, a warning icon points out something that is critical to the process.

This icon flags a piece of text that is technical in nature but is not critical to reading the book. You could actually skip over this text if you are short of time. However, if you are a curious sort, you won't want to miss this.

Here's where I introduce a new term to you. Most of the terms associated with a lingo icon are also noted in the Glossary.

I use this icon to point out information that you may want to take note of, but this information is not always critical to perform a task. This information is also not technical in nature. On the icon scale, the Note icon is between Warning and Technical Stuff.

Part I
An Introduction to Microsoft SQL Server 7

"One of the first things you want to do before installing SQL Server is fog the users to keep them calm during the procedure."

In this part . . .

I talk about the features of Microsoft SQL Server 7 and
give you an overview of how to use the tools that
come with this software. Also, I show you how to install
SQL Server 7. If all this isn't enough, I show you how to
compare Microsoft SQL Server with Microsoft Access, in
case you are not sure which product to use.

Chapter 1

A Quick Tour of Microsoft SQL Server 7 Tools

SQL Server 7 is the best release of SQL Server yet. Not only does it extend the tradition of being a very high performance relational database management system (RDBMS) at an extremely reasonable price, but it just keeps getting better. In this chapter, I show you how SQL Server keeps getting better by outlining the new features of SQL Server 7 and tools. These tools include everything from designing the database to running queries to importing data.

What's New in SQL Server 7?

SQL Server 7 introduces many new features, and in my humble opinion, these new features make Microsoft the top RDBMS vendor. I place these new enhancements in three different categories:

✔ Administrative enhancements

✔ Architectural enhancements

✔ Developmental enhancements

Administrative enhancements

Administrative enhancements lower the cost and burden of performing administrative functions, such as configuring and maintaining the system. Table 1-1 lists the administrative enhancements found in SQL Server 7.

Table 1-1	Administrative Enhancements of SQL Server 7
Feature	*Description*
On-demand disk	Automatically grows and shrinks the database size.
On-demand memory	Automatically allocates the required memory.
No maximum settings	SQL Server no longer requires any maximum settings for connections, locks, or open objects. Advanced settings will allow you to set maximum configurations for these settings so that you do not run into hardware resource problems.

Architectural enhancements

An architectural enhancement is one that affects the way SQL Server works fundamentally. Basically, an architectural enhancement is what makes up the Microsoft SQL Server 7 product. These types of enhancements are generally the most important because they affect performance. Table 1-2 lists the architectural enhancements found in SQL Server 7.

Table 1-2	Architectural Enhancements of SQL Server 7
Feature	*Description*
Auto-update of statistics	Automatically updates statistics by sampling rows and tables, as well as non-indexed columns.
Auto-recompilation of plans	A query execution plan is automatically recalculated for best performance.
Dynamic locking	Automatically determines the type of locking used, based on overhead cost of a query.
General speed increases	Microsoft has greatly sped up many areas of processing, such as redesigning the query processor, a new index design, and the way text and image data is stored.
Complex query support	Support for complex queries includes query parallelism, hash and merge joins, and multi-index operations.

Feature	Description
Recursive triggers	Recursive triggers have been added so that a trigger can call itself.
Local cursors	Local cursors aid in better performance.
Relaxed limits	Limits have been relaxed so that the number of tables per query and the number of columns per table have been increased.
Distributed query	Support for SQL Server to SQL Server data sources and SQL Server to OLEDB data sources has been added. This allows for true heterogeneous queries.
Pages	Pages have been expanded from 2K in size to 8K.
Extents	Extents have been expanded to 64K in size.
Mixed extents	Extents can now support multiple tables to save on space.
Native operating system	Native operating system files are now supported.
Filegroups	Groups of files can be placed into a filegroup for ease of maintenance and backups.
Very Large Database (VLDB) support	SQL Server 7 now has improved support for VLDBs.
Security	SQL Server 7 supports Windows NT groups and the new SQL Server 7 roles. This makes SQL Server 7 completely integrated with Windows NT.
Unicode support	SQL Server 7 fully supports Unicode.
Windows 95	SQL Server 7 now runs on Windows 95 and higher. However, some of the enterprise functionality is not supported in Windows 95.
64-bit memory	SQL Server 7 supports 64-bit memory, which is used in Windows NT 5.0.
Improved replication	SQL Server 7 now includes support for multisite replication and enhanced monitoring.

Developmental enhancements

Developmental enhancements are generally the most interesting type of enhancement — and they make accessing and querying SQL Server 7 easier. (Any time your job becomes easier, it's interesting!) Table 1-3 lists the developmental enhancements found in SQL Server 7.

Table 1-3	Developmental Enhancements of SQL Server 7
Feature	*Description*
New transact-SQL statements	Some new transact-SQL statements include ALTER PROCEDURE, ALTER TRIGGER, ALTER VIEW, and ALTER TABLE. Prior to these new statements, you had to drop and create procedures, triggers, views, and tables. Now you can just alter them.
Interfaces	SQL Server 7 supports ADO, ODBC, OLE DB, and SQL-DMO.
New tools	New tools in SQL Server 7 include Microsoft Management Console (Enterprise Manager), SQL Server Agent, SQL Server Query Analyzer, SQL Server Profiler, Data Transformation Services, Index Tuning Wizard, Microsoft English Query, and Microsoft OLAP Services.
Data types	Char, varchar, binary, and varbinary datatypes can now store up to 8,000 bytes of information, up from 255.

SQL Server Service Manager

SQL Server 7 runs in the background either on Windows NT, Windows 95, or Windows 98. Because SQL Server 7 runs in the background it's called a service, and you need some type of program to administer the starting and stopping of the service. If you're familiar with Windows NT, you know that it handles services differently than Windows 95 or Windows 98, but the tools used to control the service is the same.

For more information about Windows NT services, refer to *Windows NT 4 For Dummies* by Andy Rathbone and Susan Crawford (from IDG Books Worldwide, Inc.).

In either Windows NT, Windows 95, or Windows 98, there are three SQL Server services. The services are:

✔ **MSSQLServer:** Starts and stops SQL Server 7

✔ **SQLServerAgent:** Starts and stops the agent that controls scheduling features of SQL Server 7

✔ **MSDTC:** Starts and stops the Microsoft Distributed Transaction Coordinator

The program that starts and stops either SQL Server 7 or the SQL Server Agent is called the SQL Server Service Manager. Before you can continue with any example in this book, SQL Server must be running. To start the SQL Server Service, follow these steps:

1. **Choose Start⇨Programs⇨Microsoft SQL Server 7.0⇨Service Manager to start the SQL Server Service Manager (see Figure 1-1).**

Figure 1-1:
The SQL
Server
Service
Manager.

2. **Choose the MSSQLServer service in the Services drop-down list box.**

3. **Double-click the Start/Continue button.**

   After you double-click the Start/Continue button, the service shown in the Services drop-down list starts, which could take up to a couple of minutes, depending on the speed of your computer and the amount of memory you have.

   If you want to use the scheduling services for SQL Server 7, you need to ensure that the SQLServerAgent service is running. Start the SQLServerAgent service by choosing the service in the Services drop-down list and click the Start/Continue button.

SQL Server Enterprise Manager

The SQL Server Enterprise Manager is an application that comes with SQL Server 7 that enables you to control all aspects of your schema. To start the SQL Server Enterprise Manager, choose Start⇨Programs⇨Microsoft SQL Server 7.0⇨Enterprise Manager (see Figure 1-2).

The SQL Server Enterprise Manager enables you to control and manipulate databases, tables, indexes, users, and much more. As a matter of fact, you may quickly find that the SQL Server Enterprise Manager is the tool you use most often.

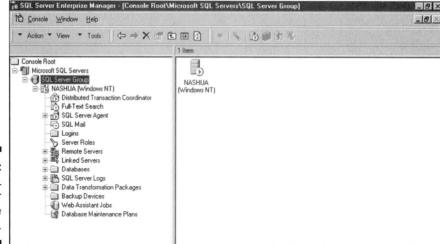

Figure 1-2:
The SQL
Server
Enterprise
Manager.

Many chapters in this book show specifically how to use the different aspects of the SQL Server Enterprise Manager, so I'll leave you with this brief introduction (this way you're forced to read the rest of my book).

Tracing Problems with SQL Server Profiler

The SQL Server Profiler is an excellent tool to use to help you trace problems with SQL Server, such as login problems. Profiler is also a great tool to help you monitor the activity that's taking place on the server in real-time. SQL Server Profiler works by running in the background while users connect to SQL Server and go about their everyday lives. SQL Server Profiler listens for specific events, such as logins and database transactions, that you specify. An *event* is an action that occurs within SQL Server 7. SQL Server 7 responds to these events by trapping them. When it traps the event, SQL Server 7 reacts in a way that you define. When SQL Server Profiler responds to these events, it displays them to the Profiler screen, and optionally writes the results to a file and/or a table. To start the SQL Server Enterprise Manager, choose Start⇨Programs⇨Microsoft SQL Server 7.0⇨Profiler (see Figure 1-3).

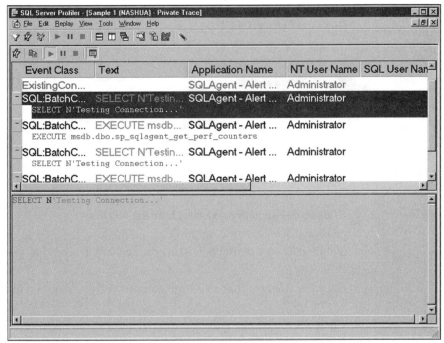

Figure 1-3:
The SQL
Server
Profiler.

The SQL Server Profiler enables you to store different configurations relating to what you want to trace. For example, one such configuration may be to trace the logins into SQL Server. Another configuration may be to trace all the locks on a given table. These different configuration choices are known as *traces.* You can store and reuse multiple traces within the SQL Server Profiler.

SQL Server Profiler is also the tool that will allow you to capture events on a production server and replay them on a development server so you can look for problems. A captured trace is also the prerequisite for the Index Tuning Wizard.

Opening and running an existing trace

You can store trace configurations so that you can recall them later. To open an existing trace, follow these steps:

1. **Choose Start⇨Programs⇨Microsoft SQL Server 7.0⇨Profiler to start the SQL Server Profiler (refer to Figure 1-3 in the previous section).**

2. **Choose File⇨Run Traces to bring up the Start Selected Traces dialog box (see Figure 1-4).**

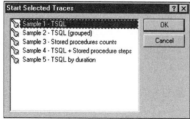

3. **Choose one or more existing trace(s) to run.**

   SQL Server 7 comes preinstalled with some sample traces. The Start Selected Traces dialog box also contains any traces that you saved previously.

   Click the trace(s) that you want to open. You can open multiple traces at one time.

4. **Click OK to run the trace(s).**

   Clicking the OK button runs the trace(s). Running the trace means that SQL Server 7 is listening for the events that have been defined in the trace.

Creating a new trace

You can define your own traces. The traces that you define contain the events you want SQL Server 7 to listen for and respond to. To create a new trace, follow these steps:

1. **Choose Start⇨Programs⇨Microsoft SQL Server 7.0⇨Profiler to start the SQL Server Profiler (refer to Figure 1-3).**

2. **Create a New Blank Trace by clicking the File⇨New⇨Trace menu option.**

   In addition, you can click the New Trace toolbar icon. Or you can press the shortcut keys, CTRL+N.

   Each method brings up the Trace Properties dialog box, consisting of four tabs (General, Events, Data Columns, Filters), which allows you to configure the new trace (see Figure 1-5). The General tab is shown by default.

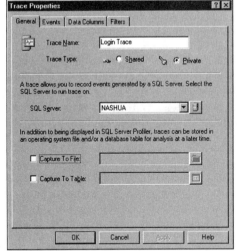

Figure 1-5:
The Trace
Properties
dialog box
showing the
General tab.

3. Fill in the desired data for the four tabs.

Create a new trace by filling in four tabs of data. The following four
sections outline how to do this. Click OK when you are finished entering data to save the new trace.

Defining general information

Supply data that describes the trace as a whole in the General tab. General
data includes information like the name and trace properties.

Click the General tab to make sure that it's selected. Then supply data for
the following fields in the General tab:

- **Trace Name:** Give the trace a name, such as **Login Trace**. Use a name
  that describes the purpose of the trace.

- **Trace Type:** Choose the option button indicating whether this trace is
  Shared or **Private**. A Shared trace can be used by all Windows NT
  users. A Private trace can be accessed only by the user who created it.
  Private is the default.

- **SQL Server:** Choose the SQL Server from the drop-down list that the
  trace you are defining belongs to. By default, the current server is
  shown.

✔ **Capture To File:** Check this box if you wish to store the results of the trace to a file for later analysis, in addition to displaying the results in the profiler itself. Checking this box enables a button allowing you to select a file.

✔ **Capture To Table:** Check this box if you wish to store the results of the trace to a table, also in addition to displaying the results in the profiler itself. Checking this box enables a button, allowing you to select a table name within the database chosen in the SQL Server drop-down list.

Entering events

Choose the events you want to trap with the trace. Events are stored in nine different categories:

✔ Error and Warning

✔ Locks

✔ Misc.

✔ Objects

✔ Scans

✔ SQL Operators

✔ Stored Procedures

✔ Transactions

✔ TSQL

To choose events, make sure that the Events tab is selected by clicking it (see Figure 1-6). Then select data for the following fields in the Events tab:

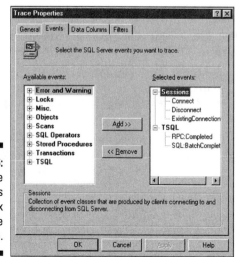

Figure 1-6:
The Trace
Properties
dialog box
showing the
Events tab.

✔ **Available events:** The events listed in this list box are divided into categories. You can click the plus sign to expand a category to see the specific events under a category. You can select an entire category by selecting (highlighting) the name of the category and then clicking the Add button. You can also select an individual event by expanding the category, selecting the individual event, and then clicking the Add button.

✔ **Selected events:** The events listed in this list box have been selected for use with your trace. To remove an event, highlight it and click the Remove button. You can remove an entire category by selecting (highlighting) the name of the category and then clicking the Remove button. You can also remove an individual event by expanding the category in the Selected events list box, and then clicking the Remove button.

Entering capture data

After the event is trapped, you decide which data the trace needs to provide back to you. This data, called *capture data,* is specified on this tab. Click the Data Columns tab to make sure that it's selected (see Figure 1-7).

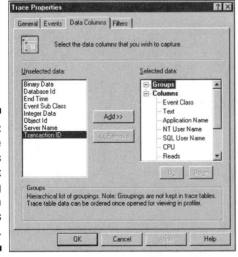

Figure 1-7: The Trace Properties dialog box showing the Data Columns tab.

Then supply data for the following fields in the Data Columns tab:

✔ **Unselected data:** The data listed in this list box is a list of all possible data that can be captured by the event. To select the item, highlight it and click the Add button.

✔ **Selected data:** The data listed in this list box has been selected from the Unselected data list box, and is a list of all data items the event captures. To remove the item, highlight it and click the Remove button.

Entering filter data

Filter data is how you instruct the trace to determine the criteria for the events to capture. The trace will return data specified in the Data Columns tab only when all the criteria specified on this screen is matched. For example, if you wish for the trace to return specific columns of data only when the Windows NT User Name is tmann (that's my username), you can indicate this.

This filter data is specified on (as you would expect) the Filters tab. This tab can look quite confusing when you first see it. However, it's not as bad as it looks. (Click the Filters tab to make sure that it's selected, as shown in Figure 1-8.) Then select and enter data for the Trace event criteria list. Select from the hierarchical list of available events to monitor. These events, when the criteria is matched, generate the trace. The Trace event criteria box presents a tree that you can use to drill-down to see the events available. In addition, you can see whether an event has a value to be included and/or excluded from the criteria.

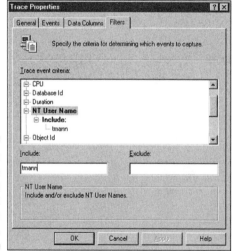

Figure 1-8:
The Trace
Properties
dialog box
showing the
Filters tab.

In addition, you can opt to include or exclude specific values for event criteria, as well as minimum or maximum values for other criteria. The only way to know what you can specify for a specific event is to click the event.

When you click the event, you see the screen visually change to allow you to specify the values for the event. For example, the NT User Name event allows you to specify whether to include or exclude names (as shown in Figure 1-8). The Object ID event does not allow for include or exclude fields, but only a value that you specify.

SQL Server Query Analyzer

The SQL Server Query Analyzer is a tool that comes with SQL Server 7 that allows you to issue any SQL Statement to SQL Server. In addition, the results can be displayed in a tabular format or a grid format. To start the SQL Server Query Analyzer, choose Start⇨Programs⇨Microsoft SQL Server 7.0⇨Query Analyzer (see Figure 1-9).

SQL Server Analyzer enables you to view an execution plan for a query, which is beneficial because you may be able to improve performance by constructing queries in a different way. See Chapter 9 for more of a discussion on the SQL Server Query Analyzer.

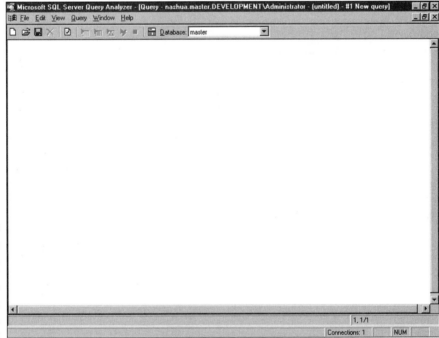

Figure 1-9:
The SQL
Server
Query
Analyzer in
all its glory.

Microsoft English Query

Microsoft English Query is a tool that comes with SQL Server 7 that allows you to issue queries by using English statements — instead of supplying SQL statements to SQL Server. To start Microsoft English Query, choose Start➪Programs➪Microsoft English Query (see Figure 1-10).

Figure 1-10:
The Microsoft English Query, ready for English statements.

By specifying in English what you want SQL Server to do, Microsoft English Query translates your English sentences into SQL and issues your requests to the server. This method is a great alternative to having to learn SQL. However, if you do want to take a look at SQL, I give you a great overview of the SQL language in Chapter 8.

I hate to burst your bubble, but please note that I don't discuss Microsoft English Query in detail in this book. You have to know a lot to set it up, and it would be way too large of a topic to cover in this book. It really needs its own book. (Now that's an idea. . . .)

SQL Server Performance Monitor

The SQL Server Performance Monitor is a tool that allows you to monitor the performance of SQL Server, as the name suggests. This tool is available only if you are running SQL Server 7 on Windows NT 4.0 or higher. Performance Monitor isn't available for Windows 95 because the SQL Server Performance Monitor extends the ability of the performance monitor already built into Windows NT.

To start the SQL Server Performance Monitor, choose Start➪Programs➪ Microsoft SQL Server 7.0➪Performance Monitor (see Figure 1-11).

When you install Microsoft SQL Server 7 onto a Windows NT Server 4.0 computer, the setup automatically integrates the Performance Monitor (PERFMON.EXE) to SQL Server. The Performance Monitor is a tool that comes with Windows NT to allow you to view and monitor the performance of a specific process or application running on Windows NT.

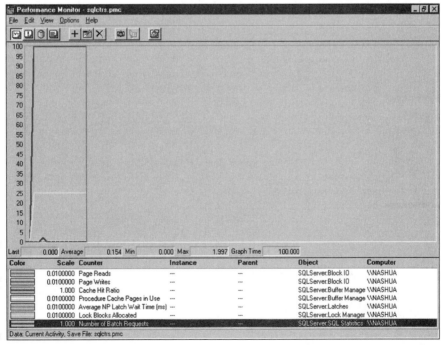

Figure 1-11: The SQL Server Performance Monitor.

Twenty-four Magical Wizards

Along with the great tools I show you in this chapter, some extremely helpful wizards come with SQL Server 7 as well. All the wizards are launched by first running the SQL Server Enterprise Manager. To start the SQL Server Enterprise Manager, choose Start⇨Programs⇨Microsoft SQL Server 7.0⇨ Enterprise Manager. After the Enterprise Manager is running, choose the Tools⇨Wizards option from the Enterprise Manager toolbar. This command brings up the Select Wizard dialog box containing all possible wizards in SQL Server 7 (see Figure 1-12).

I don't want to disappoint you too much, but in this book, I don't cover each and every wizard. I cover a bunch of them, but I don't want this book to be 1,000 pages (and I'm sure you don't want to pay for 1,000 pages).

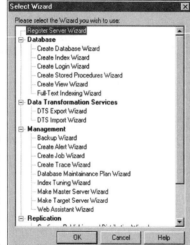

Figure 1-12:
Select a
wizard in
the Select
Wizard
dialog box.

The following wonderful wizards are available in Microsoft SQL Server 7:

Backup Wizard
Configure Publishing and Distribution Wizard
Create Alert Wizard
Create Database Wizard
Create Index Wizard
Create Job Wizard
Create Login Wizard
Create Publication Wizard
Create Stored Procedures Wizard
Create Trace Wizard
Create View Wizard
Database Maintenance Plan Wizard

DTS Export Wizard
DTS Import Wizard
Full-Text Indexing Wizard
Index Tuning Wizard
Make Master Server Wizard
Make Target Server Wizard
Publication Filtering Wizard
Pull Subscription Wizard
Push Subscription Wizard
Register Server Wizard
Uninstall Publishing and Distribution Wizard
Web Assistant Wizard

Help Me, Help Me!

What if you need additional help beyond what I show you in the book? Well,
fortunately, Microsoft thought of that. A very easy-to-use help system is
available, called Books Online. If you are new to Books Online, you'll find
that you can't live without it.

To start Books Online, choose Start⇨Programs⇨Microsoft SQL Server 7.0⇨
Books Online (see Figure 1-13).

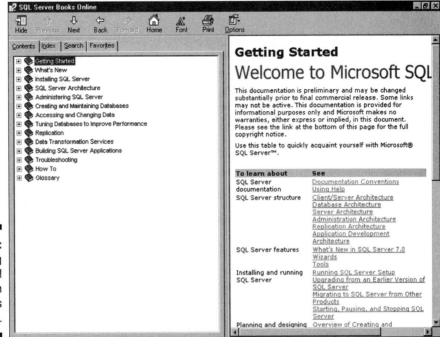

Figure 1-13:
Getting
additional
help with
Books
Online.

Expanding the tree

In almost every chapter throughout this book, I mention, "expand the tree." How do you do this? To expand the tree, click the highest level plus sign (+). The plus sign is located just to the left of the text describing the level in the tree. This plus sign indicates that there are items listed within its hierarchy. *Hierarchy* is a way of categorizing and grouping related items under a specific topic. Those topics may have subtopics that, in turn, have other subtopics. This very much follows an outline format.

Clicking the plus sign expands the tree to show the current level and all of the immediate *child* items. These child items may show other child items, and if they do, the child item will have a plus sign shown to the left of the text describing the level in the tree. If an item doesn't have a plus sign, the currently selected item has no child entries. This is sometimes referred to as a leaf entry, or simply, a leaf. A *leaf* entry is one that cannot be expanded any further.

To use Books Online, you can navigate the left side of the screen by expanding the tree to get to the topic you want. Also, you can search on any keyword by clicking either the Index or Search tabs and typing in the word(s) to search on, and then pressing Enter.

Chapter 2

Installing Microsoft SQL Server 7

• •

In This Chapter

▶ Satisfying the minimum installation requirements

▶ Figuring out other stuff you must have

▶ Setting up server and client software

▶ Installing Microsoft English Query

▶ Getting OLAP services to leap onto your hard drive

• •

*I*nstalling Microsoft SQL Server 7.0 is a piece of cake. You must choose a
few options along the way, but it is simple, and I'm going to show you
how to do it.

Microsoft SQL Server 7.0: The Minimum Requirements

As Microsoft adds more features to SQL Server, adding more disk space and
memory is also necessary. To install and run Microsoft SQL Server 7, you
need to satisfy this list of the minimum requirements:

✔ Computer hardware

- Intel 486/33 MHz or higher

- DEC Alpha AXP

✔ Peripherals

- CD-ROM drive

- Networking card on client and server

✔ Operating system

- Microsoft Windows NT 4.0 or higher, with Service Pack 3 installed

- Microsoft Windows 95 or higher (like Windows 98)

✔ Memory

- An absolute minimum of 32MB. I recommend at least 128MB

✔ Disk space for new installation

- 50MB for client utilities only

- 90MB for a compact installation

- 148MB for a typical installation

- Additional disk space is required for your data (I recommend dedicating at least a 1GB drive for installation of SQL Server.)

✔ Disk space for an upgrade installation

- 148MB plus 1.5 times the amount of disk space required for your SQL Server 6.*x* databases

✔ Networking

- Any Windows NT or Windows 95 or higher networking protocol, depending on the protocol used by your organization

Do I Need Anything Else?

Actually, you do need more than just the minimum requirements indicated in the preceding section. Before SQL Server 7.0 can be installed, you must have Internet Explorer 4.01 installed. Also, if you are using Windows NT 4.0 Workstation or Server edition, you must have service pack 3 installed, as well as the mini service pack. If you are using Windows NT 4.0 Enterprise edition, in addition to the requirements for Windows NT 4.0 Workstation or server, you must have the clustering hot fix installed.

Okay, this all sounds like a lot, but don't shoot the messenger. I'm just telling you what Microsoft requires. Fortunately, SQL Server 7.0 will not run Setup if you don't have all of the prerequisites. This makes it so that you don't have to check your machine first for all those pesky service packs.

If your CD-ROM is configured to automatically run when a disc is inserted, the Setup program runs automatically. This program shows a series of dialog boxes to install these components for you. All these options are listed under **Install SQL Server 7.0 Prerequisites,** which appears immediately as an option. Simply click this option, and you're on your way to installing all the prerequisites.

If your CD-ROM is not configured to run automatically, you must run the desired programs from the command line. To run a program from the command line, choose the Start⇨Run menu option. Then type **d:**, followed by the program you wish to run. If **d** is not the letter corresponding to your CD-ROM drive, substitute your drive letter for **d**. Use Table 2-1 to know what program you need to run from the CD-ROM to install the prerequisites you need.

Table 2-1	Location of Prerequisite Files on CD-ROM
Prerequisite	*CD-ROM File*
Internet Explorer, version 4.01	x86\other\ie4\ie4setup
Windows NT 4.0 service pack 3	Not on SQL Server 7.0 CD-ROM
Windows NT 4.0 mini service pack	x86\other\minisp\hotfix
Windows NT 4.0 clustering hot fix	x86\other\nt4clstr\clusfixi

Installing the Goods on the Server

Microsoft has made installing SQL Server 7.0 easy. Installation is performed by answering questions in a series of steps. Most of the time, you simply accept all the defaults presented in these steps and the installation program does the rest. This section guides you through installing Microsoft SQL Server 7.0 on your server. After you install SQL Server 7, you need to install the client-side software to access the server from any client computer.

The installation process can take up to 15 minutes, depending on the speed of your computer.

Some of the SQL Server 7.0 features are not available when running SQL Server 7.0 on Windows 95 or Windows 98. Enterprise-wide features are not available because, under Windows 95 or Windows 98, SQL Server 7.0 is considered to be for a single user. Therefore, it's recommended that you run SQL Server 7.0 on Windows NT 4.0 or higher. The examples I use in this chapter are for installing Microsoft SQL Server 7.0 with Windows NT 4.0.

To install Microsoft SQL Server 7.0, follow these steps:

1. **Start the Setup program.**

   Place the SQL Server 7.0 CD-ROM into the CD-ROM drive. If your CD-ROM is configured to run automatically when a disc is inserted, the Setup program runs automatically, showing a series of dialog boxes to allow you to set up different components. If the Setup program runs automatically, click the following series of buttons:

   • Install SQL Server 7.0 Components

   • Database Server

   • Desktop, Standard, or Enterprise, as you desire

If your CD-ROM is not configured to run automatically when a disc is inserted, choose the Start⇨Run menu option. Then type **d:\setup**. If **d** is not the letter corresponding to your CD-ROM drive, then substitute your drive letter for **d**. For more information about auto-insert notification, refer to *Windows 95 For Dummies* by Andy Rathbone and *Windows NT 4 For Dummies* by Andy Rathbone and Susan Crawford (both published by IDG Books Worldwide, Inc.).

In either case, the Setup program begins with a Welcome dialog box (see Figure 2-1). After you read the Welcome dialog box, click Next.

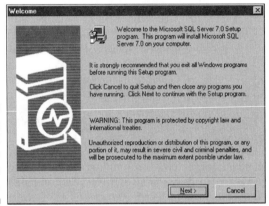

Figure 2-1:
Where it all begins; the Welcome dialog box.

2. **View the Software License Agreement dialog box; accept the agreement by clicking Yes.**

   You must accept this agreement to install SQL Server. Read the agreement carefully.

   The agreement is written in a series of pages. Scroll down to read all the agreement until you reach the end. After you get to the bottom of the agreement, Click the Yes button.

3. **From the User Information dialog box, specify your name, your company name, if applicable, and the Serial Number. Then click Next.**

   • **Name:** Enter your name. This field is required.

   Note: Many organizations don't want you to type your actual name in the Name field because you can't change the name in the Name field without completely reinstalling SQL Server. If you leave the company, or get laid off (not that that would ever happen, right?), the company would have an administrative nightmare on its hands. Often, the name of the company is entered in both the Name and Company fields.

- **Company:** Type the name of your company. This field is optional.

- **Serial:** Type the serial number of the product, which is found on either the CD case or the actual CD itself. This field is required.

4. **From the Setup Type dialog box (see Figure 2-2), choose the installation type by choosing from the following options, and then click Next.**

   - **Typical:** Choose this option if you want to perform an installation that Microsoft has determined to contain the most common options. Typical Installation is the default option. If you are new to Microsoft SQL Server, it's probably a good idea to use this option. To continue with this example, ensure that this option is checked.

   - **Minimum:** Choose this option if you have limited disk space, such as that on a laptop computer. If you choose this option, you need to have the SQL Server 7.0 CD-ROM handy every time you use SQL Server.

   - **Custom:** Choose this option if you are an advanced user and don't want to accept the default installation as you would in the Typical option. The Custom Installation option allows the advanced user more control of the features that are installed.

Figure 2-2:
Choose
how you
want to
install SQL
Server with
the Setup
Type
dialog box.

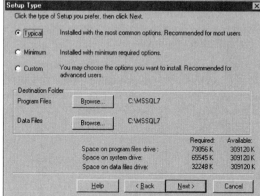

In addition, you can specify the location for the program files (SQL Server itself and all of the wizards) and for data files (your databases). By default, the Setup program tries to put the data on the C:\ drive in the MSSQL7 subdirectory. If this is okay, you're all set. If not, click the Browse button adjacent to the location you wish to change. This brings up a dialog box for you to select or enter a new location.

5. From the SQL Server Services Accounts dialog box (see Figure 2-3), specify the logon accounts by choosing from the following options and then clicking Next.

The SQL Server service is a Windows NT service that controls SQL Server. If this service isn't running, you won't be able to access SQL Server. When a SQL Server service is started, it needs a logon name and password. These fields allow you to specify these parameters:

- **Use the same account for all services. Auto start SQL Server service:** Choose this option if all three SQL Server services (SQL Server, SQL Agent, and MSDTC) are to use the same logon parameters. In addition, the SQL Server service will automatically start when the computer is booted. This option is the default. I recommend using this option.

- **Customize the settings for each service:** Choose this option if all three SQL Server services (SQL Server, SQL Agent, and MSDTC) are to have different logon parameters. To use this option, you click the services on the left part of the dialog box. As you click each service, you can specify the settings for each service on the right.

- **Use the Local System account:** Choose this option if the specified service(s) is (are) to have access only to the SQL Server that's installed on the local computer. This option is limited in functionality. For example, if you choose this option, the SQL Server service can't perform replication.

- **Use a Domain User account:** Choose this option if the service(s) is (are) to have access not only to the SQL Server you're installing now on the local computer but also to other servers and files on the network, as well. If you choose this option, you must supply the user name and password for access to the local SQL Server and other resources. If this option is selected, type the Username and Password in the text boxes provided. This option is the default option.

So you want to set up a Domain User account?

A Domain User account must meet these requirements:

- ✔ The account must be a member of the **Administrators** local group.

- ✔ The account should have the **Password Never Expires** attribute set.

- ✔ The account should have **Log on as a service** rights set.

- ✔ All logon hours must be allowed for the account.

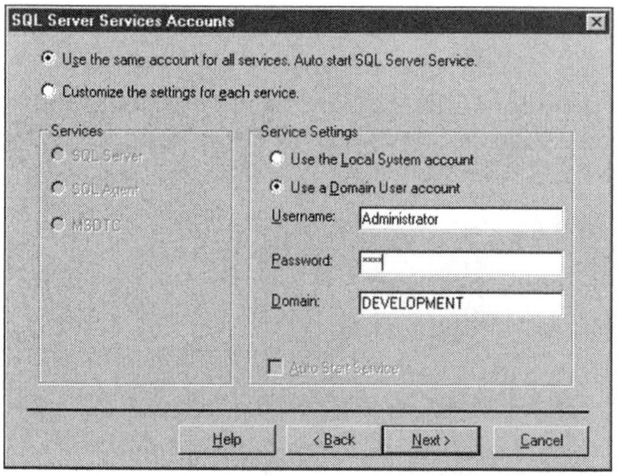

Figure 2-3:
Specify
how to
logon with
the SQL
Server
Services
Accounts
dialog box.

6. **From the Start Copying Files dialog box, click Next when you are ready to continue.**

7. **Congratulations, you did it. SQL Server 7.0 is now set up on your server. Click Finish.**

What About Your Clients?

After you install the Server software, you must also install client-side software to connect to SQL Server 7. Without it, a client computer can't use SQL Server 7. However, the client can use the utilities that come with SQL Server 7.0 to access the server on the same machine as SQL Server itself. The setup procedure that I show in this section uses an Intel-based (or compatible) computer.

A client computer needs to have a *db-library* (or database library) installed to act as a conduit to connect to SQL Server for a given protocol, called a *net-library* (or network library). You always need to install the db-library and a net-library for management tools to be used with Microsoft SQL Server 7.0.

To install Microsoft SQL Server 7.0 client-side software, follow these steps:

1. **Follow exactly the same procedure in the preceding section, "Installing the Goods on the Server," up to Step 4 (that I summarize here):**

   • Start the Setup program.

   • View the Software License Agreement dialog box; accept the agreement by clicking Yes.

   • From the User Information dialog box, specify your name, your company name, if applicable, and the Serial Number. Then click Next.

2. In the Setup Type dialog box, choose the Custom option (refer to Figure 2-2) and click Next.

3. In the Select Components dialog box, choose the components you wish to install (see Figure 2-4) and then click Next.

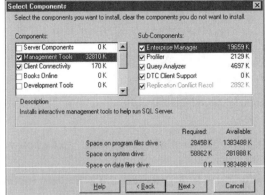

Figure 2-4: Choosing the components you want to install.

To install an option, make sure that there is a check mark in the box shown to the left of each option. Ensure that only these options are chosen:

- **Management Tools:** This option installs all the management tools that can be used with SQL Server 7.0. You don't have to install all the tools. After you click the Management Tools option, you see a list of sub-components on the right-hand part of the dialog box. Uncheck any tool that you don't want to install.

- **Client Connectivity:** This option installs all the client protocols and libraries necessary to connect to SQL Server 7.0

4. From the Start Copying Files dialog box, click Next when you are ready to continue.

5. SQL Server 7.0 client utilities are now set up. Click Finish.

In Plain English: Installing Microsoft English Query

In addition to installing Microsoft SQL Server 7.0 on the server and installing the client software, you can install the Microsoft English Query. The Microsoft English Query is a tool that allows you to query your database by specifying sentences in English instead of SQL. I don't show you how to use English Query in this book — for me to show you how to use English Query, the book would be much larger than it is now, and I wouldn't want you to hurt yourself.

To install Microsoft English Query, follow these steps:

1. **Start the Microsoft English Query Setup program.**

   Place the SQL Server 7.0 CD-ROM into the CD-ROM drive. If your CD-ROM is configured to run automatically when a disc is inserted, the Setup program runs automatically and shows a series of dialog boxes to allow you to set up different components. If the Setup program runs automatically, click the following series of buttons:

   • Install SQL Server 7.0 Components

   • English Query

   If your CD-ROM is not configured to run automatically when a disc is inserted, choose the Start⇨Run menu option. Then type **d:\mseq\x86\setup**. If **d** is not the letter corresponding to your CD-ROM drive, substitute your drive letter for **d**.

   In either case, the English Query Setup program begins.

2. **After the English Query Setup Welcome dialog box appears, click Continue.**

3. **Specify the destination folder and then click OK (see Figure 2-5).**

   By default, the system installs English Query in **C:\Program Files\Microsoft English Query**. If you want to change this folder designation, click Change Folder and choose a different folder.

Figure 2-5:
Choosing
the
destination
folder.

4. **Choose the type of installation you want to perform by clicking the desired button (see Figure 2-6).**

   I recommend that you install all options by clicking the Complete button. The installation then begins. If you are an experienced user, you may want to click the Custom button. Clicking the Custom button enables you to choose specific components you may want to install.

Figure 2-6:
Choose the
English
Query
installation
type.

Why Would I Need to Install Decision Support (OLAP) Services?

Microsoft SQL Server 7.0 now comes with OLAP services. *OLAP* stands for Online Analytical Processing. OLAP is a set of decision support services that are used in enterprise-wide computing. These decision support services (also known as DSS) allow for better reporting and data modeling, designed specifically for decision support applications. Decision support applications are sometimes referred to as *data warehousing applications*.

If you plan to utilize DSS, you need to install Microsoft Decision Support services, so follow these steps:

1. **Start the Microsoft SQL Server 7.0 Decision Support Services Setup program.**

   Place the SQL Server 7.0 CD-ROM into the CD-ROM drive. If your CD-ROM is configured to run automatically when a disc is inserted, the Setup program runs automatically and shows a series of dialog boxes to allow you to set up different components. If the Setup program runs automatically, click the following series of buttons:

   • Install SQL Server 7.0 Components

   • Decision Support Services

   • Install Decision Support Services

If your CD-ROM is not configured to run automatically when a disc is inserted, choose the Start⇨Run menu option. Then type **d:\msdss\install\setup**. If **d** is not the letter corresponding to your CD-ROM drive, substitute your drive letter for **d**.

In either case, the Microsoft SQL Server 7.0 Decision Support Services Setup program begins.

2. **After the Microsoft SQL Server 7.0 Decision Support Services Setup Welcome dialog box appears, click Next.**

3. **Accept the License Agreement by clicking Yes.**

   Read the entire license agreement by scrolling down the list. You must accept the license agreement before you can continue. Click the Yes button when you are ready to continue.

4. **Specify the data folder location and then click Next (see Figure 2-7).**

   By default, the system installs Decision Support Services in **\Program Files\Microsoft DSS\Data**. If you want to change this folder designation, click Browse and choose a different folder.

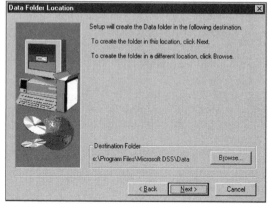

Figure 2-7:
Choosing
the data
folder
location.

5. **Specify the components you wish to install and then click Next (see Figure 2-8).**

   By default, the most common components are already checked for you.

6. **Select the program folder you wish the files to be installed into and click Next.**

   By default, **Microsoft Decision Support Services** is selected. If you wish to change the default, simply type in a new program folder name. After you click the Next button, the files are copied to your hard drive. You are prompted to restart your computer to complete the installation. That's all there is to it!

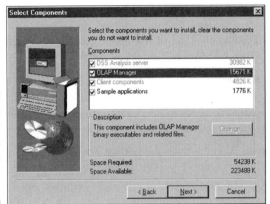

Figure 2-8:
Choosing
the DSS
components
you want to
install.

Chapter 3

Why Not Just Use Microsoft Access?

*O*ften, I have heard developers say, "Just use Access. . . . " Access is Microsoft's desktop database that can be shared across multiple users. This means that multiple users can access a single Microsoft Access database. Although it's true that sometimes it's difficult to choose a Microsoft product, you may find some definite reasons why you may want to use Access over SQL Server, and vice versa.

In this chapter, I show you some of the similarities and differences between Microsoft Access and Microsoft SQL Server. This chapter helps you decide when to use each of the products. The comparisons I make in this chapter are between Access 97 and SQL Server 7. I also recommend which product to use, based on certain criteria, which I also discuss.

When writing this chapter, I attempted to remain objective. I have used Access for many years and I like it very much. It has been great for developing small applications and prototyping.

My overall opinion (in my *humble* opinion, that is):

✔ SQL Server is better suited for enterprise-wide support and large databases. It supports distributed transactions, as well as triggers and stored procedures.

✔ Access is better for desktop database development. It has many more wizards for rapid development. Access also sports a development environment and report writing.

A Database Is Only as Good as Its Installation

Installation for both Microsoft Access and Microsoft SQL Server is relatively simple. However, you need to know a little more information when installing SQL Server than when installing Access, such as passwords, server names, servers that provide authentication, and size of databases.

When you install Microsoft SQL Server, you need to be somewhat familiar with what a service is. Basically, a *service* is a process or program that runs in the background (you don't know it is running) that allows other programs to access certain information or perform some function. For example, a user cannot dial into or out of Windows NT Server unless the Remote Access Service (RAS) is running in the background to allow such an operation.

Because Access is based on a file system, you need to know the drive and directory where you want the files to be located when installing Access. Access is not based on services, like SQL Server is. Therefore, installation is as easy as installing any other Microsoft product, such as Word, Excel, Money, and Flight Simulator. If you were to choose a product based solely on its ease of installation, I recommend using Access over SQL Server (although SQL Server is not exactly rocket science).

Resource Requirements (It's a Good Thing Memory and Disk Space Are Cheap!)

Table 3-1 shows that many more resources are required to run SQL Server than Access. However, the price of PCs has come down so dramatically that this isn't as crucial a factor as it once was. The price of memory and disk space has come down dramatically, as well — so none of these factors alone should determine which product you choose.

Table 3-1 outlines the requirement differences between SQL Server and Access.

Table 3-1	SQL Server versus Access	
Requirement	**SQL Server**	**Access**
Platform	PC, DEC Alpha, AXP, MIPS Rx4000	PC Only
Minimum processor	486/33MHZ	486

Requirement	SQL Server	Access
Minimum memory (Win 95/98)	32MB	12MB
Minimum memory (Win NT)	32MB	16MB
Approximate disk space	150MB	60MB
CD-ROM required	Yes	Yes
Display adapter	VGA	VGA
Operating system	Windows 95/98 or Windows NT 4.0 (SP3) or later	Windows 95/98 or Windows NT 3.5.1. (SP5) or later

What about Web Support?

Accessing the Web is extremely important in today's society. It provides a vast, endless resource of information. Most of the important features of web creation (publishing to the Web) is supported in both SQL Server and Access. However, Access supports a couple of additional options that may make it a more attractive product to you, if Web features are a major consideration.

Table 3-2 outlines the Web-related differences between SQL Server and Access.

Table 3-2   Web Differences between SQL Server and Access

Feature	SQL Server	Access
Publish to Web	Yes	Yes
Import HTML tables	No	Yes
Hyperlink datatype	No	Yes

Database Object Support

SQL Server and Access both have the major object-related support features, primarily because of the nature of a relational database. These features (as shown in Table 3-3) are what makes a relational database a relational database. However, a couple of major features that are missing in Access are the support for triggers and stored procedures. If you're building an Enterprise-Wide Client/Server database, expect to use triggers and stored procedures almost all the time. If you base your decision on a product solely on the database objects that it supports, I recommend that you go with SQL Server.

Table 3-3 illustrates the database object-related differences between SQL Server and Access.

Table 3-3	Database Object-Related Differences between SQL Server and Access	
Feature	*SQL Server*	*Access*
Transaction support	Yes	Yes
Heterogeneous joins	Yes	Yes
Validation rules	Yes	Yes
Default values	Yes	Yes
Triggers	Yes	No
Stored procedures	Yes	No
Referential integrity through triggers	Yes	No
Referential integrity (Declarative)	Yes	Yes
Cascading updates	Yes	Yes
Cascading deletes	Yes	Yes

Backing Up Data

SQL Server supports backing up data better than Access does, primarily because each SQL Server database is a set of files. If there are sets of files, you must know where they are physically located to back them up. Because keeping track of these files can be difficult, Microsoft built in lots of support to help you.

However, in Access, each database is stored as one file. This may be more manageable because of the lower number of physical files. Therefore, there is not as much support in Access for backing up. You back up an Access database just as you would a Word document — or any other single file. If you base your decision on a product solely on the backup support, I recommend that you go with SQL Server.

Table 3-4 shows the backup-related differences between SQL Server and Access.

Table 3-4	Backup-Related Differences between SQL Server and Access	
Feature	*SQL Server*	*Access*
Automated backups	Yes	No
Transaction log backup	Yes	No
Automatic recovery	Yes	No
Backup and restore on a single table	Yes	No
Scheduled replication	Yes	Yes
Table level replication	Yes	Yes
Row level replication	Yes	Yes
Field level replication	Yes	No
Transactional replication	Yes	No

Maximum Capacities and Other Support

The most important features listed in this category relate to the capacity of the product. SQL Server supports much larger databases. Additionally, SQL Server supports many more simultaneous connections. If you base your decision on these factors, go with SQL Server.

Table 3-5 outlines capacities and other differences between SQL Server and Access.

Table 3-5	Capacities and Other Differences between SQL Server and Access	
Feature	*SQL Server*	*Access*
Integrated Development Environment	No	Yes
Database Wizards	Yes	Yes
Design Tools	Yes	Yes
Query Wizards	Yes	Yes
Distributed database support	Yes	No

(continued)

Table 3-5 *(continued)*

Feature	SQL Server	Access
Maximum database size	1,048,516 Terabytes	1.2 Gigabytes
Very Large Database Support (VLDB)	Yes	No
Maximum number of connections	32,767	255
Built-in security	Yes	Yes
Built-in encryption	Yes	Yes
Processing	On server	On client
Reporting	None	Built-in
OLAP support	Yes	No
Data warehouse support	Yes	No

Part II
Database Design

The 5th Wave   By Rich Tennant

"OK, make sure this is right. 'Looking for caring companion who likes old movies, nature walks and quiet evenings at home. Knowledge of creating SQL Server objects and manipulating stored procedures, a plus.'"

In this part . . .

1 show you how to design your databases. I discuss all the main objects that relate to databases so you can get up and running fast. I even show you how to use stored procedures. One other thing that Microsoft SQL Server 7 gives you is extended procedures, and I tell you about these, too, of course.

Chapter 4

Understanding the Relational Data Model

*M*icrosoft SQL Server is a relational database. A *relational database* is one that's organized in a series of two-dimensional tables. These tables relate to one another based on *fields* (or columns) in the tables. The fields between tables that relate to each other are known as *keys.* A relational database is based on a relational model.

In this chapter, I describe the relational model, how it works, and what you need to know to design great databases. I don't go into great detail on process of creating the database objects. If you are looking for detail about how to create these database objects (more than just a narrative and nice pictures), see Chapters 5 and 6.

Schema Objects

The relational database is made up of objects. All of the database objects that comprise the database are referred to as the *schema*. These objects include tables, indexes, and other types of objects that will be discussed throughout this section. Surprisingly enough, a database object, or schema object, is also the database itself. The design of all these objects makes up the data model. By design, I mean how you structure the tables and other objects to store data.

A schema starts with a database. That database contains one or more tables, which contains one or more columns (see Figure 4-1).

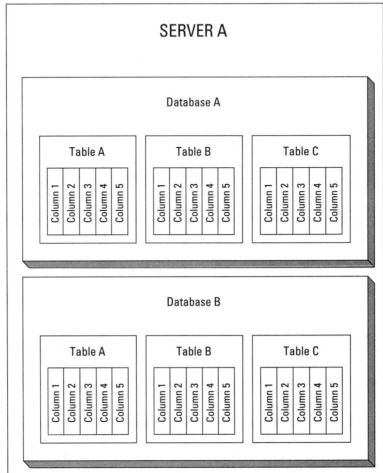

Figure 4-1:
Relationship
between
databases,
tables, and
columns.

Keys

A *key* identifies and defines a specific set of one or more columns in a table. There are two types of keys:

- ✔ Primary keys
- ✔ Foreign keys

Primary keys

A *primary key* is one or more columns in a table that uniquely identifies how records are stored in that table. You can think of a primary key as a way to locate data entries in a table. These data entries are called *records*. A primary key is used by the database to enforce uniqueness of records within a table. You want to enforce uniqueness so that you don't store duplicate records.

To help you understand primary keys, consider my example in Figure 4-2.

The Customer ID is the primary key

Figure 4-2:
A typical
customer
table!

CUSTOMER : Table		
Customer ID	Last Name	First Name
1001	Jones	Fred
1002	Smith	Linda
1003	Smith	Fred

Record: 1 of 3

Because the Customer ID column is unique per customer, the Customer ID column defines the primary key. You cannot define the Customer ID and Last Name columns as the primary key because the last name of Smith appears more than once. This goes against the primary key definition. In other words, it is said to *violate* the primary key. SQL Server will not allow you to violate the primary key. You also cannot define the Customer ID and First Name columns as the primary key because the first name of Fred appears more than once. Therefore, you must know how the data is stored in the table helps to define the primary key. The only possible way to define a primary key in this table is the Customer ID column.

However, in the following example, Customer ID no longer identifies a unique row (see Figure 4-3).

Figure 4-3:
Customer ID
and Order
ID are the
primary key,
not just
Customer ID.

CUSTOMER : Table			
Customer ID	Order ID	Last Name	First Name
1001	100	Jones	Fred
1002	100	Smith	Linda
1003	100	Smith	Fred
1001	101	Jones	Fred
1002	101	Smith	Linda
1003	101	Smith	Fred

Record: 1 of 6

The table in Figure 4-3 needs to have a primary key containing Customer ID and Order ID because the combination of these two columns uniquely identifies records (the data) in the table. In this example, the reason why the primary key is Customer ID and Order ID is because the values in the Customer ID column are not unique. Likewise, the values in the Order ID column are not unique. There are duplicate values in each of the columns. However, if the primary key is Customer ID and Order ID, the combination of these columns contains unique values.

A quick design note: The values for the Order ID column start at 100 for *each* customer and are incremented every time a customer places an order. If a new Order ID was generated every time *any* customer placed an order, then Order ID would contains unique values. That would define Order ID as the primary key.

Just because you know what the primary key is doesn't mean that SQL Server does. You need to actually define the primary key for SQL Server. Define the primary key at one of two different times:

- ✔ By specifying when you create the table with SQL
- ✔ By specifying after you create the table with SQL or the Enterprise Manager

Foreign keys

A *foreign key* is one or more columns in a table whose values in those columns match the values in the primary key of another table. A foreign key is used by SQL Server to ensure that the value in the table containing the foreign key actually matches the value in the table containing the primary key. This is known as referential integrity. *Referential integrity* maintains the integrity of data between one or more tables that relate to each other. If you use SQL Server to manage your relationships, this is called *declarative referential integrity,* or DRI. DRI allows SQL Server to enforce your relationships through foreign keys. Look at Figure 4-4 to see how the foreign key in the Orders table (Customer ID column) enforces the referential integrity in the Customers table (Customer ID column). In Figure 4-4, the primary keys are shown in bold. The foreign key relationship is defined by the arrow shown in the diagram. The arrow "points to" the foreign key. The symbols shown above the arrow indicate the type of relationship (one-to-many). For more information, see "Relationships" later in this chapter.

Figure 4-4:
Foreign
keys
enforce
referential
integrity.

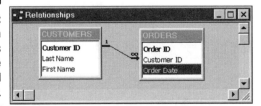

You need to define the foreign key to let SQL Server know how to enforce referential integrity. Define the foreign key at one of two different times:

- ✔ By specifying when you create the table with SQL
- ✔ By specifying after you create the table with SQL or the Enterprise Manager

For more information about creating a foreign key, see Chapter 5.

Rules

A *rule* is a database object that you attach, or *bind,* to a column in a table. A rule indicates to SQL Server what values are valid and whether you can insert or update it into the column. You can also apply a rule to a user-defined type.

You define a rule with a name, like any other database object, and a condition. The condition can be any expression that you enter in the WHERE clause of a SQL statement.

You can create a rule at one of two different times:

- ✔ By specifying when you create the table with SQL
- ✔ By specifying after you create the table with SQL or the Enterprise Manager

For more information about creating rules, see Chapter 6.

Defaults

A *default* is a database object that indicates a value for a column so that if a value is omitted or null, a value is still inserted or updated for that column.

You can create a default in one of three ways:

- ✔ By using the SQL Server Enterprise Manager
- ✔ By specifying when you create the table with SQL
- ✔ By specifying after you create the table with SQL or the Enterprise Manager

For more information about creating defaults, see Chapter 5.

Triggers

A *trigger* is a database object that SQL Server automatically executes when you insert, update, or delete data from a table. You define a trigger for a specific action. You can't define a single trigger for the insertion, update, and deletion at the same time, though. If you need three different actions, you need to define three different triggers.

Triggers can be very useful for referential integrity. You can, for example, define a trigger so that every time you insert a value into table A, columns of data are also updated in table B.

The nice thing about triggers is that they're automatic. After you successfully insert, update, or delete data from a table, the trigger fires. A SQL statement is then executed, and you get to define this SQL statement.

For more information about creating triggers, see Chapter 6.

Indexes

An *index* is a database object that helps speed queries by either instructing SQL Server to physically put the records in a table in order, or by providing an execution path so that SQL Server (actually the optimizer) knows how to run the query.

Indexes can help or hurt query performance, depending on the situation. However, Microsoft improved the optimizer in SQL Server 7. This improvement means that if the SQL Server optimizer determines that an index may adversely affect the performance of the query, SQL Server will do a table scan. A *table scan* occurs when SQL Server looks up all records by reading the table into memory and testing to discover which records match the specified criteria. In this case, SQL Server doesn't use an index to run a query.

For more information about creating indexes, see Chapter 5.

There are two types of indexes:

- ✔ Clustered
- ✔ Non-clustered

A *clustered* index is an index that stores the data physically on the disk in order, based on your primary key. This allows for greater access speed to your data because SQL Server can get right to the row(s) you need if they are stored in order. There can be a maximum of one clustered index on a table — the data in a table can be physically stored in order one way, unless your primary key changes.

A *non-clustered* index is one which is not physically stored in order of the primary key, but is stored in such a way that the index points to the location of the data in the table. This allows for fast retrieval, but not as fast as a clustered index.

What Is a Relational Model?

Notice how much data is repeated in the table in Figure 4-5. The customer names, order numbers, and prices are all repeated. This repetition of data is affected by the relational model. A relational model (sometimes called a data model or a relational data model) defines the way you design your database. This means that the way you layout your databases, tables, and columns defines your relational model.

	Customer ID	Last Name	First Name	Order Num	Line Num	Stock Num	Price
▶	1001	Jones	John	100	1	33343G	100
	1001	Jones	John	100	2	54544A	50
	1001	Jones	John	100	3	84763B	65
	1001	Jones	John	100	4	33232B	45
	1002	Riggs	Linda	101	1	54544A	50
	1002	Riggs	Linda	101	2	84763B	65
	1002	Riggs	Linda	102	1	33234T	75
	1003	Smith	Fred	103	1	54544A	50
	1003	Smith	Fred	103	2	33234T	75
	1003	Smith	Fred	103	3	84763B	65
*							0

Figure 4-5: Diagram showing redundant data.

To break this table into parts so that data is not repeated is called *normalization*. To normalize a table, you need to follow five rules:

- ✔ **Eliminate repeating groups.** This means that a separate table must be used for each set of related attributes. Each separate table must have a primary key. Primary keys are described earlier in this chapter.

- ✔ **Eliminate redundant data.** If an attribute depends on part of a multi-valued key, move it to a separate table.

- ✔ **Eliminate columns not dependent on a key.** If attributes do not contribute to a description of a key, move them to a separate table.

- ✔ **Isolate independent multiple relationships.** No table can contain two or more relationships that are not directly related.

- ✔ **Isolate semantically related multiple relationships.** Sometimes practical constraints on information justify separating logically related many-to-many relationships. For more information about many-to-many relationships, see "Relationships" later in this chapter.

The table in Figure 4-6 shows the normalized table from Figure 4-5. To normalize the table in Figure 4-5, you would reconstruct it by creating four tables (CUSTOMERS, ORDERS, STOCK, and PRICES) and enforcing these relationships:

CUSTOMERS.Customer ID -> ORDERS.Customer ID

ORDERS.Order Num -> STOCK.Order Num

STOCK.Stock Num -> PRICES.Stock Num

In the preceding list of relationships, I show the relationships in the format of TABLE.COLUMN — the table name is followed by a period, followed by the column name.

Figure 4-6:
Diagram showing normalized tables.

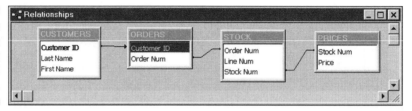

 You may think it simple enough to normalize the tables in a database. However, nothing is ever easy! Every time you split your data model from one table to two tables, a query will take longer to execute. This is called a *performance hit* — a very common term in database terminology. In the example in Figure 4-5, the database is large because so much data is repeated. On the other hand, in the example in Figure 4-6, the queries to access the data will take longer to execute, even though the database is smaller.

Designing the Model

The data model, sometimes referred to as the *schema,* is very important because it defines how your data is stored. Defining your data model can be a very difficult task because every situation is different. However, I can show you some things to keep in mind, along with some tips and tricks.

The data model physically reflects how your data will be stored into tables. It is always a good idea to design your data model on paper first. If you design your data model as you are creating the tables, you will invariably have to change it.

Before designing the model, you must understand what your client needs. If you don't know, there's no way you can design the model. More often than not, you must first sit down with your client and document the user's requirements. It can also be helpful to create a prototype. A prototype is generally created using some tool that can create screens. Visual Basic is such a tool, used for fast prototyping.

One of the main reasons for prototyping your application is that it will show all fields on a screen. Generally, every field on a screen corresponds to a column in a table in a database.

The diagram in Figure 4-7 shows a dialog box that I generated in Visual Basic. It simulates a dialog box similar to that which you may show to a customer to make sure that you are capturing the data that the customer wants. The dialog box is used to present customer information.

Figure 4-7:
A prototype
Customer
Information
dialog box.

Based on the dialog box shown in Figure 4-7, you know that you at least need one table — call it the Customer table — and you know that you need the following fields:

Customer ID
Last Name
First Name
Middle Initial
Company Name
Address 1
Address 2

    City
    State
    Zip
    Phone
    Fax

Looking at these fields, it becomes obvious that Customer ID is the primary key to the table because the Customer ID uniquely identifies the customer. It doesn't make sense for any other field to be the primary key. For example, First Name doesn't make sense to be the primary key because many people in the database may have the same first name. The same theory applies to every column in the table.

Although this model may seem easy so far, we're not finished with this dialog box. Notice that there is a drop-down list of states. Where does this list come from? It can't come from the Customer table because there may be customers in the database from only one state. If this were the case, the drop-down list of states would contain only one state. Therefore, it makes sense to create another table that contains only a list of all states. Creating a separate table that contains every state ensures that when you take an order, you can choose the correct state for a customer.

This type of table is called a look-up table. A *look-up table* is one whose sole purpose is to provide a valid list of values from which to choose your data. If the table were not used, it would not affect the ability of the data model to perform its function.

I'll call the look-up table States. The States table needs only one field:

    State

In addition to the two tables I discuss so far, in an order-taking system, you need to have an Orders table to store the order information taken and to input into the dialog box shown in Figure 4-8. I constructed this dialog box, too, in Visual Basic.

Figure 4-8 shows a basic dialog box that contains many fields, most of which are read-only. A *read-only* field displays data on the dialog box but doesn't allow you to type any data into it. The following fields on the dialog box are read-only:

    Order Date
    Customer ID
    Name
    Description
    Unit Price
    Ext. Price
    Sub-Total

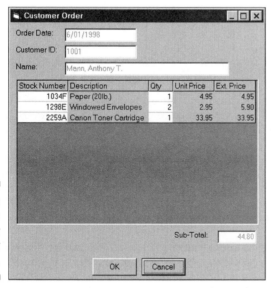

Figure 4-8:
A prototype
Customer
Order
dialog box.

The only two fields that are enterable, or known as *read-write*, are:

Stock Number
Qty

Knowing which fields are read-only is important because these fields can come from the database or they can be derived. A *derived field* is one that can be calculated or formulated, and not actually stored in the database. For example, notice that the value in the Name field in Figure 4-8 is my name, Anthony T. Mann, and is a derived field because my name is not stored in the database in one field. Names are stored in the Customer table under the three fields, Last Name, First Name, and Middle Initial.

Not all read-only fields are derived. The Customer ID field is read-only, not derived, and comes from the Customer table. The Order Date field is read-only and derived. It isn't derived from one or more database fields, but is derived from the computer's clock.

Notice that the date in the Order Date field uses a four digit year. It's a good idea to use a four digit year to account for any year 2000 issues before they start.

Now, look once again at Figure 4-8. The data stored from this dialog box needs to go into a table. Because it stores order information, I call the table Orders. The following columns are needed in the Orders table:

Order Date
Customer ID
Stock Number
Qty

These are the only columns needed in this table. Why, you may ask? Look at each of the other fields shown in Figure 4-8. Name is a derived field. Look up the Name by using a join in the Customer table. The Customer table contains the Customer ID, Last Name, First Name, and Middle Initial.

The Description field is not derived, but is looked up in another table for stock information. Along with the stock information is the price of each unit. Therefore, when the user types a quantity, the system looks up the unit price and calculates, or derives, the Ext. (Extended) Price. Sub-Total is a derived field that is calculated based on all of the Ext. Price values.

It's a good design tip to know that if a derived field can be derived every time from the values in the database, you probably don't want to store it in the database. Ext. Price is such a field. On the other hand, Order Date is not such a field. The client program written in Visual Basic automatically fills in the current date when the order is taken, but it needs to be stored so that reports can be generated based on date.

The stock information is stored in a separate table, mainly because if we follow rule number two in the five rules of data normalization shown earlier (see "What Is a Relational Model?"), you'll see no repeating data. If the stock information is stored in the Orders table, much of the data may be repeated, such as Description, which greatly increases the size of the database. We don't want that!

I propose storing the stock information in a table called, what else, Stock. The Stock table contains these columns:

Stock Number
Description
Unit Price

The primary key for the table is Stock Number because it uniquely identifies a row in the Stock table.

To put it all together, have a look at Figure 4-9, which shows the relationship between all three tables I have discussed in this section. It isn't possible to teach you everything I've learned about database design over the years in one chapter, but I wanted to give you a good overview as to not only the technique, but a method to the madness as well.

Figure 4-9:
The
relationship
between
the
CUSTOMERS,
ORDERS,
and
STATES
tables.

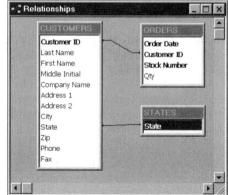

The concepts that I've discussed in this section, "Designing the Model," could prompt for many questions in your mind. One question may be, "Why don't you store the Unit Price in the Orders table?" The reason for this is that for my example, I have decided that there are no price overrides. If there were, the override price would need to be stored somewhere.

Another question you may ask is, "What about sales tax?" It's true that this example did not take sales tax into account. It isn't intended to be a real-world database, but only a lesson.

One final question could be, "What happens if someone places an order outside the United States?" The example that I presented takes into account only orders within the United States. You can easily expand it to take international orders into account.

Another way to design your data model is to design an entity relationship diagram based on data flow and the business process model. This way to design the data model generally works if your clients know exactly what they want. However, many times, your clients will need to see a screen prototype because they can't visualize the application based on an entity relationship diagram or business definitions.

Datatypes

Every column in every table must be declared as a certain type of data, known as a *datatype*. A finite number of datatypes are available in SQL Server 7. However, you can create your own. The next few pages outline both of these cases.

Standard datatypes

Microsoft SQL Server 7 comes standard with 20 different datatypes. These almost always suit your needs. However, if not, refer to the next section, "User-defined datatypes."

Table 4-1 shows the standard datatypes available in SQL Server 7. In the future, if you need a quick reference to these datatypes (as I know you will), you can find them on the Cheat Sheet at the front of the book.

Table 4-1	Suggested Database Object Prefixes
Datatype	*Explanation*
Binary	Holds up to 8,000 bytes of binary data. Binary data is any data that is stored in a stream of 1s and 0s. The data stored in a Binary column must be fixed in length.
Bit	Used to hold either a 1 or a 0, commonly used as a True/False or Yes/No indicator, or a flag that indicates that something is "switched on or off." A bit datatype takes 1 byte in storage.
Char	Holds up to 8,000 bytes (characters) of data. The data stored in a Char column must be fixed in length.
Datetime	Stores a date and time value. A Datetime column takes two 4-byte integers of storage. The date range available in the 4-byte configurations are between 1/1/1753 and 12/31/9999. The time range spans the full range of the clock, accurate to within 3/100 of a second.
Decimal	Stores numeric data. The storage space required for the Decimal datatype range is from 2 to 17 bytes, depending on the precision and scale of the data. Precision indicates the number of digits required by the number. Scale indicates the number of decimal places required by the number.
Float	Stores numeric data with floating-point numbers. The range of data that can be stored is from $2.23E - 308$ to $1.79E\ 308$ for positive numbers. The range of data that can be stored is from $2.23E\ -308$ to $-.79E\ 308$. The amount of space required to store a Float datatype is 8 bytes.
Image	Stores binary data represented by an image. The Image datatype can store more information than a Binary datatype, but requires more space. An Image datatype holds variable-length binary data. The amount of space required varies, based on the amount of data. It can store more than 2GB (gigabytes) of binary data.

Datatype	Explanation
Int	Stores whole number integers in the range of -2,147,483,648 to +2,147,483,647. The Int datatype requires 4 bytes to store data.
Money	Stores monetary values in the range of -922,337,203,685,477.5808 to +922,337,203,685,477.5807. The Money datatype requires 8 bytes to store data.
nChar	Holds up to 4,000 bytes (characters) of Unicode data. The data stored in an nChar column must be fixed in length. Unicode data is used for international characters.
nText	Stores variable-length Unicode character data. The nText datatype can store up to 1,073,741,823 bytes (or characters).
Numeric	Same as the decimal datatype, but the Numeric datatype is preferred.
nVarchar	Holds up to 4,000 bytes (characters) of Unicode data. The data stored in an nVarchar column is variable-length. Unicode data is used for international characters.
Real	Stores numeric data with floating-point numbers. The range of data that can be stored is from 1.18E — 38 to 3.40E 38 for positive numbers. The range of data that can be stored is from -1.18E — 38 to -3.4E 38. The amount of space required to store a Real datatype is 4 bytes, which is half the size (and range) of the Float datatype.
Smalldatetime	Stores a date and time value. A Datetime column takes 4 bytes of storage. The date range available is between 1/1/1900 and 6/6/2079. The time range spans the full range of the clock, accurate to within one minute.
Smallint	Stores whole number integers in the range of -32,768 to 32,767. The Smallint datatype requires 2 bytes to store data.
Money	Stores monetary values in the range of -214,748.3648 to 214,748.3647. The Money datatype requires 4 bytes to store data. Decimal places are rounded to two places.
Sysname	Used to store the name of system tables. The Sysname datatype is automatically defined as being varchar(30) and therefore takes no more than 30 bytes to store.
Text	Stores variable-length character data. The Text datatype can store up to 2,147,483,647 bytes (or characters).
Timestamp	Stores binary data representing the current date and time. The data in a Timestamp column is automatically inserted or updated every time the data in a row is changed.

(continued)

Table 4-1 *(continued)*	
Datatype	Explanation
Tinyint	Stores whole numbers in the range from 0 to 255 and requires only 1 byte to store.
Uniqueidentifier	Stores a globally unique identifier. The Uniqueidentifier datatype requires 16 bytes of storage.
Varbinary	Holds up to 8,000 bytes of binary data. Binary data is any data that is stored in a stream of 1s and 0s. The data stored in a varbinary column is variable-length.
Varchar	Holds up to 8,000 bytes (characters) of data. The data stored in a Varchar column is variable-length.

User-defined datatypes

If one of the datatypes listed in the "Standard datatypes" section earlier in this chapter doesn't suit your needs, you can create your own. User-defined datatypes are also known as UDTs.

When I say *create your own,* I don't mean that you can create a datatype, like extremelysmalldatetime, and have that built into SQL Server. You create your own datatype by using the SQL Server Enterprise Manager. The only thing that creating your own datatypes does is to configure the properties of a standard datatype. These configured datatypes can be wrapped into a new datatype so that you don't have to configure it again.

As an example, suppose you wanted to create a new datatype called Address. The Address datatype would actually be a varchar datatype, but with the length set to a value of 30. After you create the datatype, you can then use it in the database where it was created. The only thing a UDT saves is a little bit of time.

To create a UDT, follow these simple steps:

1. **Choose Start⇨Programs⇨Microsoft SQL Server 7.0⇨Enterprise Manager to start the SQL Server Enterprise Manager.**

2. **Expand the tree so that you see the User Defined Datatypes folder.**

   For more information about expanding the tree, see Chapter 1.

3. **Highlight the User Defined Datatypes folder.**

   After highlighting the User Defined Datatypes folder, notice the list of User Defined Datatypes (UDTs) on the right-hand part of the screen. If you have not created any UDTs, none will be listed (see Figure 4-10).

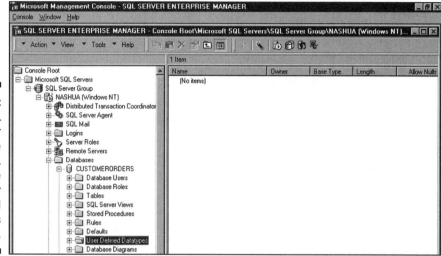

Figure 4-10:
The SQL
Server
Enterprise
Manager,
showing the
User
Defined
Datatypes
folder.

4. **Choose the Action⇨New User Defined Datatype menu option to bring up the User Defined Datatype Properties dialog box.**

Alternatively, you can use the mouse to right-click anywhere on the right-hand part of the screen and select the New User Defined Datatype menu. Also, you can right-click the User Defined Datatypes folder in the tree and select the New User Defined Datatype menu.

Whatever method you choose to create a new User Defined Datatype, each brings up the User Defined Datatype Properties dialog box (see Figure 4-11).

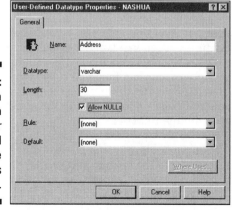

Figure 4-11:
Create a
datatype in
the User
Defined
Datatype
Properties
dialog box.

5. **Fill in the desired fields on the User Defined Datatype Properties dialog box.**

   Fill in these fields:

   - **Name:** This is the name of your new datatype. Enter something like **Address**.

   - **Datatype:** Select from the drop-down list of available datatypes. These are all standard datatypes. For example, choose **varchar**.

   - **Length:** Type the length for you new datatype, if you wish to change it from the default value. For example, enter **30**.

   - **Allow NULLs:** Check this box if your new datatype is to allow null values.

   - **Rule:** Select from the drop-down list of defined rules if the rule is to apply to your new datatype. This isn't mandatory, and **(none)** is the default value.

   - **Default:** Select from the drop-down list of defaults if the default is to apply to your new datatype. This isn't mandatory, and **(none)** is the default value.

6. **Click OK to save your new User Defined Datatype.**

The "Tier" Buzzword

You may have heard the term tier. A *tier* is a database term that indicates a specific level of business functionality that's encapsulated into a single object or set of objects. A tier is not created in SQL Server 7.0, but it's important to understand the concept anyway because you can't be proficient with SQL Server 7.0 and not know how tiers are related to it.

A very typical situation is what you may find in Figure 4-12. It shows a 4-tier application. The client application written in a language like Visual Basic is the first tier. The last tier is always the database itself. The middle tiers for which there is no limit to the number, contain business logic. Figure 4-12 shows two middle tiers, one which calls the other. Such functionality could be customer-related functionality in one middle tier (tier 2), and order-related functionality in another middle tier (tier 3).

The main advantage to this 4-tier application is that if the business rules change, a developer only has to change the object representing the tier, and not the database. An alternative representation of the 4-tier application is not to have one object call another, but to have the client tier (tier 1) call either tier 2 or tier 3. There are no limits to the design, and I can't show them all to you. However, I give you a good overview of some of the concepts. This way when your boss asks you, you can look like a smartie.

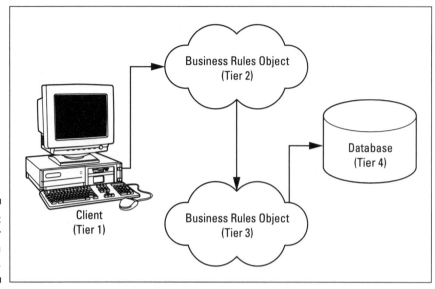

Figure 4-12:
A 4-tier
application
architecture.

Naming Conventions

You need to take naming conventions into account when you design your database. A *naming convention* is a consistent way to name your database objects. No mandatory way exists that you need to use to name your columns. I present some possibilities that aren't set in stone. Many organizations already publish a list of conventions that are acceptable. The main thing to keep in mind when using naming conventions is that they are for consistency.

Without a naming convention, if you ask someone how they would name a table that contains customer information, you may get these six responses:

- CUSTOMER
- Customer
- Customer_Info
- CUSTOMERS
- TAB_CUSTOMER
- CustInfo

As you can see, it's important to have some type of convention so that all objects don't appear to have been named haphazardly. You need to keep these things in mind:

- ✔ Do your objects contain spaces?
- ✔ Do you prefix your objects with a code identifying the type of object?
- ✔ Are your objects mixed uppercase and lowercase, uppercase only, or lowercase only?
- ✔ Do you use plurals in your object names?
- ✔ Do you allow underscore characters in your object names?
- ✔ Do you limit the number of characters in an object name?

Because coming up with a naming convention is sometimes difficult, all I can do is let you know the naming convention that I use. Note that the naming conventions I show in the rest of this section are how I would construct a production database, which is many times different than the examples I show throughout the book.

Here are my own naming conventions:

- ✔ I do not use spaces in any of my object names (even though I show them for clarity in my examples in the book).
- ✔ I do prefix all my objects with the type of object it is. For example, I prefix all table names with **TAB**. Table 4-2 shows the prefixes I use.

Table 4-2	Suggested Database Object Prefixes
Prefix	*Database Object*
CSP_	Custom Stored Procedure
CXP_	Custom Extended Procedure
DEF_	Default
FK_	Foreign Key
IDX_	Index
PK_	Primary Key
RUL_	Rule
SCH_	Schema
TAB_	Table
TRG_	Trigger
UDT_	User-Defined Type
VEW_	View

✔ All my table names are in uppercase, but all other objects can be in mixed case. For example, I may name a table **TAB_CUSTOMER**, but an index would be named **IDX_PrimaryIndex**.

✔ I never use plurals in my object names. For example, I may name a table **ORDER**, not **ORDERS**. I realize that **ORDERS** may make more sense, but by using the convention of no plural names, it's easier to create SQL statements. You don't need to remember which tables are plural and which ones are not.

✔ I do use underscore characters in my object names, but only after the prefix. After that, I use mixed cases, where it makes sense. For example, a trigger used to update a customer's address would be named something like **TRG_UpdateAddress**.

✔ I don't limit the number of characters in an object name. I try to make the name as short as possible, but I don't abbreviate. SQL Server 7 can handle very long names. Therefore, there's no need to truncate them if it isn't necessary. For example, I would name a column in a customer table **LastName**, not **LstNme**. I have seen many companies truncate names in this way. My feeling is, what's the point? In this example, truncating the name saves only two characters.

Relationships

A relationship defines how a column in one table relates to a column in another table. A relationship is defined within the database itself. If a relationship is defined, SQL Server can automatically enforce referential integrity with the definition.

The following types of relationships are available:

✔ One-to-one
✔ One-to-many
✔ Many-to-many

I outline these relationships throughout the rest of this chapter.

One-to-one relationships

A one-to-one relationship indicates that a row in table A can have at most one matching row in table B. Also, a row in table B can have at most one matching row in table A. This type of relationship is not used very often. Primarily, a one-to-one relationship defines the relationship between primary keys in two tables.

So, how about an example? Suppose you have two tables (with the columns shown in parentheses), as follows:

- ✔ Employees (Employee ID, Last Name, First Name, Address, City, State, Zip, Phone)
- ✔ Salaries (Employee ID, Salary)

The preceding tables each must have its primary key defined as Employee ID. This is because you cannot have more than one employee with the same ID.

If you define a relationship between the Employee ID column in the Employees table and the Employee ID column in the Salaries table, this would be a one-to-one relationship — one Employee ID in the Employees table can have at most one value in the Employee ID column in the Salaries table. Likewise, one Employee ID in the Salaries table can have at most one value in the Employee ID column in the Employees table.

Many times, as in the one-to-one relationship that I've shown, you can simply combine the tables. Because the primary key is the same in each table, you can decide which table you wish to keep and transfer the non-primary key columns from the other table into that table. For example, if you want to keep the Employees table, you can simply add the Salary column to the Employees table and get rid of the Salaries table.

If you are going to delete a table, make sure you update the remaining table with the data from the table you are going to delete.

One-to-many relationships

A one-to-many relationship indicates that a row in table A can have many matching rows in table B. However, a row in table B can have only one matching row in table A. This type of relationship is extremely common.

An example of a one-to-many relationship is the example used in the earlier section, "Foreign keys" in this chapter (refer to Figure 4-4). A Customer ID column in the CUSTOMERS table can have at most one value and a Customer ID column in the ORDERS table can have many values. This is where the one-to-many comes in. Also, note in Figure 4-4 that there is a 1 next to the Customer ID column in the CUSTOMERS table and an ∞ symbol (indicating infinite, or many) next to the Customer ID column in the ORDERS table. This identifies the relationship visually.

Many-to-many relationships

A many-to-many relationship indicates that a row in table A can have many matching rows in table B. Also, a row in table B can have many matching rows in table A. Generally, it is a good idea to stay away from many-to-many relationships. If you have this type of relationship on two tables, it can make it very difficult (if not impossible) to enforce referential integrity. It can also make the tables difficult or impossible to optimize for performance. A many-to-many relationship results in data that contains all possible combinations of all data in each of the tables. This type of data result is called a *Cartesian product*. Cartesian products are extremely slow.

An example of when you would have a many-to-many relationship is if you have these two tables (with column names in parentheses):

  ✔ Computers (Manufacturer ID, Model)
  ✔ Vendors (Supplier ID, Manufacturer ID)

This is a many-to-many relationship because many Manufacturers in the Computers table are supplied by the Manufacturer ID column in the Vendors table. Also, many Manufacturers in the Vendors table supply computers in the Computers table.

You can turn two tables with many-to-many relationships into tables with one-to-many relationships by adding a third intermediate table, called a *resolution table*. You can name this resolution table something like **ComputerVendors** and add a couple of columns like this:

  ✔ Computers (Manufacturer ID, Model ID)
  ✔ ComputerVendors (Model ID, Supplier ID)
  ✔ Vendors (Supplier ID, Manufacturer ID)

With the addition of the third table, one Supplier ID in the Vendors table can have many values in the ComputerVendors table. A Model ID in the ComputerVendors table can have many values in the Computers table. This is how the one-to-many relationships can be obtained.

Chapter 5

Creating Base-level SQL Server Objects

*I*n this chapter, I show you how to create base-level SQL Server objects. The term *base-level* describes the most elemental of all database objects — those that must exist for even the simplest database to function. SQL Server 7 offers you multiple ways to create these objects, and I introduce you to all of them within this chapter.

To fully understand the concepts in this chapter, you may want to refer to Chapter 4 for an overview of databases, tables, indexes, and other database objects. Knowledge of relational databases can help you follow through the processes involved in creating base-level SQL Server objects.

Building Databases

A database, the most elemental of objects that you can have on a database server, acts as a container for other objects. You can create a database using any of three tools: the Create Database Wizard, SQL Server Enterprise Manager, or SQL.

Using the Create Database Wizard

SQL Server 7 is equipped with many wizards, one of which is the Create Database Wizard. This handy utility guides you through a series of steps, prompting you for input along the way. (See Appendix A for a flowchart of the steps in the Create Database Wizard.) Here's how to create a database using the Create Database Wizard:

1. **To start the SQL Server Enterprise Manager, choose Start⇨ Programs⇨Microsoft SQL Server 7.0⇨Enterprise Manager.**

   The SQL Server Enterprise Manager opens, as shown in Figure 5-1.

2. **Click SQL Server Group so that you see the name of your server.**

   My server name is Nashua.

3. **From the Tools menu, click Wizards.**

   The Select Wizard dialog box appears (see Figure 5-2).

4. **Click the Create Database Wizard (under the Database category) and then click the OK button.**

   The Create Database Wizard introductory dialog box appears. Just click Next and get ready to fill in some blanks!

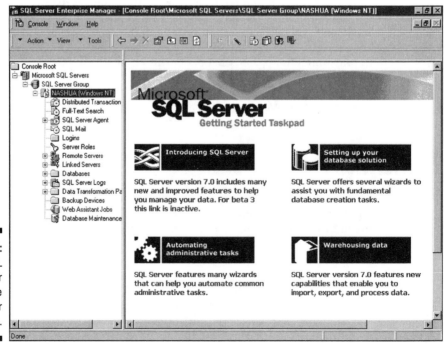

Figure 5-1: The SQL Server Enterprise Manager screen.

Figure 5-2:
The Select
Wizard
dialog box
enables you
to choose
the wizard
that you
want to
use.

5. **Fill in the appropriate Database name and Location fields (see Figure 5-3); then click Next.**

   - **Database name:** The name that you give to your database is used when you connect to the server. If you are going to use the database to track orders, you may want to call it **CUSTOMERORDERS**.

   - **Location:** When you consider where you want your database to be stored, keep in mind that the default location is in the **\data** subdirectory of wherever you installed SQL Server 7.

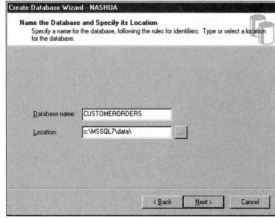

Figure 5-3:
You can
name your
database
and specify
its location
in the
Create
Database
Wizard
dialog box.

6. Name the file(s) for the database and specify its initial size; then click <u>N</u>ext.

Just like its own title suggests, the Name the database files window enables you to specify the File name and Initial size of the database.

- **File name:** By default, **_Data** is added to the end of the database name. For example, **CUSTOMERORDERS_Data** is the name of my file. You can change the file name by clicking it and typing a new name.

- **Initial Size (MB):** By default, the initial size is 1 megabyte (MB). If you want to change the number, click the proposed size and type in a new size.

7. In the Define the database file growth dialog box, choose one of the following option buttons (see Figure 5-4), and then click <u>N</u>ext.

- **<u>D</u>o not automatically grow the database files:** This option indicates to SQL Server that you do not want SQL Server to automatically increase the size of the database files. You prefer to configure the size of your databases manually.

- **<u>A</u>utomatically grow the database files:** This default option indicates to SQL Server that you do not want to manually specify the size for a database as it grows; you want SQL Server to manage this automatically. If you choose this option, a few other options become available. These options are:

    Grow the files in <u>m</u>egabytes: You can tell SQL Server the increments of growth that you want each time the database needs to enlarge; 1MB is the default value. Unless you plan to add a tremendous amount of data at one time, the default setting is fine.

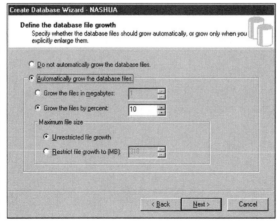

Figure 5-4:
State your
growth
information
preferences
in this
Create
Database
Wizard
dialog box.

Grow the files by percent: This option indicates to SQL Server that you want the size of the database to grow by a certain percentage, enabling a bigger chunk to be allocated each time the database gets larger. For example, suppose you set the size increase by 10 percent. If the database begins at 4MB, the next time it increases, it will enlarge by 400,000 bytes, or 10 percent in size. The next time it increases, it does so by 440,000 bytes. This is because of compounding (just like your bank statements).

Unrestricted file growth: This option, chosen by default, specifies that the file is allowed to grow until you run out of disk space.

Restrict file growth to (MB): This option specifies that the file is allowed to grow until it reaches the size that you specify in the box to the right. Because the option is very limiting, you're wise to go with the default setting instead.

8. **Name the transaction log file(s) and specify its initial size by filling in the fields and then click Next.**

   The transaction log is a file that SQL Server uses to list every change that has been made to a database within a transaction. This transaction log is how SQL Server recovers data if a transaction is not committed.

   • **File name:** By default, your file name is your database name with **_LOG** at the end. For example, **CUSTOMERORDERS_LOG** is the name of my file. You can change the file name by clicking it and typing a new name.

   • **Initial Size (MB):** By default, the initial size of each file is 1MB. You can change the size by clicking the proposed size and typing your preference.

9. **Specify whether you want to automatically grow transaction log files or explicitly enlarge them by choosing an option button (similar to the dialog box already shown in Figure 5-4); then click Next.**

   • **Do not automatically grow the transaction log files:** With this option, you can indicate that you want to configure the size of your transaction logs manually.

   • **Automatically grow the transaction log files:** By default, this option indicates to SQL Server that you do not want to manually specify the size for a transaction log as it grows, but rather have SQL Server manage growth automatically. If you choose this option, a few other options become available. These options are:

     Grow the files in megabytes: You can tell SQL Server the incremental size that you prefer for transaction log growth; 1MB is the default value. Unless you plan to add a tremendous amount of data at one time, the default setting's fine.

Grow the files by percent: This option indicates to SQL Server that you want the transaction to grow by a certain percentage, which means that a bigger chunk is allocated each time the transaction log gets larger. For example, if you choose this option and set the size increase to 10 percent, the transaction log file begins at 1MB and increases by 100,000 bytes. The next time the file increases, it does so by 110,000 bytes. Think of it as compounding — like your bank statements.

Unrestricted file growth: By default, this option specifies that the file is allowed to grow until you run out of disk space.

Restricted file growth to (MB): This option specifies that the file is allowed to grow until it reaches the size that you specify in the box to the right. The option is too limiting for practical use.

Do not automatically grow the transaction log files: This option indicates to SQL Server that you do not want SQL Server to automatically increase the size of the transaction log files automatically. You would like to configure the size of your transaction logs manually.

10. **Review the Completing the Create Database Wizard information and click the Finish button when you're satisfied with the criteria that the wizard will use to create the database (see Figure 5-5).**

    If you want to change any of the criteria that you specified in earlier steps, you can click the Back button until you reach the dialog box that you want to change.

Figure 5-5: This dialog box recaps your choices throughout the database creation process.

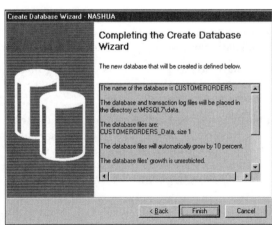

Create Database Wizard - NASHUA

Completing the Create Database Wizard

The new database that will be created is defined below.

The name of the database is CUSTOMERORDERS.

The database and transaction log files will be placed in the directory c:\MSSQL7\data.

The database files are:
CUSTOMERORDERS_Data, size 1

The database files will automatically grow by 10 percent.

The database files' growth is unrestricted.

< Back   Finish   Cancel

Relying on the SQL Server Enterprise Manager

You can use the SQL Server Enterprise Manager to create databases, as well as many other objects. To use the SQL Server Enterprise Manager for creating a database, follow these steps:

1. **Start the SQL Server Enterprise Manager by choosing Start⇨ Programs⇨Microsoft SQL Server 7.0⇨Enterprise Manager.**

2. **Expand the tree by clicking your server name, and then click Databases.**

   Notice the row of databases that appears on the right-hand part of the screen (see Figure 5-6). If you don't see a list of databases, you may have clicked on the wrong area of the tree.

 3. **Click the New Database icon on the toolbar to bring up the Database Properties dialog box.**

   You can also right-click anywhere on the right-hand side of the screen and select the New Database menu. Or you can right-click the Databases entry in the tree and select the New Database menu.

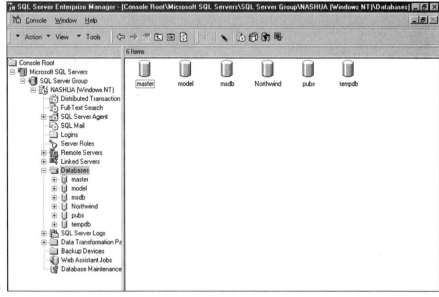

Figure 5-6: The SQL Server Enterprise Manager lists the Databases folder.

The Database Properties dialog box is used to specify properties of the new database; it consists of three tabs that enable you to type the new database's parameters and data (General, Transaction Log, and Options). The General tab shows by default.

The General tab

You can use the General tab (see Figure 5-7) to enter data that describes the properties of the database, including name, location, and size.

- ✔ **Name:** The name that you give to your database will be used each time you connect to the server. If you're going to use the database to track orders, consider calling it CUSTOMERORDERS.

- ✔ **File name:** By default, the database file name you enter will be followed by _Data.

- ✔ **Location:** You can specify where you want to store your database. The default location is in the \DATA subdirectory of wherever you installed SQL Server 7.

- ✔ **Initial Size (MB):** By default, the initial size of the database is 1MB. If you want to change the setting, click the proposed size and type a new size.

- ✔ **File group:** You can specify a file group so that all files are handled in a single set. By default, this is set to Primary. If you want to change the setting, click the File group name and select from the drop-down list of available file groups. If you want to create a new file group, simply type in the name of the group. A file group is particularly useful to allow an administrator to handle the necessary files for a database as one logical file group name.

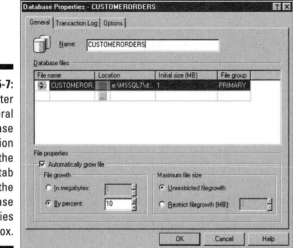

Figure 5-7: Enter general database information on the General tab of the Database Properties dialog box.

✔ **Automatically grow file:** With this check box, you can indicate to SQL Server that you do not want to manually specify the size for a database as it grows. The default option states your preference to manage file growth automatically.

✔ **In megabytes:** This option tells SQL Server that every time the size of the database needs to grow, you want it to grow in the specified incre- ments. Unless you plan to add a tremendous amount of data at one time, the 1MB default setting is fine.

✔ **By percent:** When you choose this option button, you instruct SQL Server to expand the database by a certain percentage each time it needs to grow. Every time the database gets larger, a bigger chunk is allocated. For example, if you set the increase size by 10 percent, and the database files begin at 1MB, the next increase will be by 100,000 bytes, or 10 percent. The next increase goes up by 110,000 bytes. Call it compounding — similar to your bank statements.

✔ **Unrestricted filegrowth:** Choose this option, and your file grows until you run out of disk space. This is the option chosen by default.

✔ **Restrict filegrowth (MB):** This option specifies that the file is allowed to grow until it reaches the size specified in the box to the right. It's best not to use this very limiting option.

The Transaction Log tab

The Transaction Log tab enables you to enter data that describes transac- tion properties, such as name, location, and size (see Figure 5-8).

✔ **File name:** Give your transaction log a file name. By default **_Log** is appended to the name of your transaction log.

✔ **Location:** Specify where your transaction log is to be stored. The default location is in the **\DATA** subdirectory of wherever you installed SQL Server 7. Mine is **E:\MSSQL7\DATA**.

✔ **Initial Size (MB):** Specify the initial size of the database. By default, this is 1 megabyte (MB). If you wish to change this, click the proposed size and type in the new size.

✔ **Automatically grow file:** This option indicates to SQL Server that you do not want to manually specify the size for a transaction log as it grows. You would like SQL Server to manage this automatically. This is the default option.

✔ **In megabytes:** This option indicates to SQL Server that every time the size of the transaction log needs to grow, you want it to grow in size increments specified here. One megabyte is the default value. Unless you plan to be adding a tremendous amount of data at one time, this setting is fine.

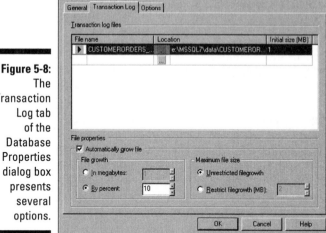

Figure 5-8:
The
Transaction
Log tab
of the
Database
Properties
dialog box
presents
several
options.

✔ **By percent:** This option indicates to SQL Server that every time the size of the transaction log needs to grow, you want it to grow by a certain percentage. This option allows for a bigger chunk to be allocated every time the database gets larger. For example, suppose you choose this option and set the size increase at 10%. If the transaction log file begins at 1MB, the next time it increases, it will increase by 100,000 bytes, or 10% in size. The next time it increases, it does so by 110,000 bytes. This is because of compounding.

✔ **Unrestricted filegrowth:** This option specifies that the file is allowed to grow until you run out of disk space. This option is chosen by default.

✔ **Restrict filegrowth (MB):** This option specifies that the file is allowed to grow until it reaches the size specified in the box to the right. This option is very limiting; you may want to avoid it.

The Options tab

You can use the Options tab to choose access rights and indicate specific database settings, as shown in Figure 5-9.

✔ **DBO Use Only:** Choose this option if you want yourself (the database owner) to be the database's only user.

✔ **Single User:** Click this box if you want one person at a time to be able to use the database.

✔ **Read Only:** Choose this option if you want the database to be read-only, which means that you can't change the database, but can use it only for reports and SELECT queries. For more information about SELECT queries, see Chapter 8.

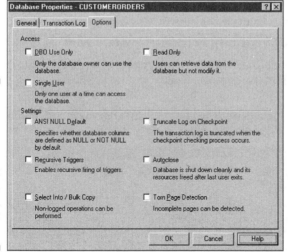

Figure 5-9:
The Options
tab of the
Database
Properties
dialog box
offers
check
boxes
galore.

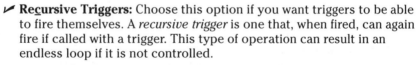

✓ **ANSI Null Default:** Choose this option if you want columns in tables to be treated as Null by default. If this option is not checked, columns in tables are treated as Not Null by default.

✓ **Recursive Triggers:** Choose this option if you want triggers to be able to fire themselves. A *recursive trigger* is one that, when fired, can again fire if called with a trigger. This type of operation can result in an endless loop if it is not controlled.

✓ **Select Into/Bulk Copy:** Click this box if you want to perform operations that will not be entered in the transaction log.

✓ **Truncate Log on Checkpoint:** Choose this option if you want the transaction log truncated every time a checkpoint operation occurs.

✓ **Autoclose:** Choose this option if you want SQL Server to automatically clean up system resources (memory, disk space, etc.) when the last user of a database exits.

✓ **Torn Page Detection:** Choose this option if you want SQL Server to automatically detect when data has not been completely written to a database. This is especially useful for detecting power outages.

Enlisting SQL Server Query Analyzer

You can use SQL Server Query Analyzer to create a new database by issuing SQL statements directly to the server. To issue the SQL statement to create a database, follow these steps:

1. **Start the SQL Server Query Analyzer by choosing Start⇨Programs⇨ Microsoft SQL Server 7.0⇨Query Analyzer.**

2. **Type the SQL statement needed to create a database.**

   To create a database through SQL, you must issue the CREATE DATABASE statement. For more information about the CREATE DATABASE statement, see Chapter 8 and follow the example below.

   As an example, a database named CUSTOMERORDERS can have a statement that looks like this:

```
CREATE DATABASE CUSTOMERORDERS
ON
(NAME = CUSTOMERORDERS_DATA,
FILENAME = "E:\MSSQL7\DATA\CUSTOMERORDERS.MDF",
SIZE = 4MB,
MAXSIZE = 100MB,
FILEGROWTH = 4MB)

LOG ON
(NAME = CUSTOMERORDERS_LOG,
FILENAME = "E:\MSSQL7\DATA\CUSTOMERORDERS.LDF",
SIZE = 1MB,
MAXSIZE = UNLIMITED)
```

This statement creates a database called CUSTOMERORDERS with an initial size of 4MB that can grow in 4MB increments up to a maximum of 100MB. Additionally, the logical name for the database is CUSTOMERORDERS_Data and is stored in a file called E:\MSSQL7\DATA\CUSTOMERORDERS.MDF.

A *logical name* is a name given to an object that you will use when you refer to that object after it is created. A logical name is different from a file name. A file name is sometimes referred to as a physical name. A *physical name* is the physical location given to an object. You generally do not refer to this physical name after the object is created. You refer to its corresponding logical name.

Also, this statement creates a transaction log with a logical name of CUSTOMERORDERS_Log. It begins with an initial size of 1MB and grows to an unlimited size. The transaction log is stored in a file named E:\MSSQL7\DATA\CUSTOMERORDERS.LDF.

You can also accept all the default values and create the database with this one line:

```
CREATE DATABASE CUSTOMERORDERS
```

Designing Tables

A table is a database object that actually stores data; a database can contain one or more tables. You can create a table with either the SQL Server Enterprise Manager or SQL, as you discover in the next sections.

Using the SQL Server Enterprise Manager

You can use the SQL Server Enterprise Manager to create and define tables with specified columns and column attributes. Here's how to accomplish this magic:

1. **To start the SQL Server Enterprise Manager, choose Start⇨ Programs⇨Microsoft SQL Server 7.0⇨Enterprise Manager.**

2. **Click the Tables folder in the Databases folder.**

   Notice the list of tables on the right-hand side of the screen. If you just created the database, the only tables that you see are system tables that are automatically created and maintained by SQL Server, as shown in Figure 5-10.

3. **Choose New Table from the Action drop-down menu.**

   Alternatively, you can right-click anywhere on the right-hand side of the screen or right-click the Tables folder, and then click New Table to bring up the Choose Table dialog box.

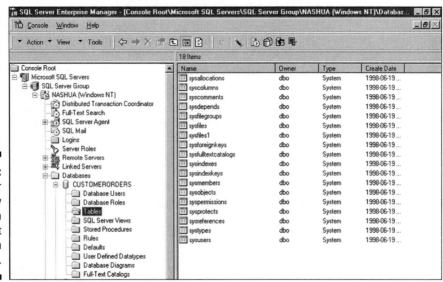

Figure 5-10: SQL Server automatically creates an assortment of system tables.

4. Type the name of your new table in the Choose Name dialog box, and then click OK.

The Design Table screen appears (shown in Figure 5-11), allowing you to configure the properties of your new table. The screen is made up of rows and columns (a table unto itself). Now follow me on this one. Every row that you see in the Design Table screen represents a column in your new table. Every column in the Design Table screen represents attributes of that column in your new table.

Figure 5-11: Configure your table's properties with the Design Table screen.

Column Name	Datatype	Length	Precision	Scale	Allow Nulls	Default Value	Identity	Identity Seed	Identity Increment	Is RowGuid
[Customer ID]	numeric	9	18	0			✓	1001	1	
[Last Name]	varchar	50	0	0	✓					
[First Name]	varchar	30	0	0	✓					
[Middle Initial]	char	1	0	0	✓					
[Company Name]	varchar	30	0	0	✓					
[Address 1]	varchar	30	0	0	✓					
[Address 2]	varchar	30	0	0	✓					
City	varchar	30	0	0	✓					
State	char	2	0	0	✓					
Zip	char	5	0	0	✓					
Phone	char	10	0	0	✓					
Fax	char	10	0	0	✓					

5. Fill in the following fields, according to your data model.

To refresh your understanding of data model design, you can review the relational data model discussion in Chapter 4.

- **Column Name:** All the fields in this row are the names of the columns in the new table. If you have one column in your new table, there will be one row in this dialog box. Likewise, if you have five columns in your new table, there will be five rows in this dialog box. Well . . . you get the picture.

- **Datatype:** This column specifies the type of data that will appear in your new table. SQL Server has 24 different datatypes available. For a description of these datatypes, see Chapter 4. You do not have to physically type the datatype. You select it from a drop-down list of available datatypes. Char is the datatype chosen by default.

- **Length:** This column specifies the length of data for the datatype chosen. You can change this value only for a datatype of binary, varbinary, char, or varchar.

- **Precision:** This column indicated the maximum number of digits used for the chosen datatype. By default, this value is zero, except for decimal and numeric datatypes, whose Precision is 18.

- **Scale:** Here, you find the number of decimal places to the right of the decimal. By default, this value is zero.

- **Allow Nulls:** Placing a check in this box enables you to omit null values when you insert data into the table.

- **Default Value:** If you want to use a default value (a value that is entered automatically if one is not supplied), enter that value in this field.

- **Identity:** You can check this box if you want the column of data to be an identity column. An *identity* column is one whose value is automatically increased by one every time a row is added. An identity column is often used as part of a primary key. A *primary key* is a term used to describe the columns whose values uniquely identify a row in a table. An identity column is useful when each value needs to be unique, such as with a Customer ID column. For more information about primary keys, refer to Chapter 4.

- **Identity Seed:** A check in the Identity box enables you to alter the number that SQL Server uses as its start value. By default, a seed value of 1 is used. This means that when the first record is inserted into the new table, a value of 1 appears in this column. Every row after is incremented by 1. Change this seed value if you want the number to begin at any value other than 1.

- **Identity Increment:** If you place a check in the Identity box, you can alter the number that SQL Server uses when it increments the value in the Identity column. The default increment value is 1. This means that when the second and subsequent records are inserted into the new table, the value entered will be the prior value plus the increment value placed in this field.

- **Is RowGuid:** Place a check in this box if you want this column to be a row global unique identifier. Only one column in a table can be identified as a global unique identifier column.

 6. **Click the Save icon on the toolbar after you finish filling in rows for every column that you want to create in your new table.**

You must carefully consider the datatype and length of your columns. For example, if you're going to store character data, decide whether you need a char or varchar datatype. A char datatype allocates the storage for the number of characters specified by length. A varchar dynamically allocates storage. As an example, you don't want to make a First Name column a char datatype because it's not always going to be the same size. On the other hand, a State column will always be two characters (if you're abbreviating). Therefore, it makes sense to use the char datatype.

Turning to the SQL Server Query Analyzer

With the SQL Server Query Analyzer, you can issue SQL statements directly to the server to create a new table. Here's how to issue the SQL statement to create a table:

1. **Choose Start⇨Programs⇨Microsoft SQL Server 7.0⇨Query Analyzer.**

2. **Type the SQL needed to create a database.**

   To create a table through SQL, you must issue a CREATE TABLE statement. For a review of the CREATE TABLE statement, see Chapter 8.

   New tables require the following basic information: number of columns in the table, their datatypes, and any properties for the columns. These properties can include determination of whether the column allows null values, if the column is an identity column, and so on.

   To create a table named CUSTOMER in the CUSTOMERORDERS database, you issue this statement:

   ```
   CREATE TABLE CUSTOMER
   ([Customer ID] numeric IDENTITY (1001,1),
   [Last Name] varchar (30) NULL,
   [First Name] varchar (30) NULL,
   [Middle Initial] char (1) NULL,
   [Company Name] varchar (30) NULL,
   [Address 1] varchar (30) NULL,
   [Address 2] varchar (30) NULL,
   [City] varchar (30) NULL,
   [State] char(2) NULL,
   [Zip] char (5) NULL,
   [Phone] char (10) NULL,
   [Fax] char (10) NULL)
   ```

Square brackets ([ ]) around column names indicate the entire column name to SQL Server — significant when you use spaces in the column name. Without the brackets, SQL Server would have a bit of trouble knowing where the column begins and ends. You don't need square brackets for column names that don't use spaces, but they can't do any damage either. I use brackets for consistency. Many software developers and database administrators advise against using spaces in column names (or any other database object). The main reason for this is that some SQL Server add-on tools might have a problem with spaces in the object names, even though SQL Server 7.0 supports them.

This SQL statement is all that's required to create the table, but it doesn't specify anything about primary keys. In that same table, the Customer ID column is the primary key. Usually, any column that's defined as an Identity column is the primary key (or at least part of the primary key). For more information about primary keys, refer to Chapter 4.

You can define the primary key at the same time you issue the CREATE TABLE statement. The same statement example can create a primary key like this:

```
CREATE TABLE CUSTOMER
([Customer ID] numeric IDENTITY (1001,1) PRIMARY KEY,
[Last Name] varchar (30) NULL,
[First Name] varchar (30) NULL,
[Middle Initial] char (1) NULL,
[Company Name] varchar (30) NULL,
[Address 1] varchar (30) NULL,
[Address 2] varchar (30) NULL,
[City] varchar (30) NULL,
[State] char(2) NULL,
[Zip] char (5) NULL,
[Phone] char (10) NULL,
[Fax] char (10) NULL)
```

Falling Back on Default Values

If you have a column in a table that requires a value (not null) and one is not specified in a SQL query, what happens? Does your query fail? What if it's a big, complex query and you don't want to recreate it? The answer is, "Yes, the query will fail." That is, unless you create a default.

A *default* is a way to indicate to SQL Server 7 what value to use for a column in a table when the value is omitted from a SQL statement. Having a default ensures that a value is always inserted or updated into a table.

The steps for creating a default in SQL Server 7 are to create the default and then bind the default to one or more columns in a table to put the default in effect. You can create a default in one of two ways. You can use the SQL Server Enterprise Manager or SQL. I outline both ways in the next few pages.

You can also specify a default value when you create a table.

DEFAULTing with the SQL Server Enterprise Manager

To use the SQL Server Enterprise Manager to create a default, follow these steps:

1. **Start the SQL Server Enterprise Manager by choosing Start⇨ Programs⇨Microsoft SQL Server 7.0⇨Enterprise Manager from the Windows menu.**

2. **Expand the tree so that you can see the Defaults entry within the desired database under the Databases entry.**

   For more information about expanding the tree, see Chapter 1.

3. **Highlight the Defaults entry by clicking Defaults.**

   When you highlight the Defaults entry, the list of defaults appears on the right-hand part of the screen. If this is your first time to create a default, the right-hand part of the screen is blank.

4. **Choose Action⇨New Default to bring up the Default Properties dialog box.**

   Alternatively, you can use the mouse to right-click anywhere on the right-hand part of the screen and choose the New Default menu. Also, you can right-click the Defaults entry in the tree and choose the New Default menu. Whatever method you choose to create a new default, each brings up a dialog box in which you can specify the properties of your new default (see Figure 5-12).

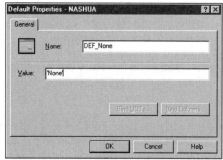

Figure 5-12: The Default Properties dialog box with a default I've entered.

To use the Default Properties dialog box, you simply fill in the fields.

- **Name:** Give your default a name.

  You should use a name that is germane to the purpose of your default. For example, if your default specifies to use a value of "None," you could use the name **DEF_None**.

- **Value:** Specify the value for your default.

  Because the value you enter here must be a string literal, you must enclose your value inside *ticks* (single quote marks). A *string literal* is a series of characters that is to be used literally. That is, exactly as you see it (without the quote marks). It will not be substituted or interpreted in any way by SQL Server. An example would be me saying, "Hello". It means the same as "Hi", but I did not say, "Hi". My string literal is "Hello".

- **Bind UDTs:** Click this button to specify how to bind your default to a user-defined type.

- **Bind Columns:** Click this button to specify how to bind your default to one or more columns in a table.

5. **Click the OK button to create your default.**

Maintaining control over defaults with SQL

You can use the SQL Server Query Analyzer to issue SQL statements directly to the server to create a new default and to bind that default to a column in a database. To issue the SQL statement to create a default, follow these steps:

1. **Start the SQL Server Query Analyzer by choosing Start⇨Programs⇨ Microsoft SQL Server 7.0⇨Query Analyzer.**

2. **Type the SQL needed to create a default.**

   You create a view through SQL by issuing the CREATE DEFAULT statement. For more information about the CREATE DEFAULT statement, see Chapter 8.

   To create a default named **DEF_None** that specifies a default value of "none," for example, you issue a statement like this:

   ```
   CREATE DEFAULT DEF_None
   AS
   "None"
   ```

   Everything after the AS clause is the actual default. A default is a string literal, but you can enclose it in either double or single quote marks (ticks). This string literal corresponds to the text that you enter in the Value field if you use the SQL Server Enterprise Manager to create your default (see Step 4 in the preceding section).

3. **Bind the default to a column in a table.**

It would be nice if a clause in the CREATE DEFAULT statement allowed you to bind the default to a column, but no such luck. You need to use the sp_bindefault system stored procedure to bind a default to a column. For more information about system stored procedures, see Chapter 7.

The system procedure is not called *sp_binddefault,* as if the two words *bind* and *default* were simply joined. Microsoft chose to leave one of the ds out.

The sp_bindefault system stored procedure follows this general syntax:

```
sp_bindefault {'default'} [, 'object_name' [,
    futureonly_flag]
```

where *default* is the name of the default you created with the CREATE DEFAULT statement and *object_name* is the name of the object to bind the default to. This object can be either a column, in the form of *table.column,* or a user-defined type. *Futureonly_flag* is a flag that can contain only one value, called futureonly. If this flag is set, then the default is only bound to columns in the user-defined type that do not already have a default bound to them.

Therefore, to bind the DEF_None default to the Address column in the EMPLOYEES table, use this statement:

```
sp_bindefault 'DEF_None','EMPLOYEES.Address'
```

Deleting Database Objects

Any of the database objects discussed in this chapter can be deleted, or dropped, by using the DROP SQL keyword.

The SQL Server Query Analyzer enables you to issue SQL statements directly to the server to drop a database object. To issue the SQL statement to delete an index, follow these steps:

1. **Choose Start⇨Programs⇨Microsoft SQL Server 7.0⇨Query Analyzer from the Windows menu to start the SQL Server Query Analyzer.**

2. **Type the SQL needed to drop the database object.**

Dropping a database object follows this basic format:

```
DROP ObjectType [Database.]Object
```

- ObjectType is the type of object, either database, table, or index.

- Database is the name of the database in which the object that you're dropping resides.

- Object is what you named the object when the object was initially created.

Therefore, if you want to drop the table CUSTOMER, you issue this statement:

```
DROP TABLE CUSTOMERORDERS.CUSTOMER
```

If you want to drop the index Index1 on the CUSTOMER table, you issue this statement:

```
DROP INDEX CUSTOMER.Index1
```

If you want to drop the database named CUSTOMERORDERS database, you issue this statement:

```
DROP DATABASE CUSTOMERORDERS
```

Chapter 6

Creating Advanced SQL Server Objects

- -

In This Chapter

▶ Establishing house rules for Microsoft SQL Server 7

▶ Making your queries fast with indexes

▶ Teaching SQL Server 7 to react to triggers

- -

*I*n Chapter 5, I show you how to create basic objects in Microsoft SQL Server 7. These objects are used in almost every SQL Server database that you create. In this chapter, I expand on the basic objects in Chapter 5 and show you more advanced objects that are often used in a well-designed database.

Because SQL Server 7 gives you multiple ways to create these advanced objects, I show all those methods to you throughout this chapter, as I do in Chapter 5.

Laying Down the Law: Setting Up Rules in SQL Server 7

A *rule* is a way to indicate to SQL Server 7 what values are valid for the insertion or updating of data. The following list shows some examples of rules:

- ✔ Allow all values from a to z, but in lowercase only.
- ✔ Allow only values from the CUSTOMER_ID column of the CUSTOMER table.
- ✔ Social Security numbers must be in the **###-##-####** format.
- ✔ Values must be a multiple of 5.
- ✔ Values must be greater than 100.

Another way to create a "rule" is to use a special type of constraint, called a CHECK constraint. CHECK constraints can apply multiple rules to a column, while only one rule can be applied to a column. CHECK constraints are specified as part of the CREATE TABLE statement.

However, these rules aren't in a form that SQL Server 7 can understand. You can't establish these rules just by saying them out loud to your computer, the way you set rules for your kids or your dogs (although my dogs don't understand rules no matter what I do). You have to jump through a few hoops to get SQL Server 7 to know the rules.

The steps for creating a rule in SQL Server 7 are to create the rule and then bind the rule to one or more columns in a table in order to put the rule in effect. You can create a rule in one of two ways. You can use the SQL Server Enterprise Manager or simply use SQL. I outline both ways in the next few pages.

When you create rules, you use a variable to serve as a placeholder for the actual value of a column. It's important to note that you can't use more than one variable in a rule because only one value at a time can be substituted when SQL Server tests the rule. You'll see what I mean later in this chapter.

Creating rules with SQL Server Enterprise Manager

To use the SQL Server Enterprise Manager to create a rule, follow these steps:

1. **Start the SQL Server Enterprise Manager by choosing Start➪Programs➪Microsoft SQL Server 7.0➪Enterprise Manager.**

2. **Expand the tree so that you can see the Rules entry within the desired database under the Databases entry.**

   For more information about expanding the tree, see Chapter 1.

3. **Highlight the Rules entry by clicking Rules.**

   When you highlight the Rules entry, notice the list of rules that appears on the right-hand part of the screen (see Figure 6-1). If this is your first time to create a rule, the right-hand part of the screen is blank.

4. **Choose Action➪New Rule to bring up the Rule Properties dialog box.**

   Alternatively, you can use the mouse to right-click anywhere on the right-hand part of the screen and choose the New Rule menu. Also, you can right-click the Rules entry in the tree and select the New Rule menu.

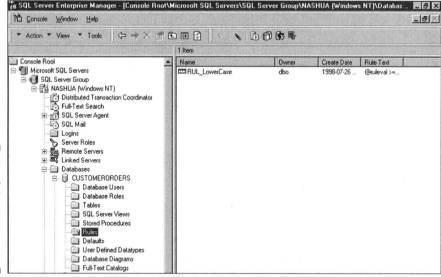

Figure 6-1:
The SQL
Server
Enterprise
Manager,
showing the
Rules entry.

Whatever method you choose to create a new rule, the Rule Properties dialog box appears, allowing you to specify the properties of your new rule (see Figure 6-2).

To use the Rule Properties dialog box, you simply fill in the fields.

- **Name:** Give your rule a name in the Name field.

  You should use a name that is germane to the purpose of your rule. For example, if your rule specifies that the only values allowed are lowercase letters, you could use the name **RUL_LowerCase**.

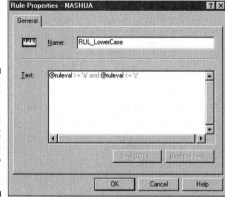

Figure 6-2:
The Rule
Properties
dialog box
with a rule
I've already
entered.

- **Text:** Specify your rule.

  Any valid SQL WHERE clause is valid here. For more information about SQL or a WHERE clause, see Chapter 8.

  For your rule that allows only lowercase letters, the following text is valid:

  ```
  @ruleval >= "a" and @ruleval <= "z"
  ```

Notice the @ruleval variable. All SQL Server variables are preceded by the @ sign. Because you have no value to test at the time you create the rule, you insert a variable in its place. You can name this variable anything you want, except @value. The @value variable name is reserved, so I use @ruleval. SQL Server substitutes the value that is attempting to be inserted or updated into the column (after you bind it) and substitutes that value for @ruleval.

- **Bind UDTs:** Click this button to bind your rule to a user-defined type.

- **Bind Columns:** Click this button to specify how to bind your rule to one or more columns in a table.

5. **Click the OK button to create your rule.**

Creating rules with SQL

You can use the SQL Server Query Analyzer to issue SQL statements directly to the server to create a new rule and to bind that rule to a column in a database. Using SQL to create the rule can be advantageous in a case where you have a friend who wants to create a rule but doesn't know how (because he or she doesn't have this wonderful book). You could write the rule, send it, and the friend can execute the SQL statement.

And another reason for you to know how to create rules with SQL: If you want to create a script that recreates all your database objects (in case of a disaster), this SQL will go into the script.

To issue the SQL statement to create a rule, follow these steps:

1. **Start the SQL Server Query Analyzer by choosing Start⇨ Programs⇨Microsoft SQL Server 7.0⇨Query Analyzer.**

2. **Type the SQL needed to create a rule.**

   You create a view through SQL by issuing the CREATE RULE statement. For more information about the CREATE RULE statement, see Chapter 8.

To create a rule named RUL_LowerCase that allows only lowercase letters in values, you type a statement like this:

```
CREATE RULE RUL_LowerCase
AS
@ruleval >= 'a' and @ruleval <= 'z'
```

Everything after the AS clause is the actual rule. This rule corresponds to the text that you type in the Text field if you use the SQL Server Enterprise Manager to create your rule (see the preceding section).

3. **Bind the rule to a column in a table.**

It would be nice if a clause in the CREATE RULE statement allowed you to bind the rule to a column. However, things are not always a one-step process, and this is one of those times. You need to use the sp_bindrule system stored procedure to bind a rule to a column. For more information about system stored procedures, see Chapter 7.

The sp_bindrule system stored procedure follows this general syntax:

```
sp_bindrule {'rule'} [, 'object_name' [,
        futureonly_flag]
```

where *rule* is the name of the rule you created with the CREATE RULE statement and *object_name* is the name of the object to bind the rule to. This object can be either a column, in the form of *table.column,* or a user-defined type. *Futureonly_flag* is a flag that can contain only one value, and that value is futureonly. If this flag is set, the rule is only bound to columns in the user-defined type that do not already have a rule bound to them.

To bind the RUL_LowerCase rule to the Employee ID column in the EMPLOYEES table, use this statement:

```
sp_bindrule 'RUL_LowerCase','EMPLOYEES.[Employee ID]'
```

Creating Indexes

An index is a database object that helps speed queries by either instructing SQL Server to physically order records in a table or providing an execution path so that SQL Server (actually the optimizer) knows how to run the query.

You can create an index by using either the Create Index Wizard or SQL in the SQL Server Query Analyzer. The next sections outline both methods.

You must be the table owner to create an index on that table.

Discovering the Create Index Wizard

SQL Server 7 features many handy utilities, including the Create Index Wizard. This wizard guides you through a series of steps, prompting you for input along the way (see Appendix A for a flowchart of the steps in the Create Index Wizard). To create a database using the Create Index Wizard, follow these steps:

1. **Start the SQL Server Enterprise Manager by choosing Start➪Programs➪Microsoft SQL Server 7.0➪Enterprise Manager.**

2. **Expand the tree so that you see the name of your server.**

   For more information about expanding the tree, see Chapter 1.

3. **Choose Tools➪Wizards.**

   The Select Wizard dialog box appears.

4. **Click Create Index Wizard (under the Database category), and then click OK to start the Create Index Wizard.**

   The Welcome dialog box sums up everything the wizard can do for you (select the database and the table that you want to index, view information about current indexes, and select one or more columns to include in the index). When you're properly impressed, click Next — the wizard presents a dialog box that requires entry of a database and a table name, as shown in Figure 6-3.

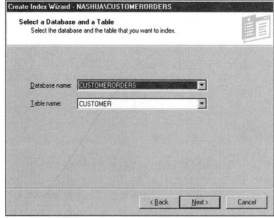

Figure 6-3:
The Create
Index
Wizard asks
you for
database
and table
names.

5. **Specify the database and table name by filling in the following fields, and then click Next:**

   • **Database name:** Select a database from the drop-down list of existing databases.

- **Table name:** From the drop-down list, select a table in which you want to create an index. The tables presented are those that belong to the name selected in the Database field.

6. **Select all the column(s) that you want to include in the index by clicking the check box in the Include in Index column to communicate your intent to the wizard, as shown in Figure 6-4; then click Next.**

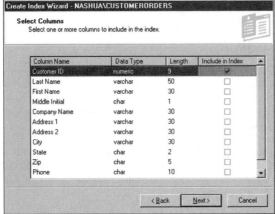

Figure 6-4:
You can choose one, two, or several columns for your index.

7. **In the dialog box that appears (see Figure 6-5), specify the index options that you prefer by filling in the following fields, and then click Next.**

- **Make this a clustered index:** Click this box if you want data to be stored in the column order you specified in Step 6. The order that the data is stored is from top to bottom, as chosen in Step 6. For more information on clustered indexes, see Chapter 4.

- **Make this a unique index:** Check this box if you want the columns specified in the earlier step to be the primary key. For more information about primary keys, refer to Chapter 4.

- **Optimal:** This default option indicates to SQL Server that you prefer automatic configuration of page size for indexes.

- **Fixed:** This option indicates to SQL Server that you want to manually identify index page fullness before creating a new page. I don't recommended choosing this option for beginners. For you beginners, it's not that I don't trust you — I just don't want you to waste disk space. If you specify a value that is too low, your index pages will not be very full and will take up more space.

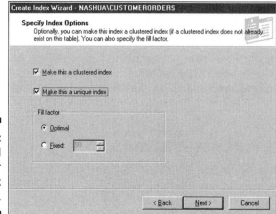

Figure 6-5:
Step up and
specify your
index
options.

8. **Now change or accept the index name and column order through the following options (shown in Figure 6-6):**

   • **Index name:** By default, an index name is already entered. You can replace this name with one of your choosing, although a change isn't likely to be beneficial because you don't use the index name on a daily basis.

   • **Columns Included:** The columns that you specified in Step 6 are listed in this box. If you want to change the order of the columns, click the column name (as shown in Figure 6-6), and then click the Move Up or Move Down buttons to position the column name where you want it.

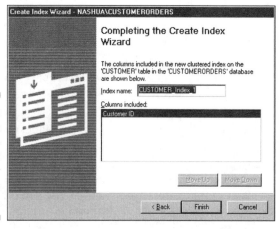

Figure 6-6:
You can
complete
the creation
of your
index in this
dialog box.

If you want to change any of the criteria that you specified in earlier steps, click the Back button until you reach the desired dialog box. When you're satisfied with your creation, click Finish. Voilà — your index awaits!

Using SQL Server Query Analyzer

With the SQL Server Query Analyzer, you can issue SQL statements directly to the server to create an index without using a wizard. Here's how it works:

1. **To Start the SQL Server Query Analyzer, choose Start➪Programs➪ Microsoft SQL Server 7.0➪Query Analyzer.**

2. **Type the SQL needed to create an index.**

   Creating an index through SQL requires issuing the CREATE INDEX statement — and Chapter 8 is a resource for review of the CREATE INDEX statement.

   When you create an index, you must specify the index name, the table that contains the index, and the columns that make up the index. As an example, suppose you want to create a basic index on the Customer ID column of the CUSTOMER table, and you want to call the index, Index1. Your statement would look like this:

```
CREATE INDEX Index1 ON CUSTOMER ([Customer ID])
```

   To create a unique clustered index using this same criteria, you would issue this statement:

```
CREATE UNIQUE CLUSTERED INDEX Index1 ON CUSTOMER
        ([Customer ID])
```

   For more information on clustered indexes, see Chapter 4.

The Safe Way to Pull the Trigger

A *trigger* is a very powerful feature that allows SQL Statements to execute when a certain event happens. These events are

✔ Insert

✔ Update

✔ Delete

Using a trigger is a great way to enforce data integrity because everything happens automatically. A trigger is also a great way to have any process occur automatically when specific conditions exist. For example, the HR Manager can be notified by e-mail when a new employee's salary is entered for more than $100,000 annually.

You can create a trigger in one of two ways. You can use the SQL Server Enterprise Manager or SQL. I outline both ways in the next few pages.

Creating triggers with the SQL Server Enterprise Manager

To use the SQL Server Enterprise Manager to create a trigger, follow these steps:

1. **Start the SQL Server Enterprise Manager by choosing Start▷Programs▷Microsoft SQL Server 7▷Enterprise Manager.**

2. **Expand the tree so that you can see the Tables entry within the desired database under the Databases entry.**

   For more information about expanding the tree, see Chapter 1.

3. **Highlight the Tables entry by clicking on Tables.**

   When you highlight the SQL Server Tables entry, notice the list of tables that appears in the right-hand part of the screen (see Figure 6-7).

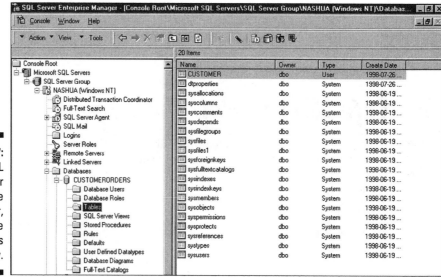

Figure 6-7: The SQL Server Enterprise Manager, showing the Tables entry.

4. **Choose Action⇨Task⇨Manage Triggers to bring up the Trigger Properties dialog box.**

   The Trigger Properties dialog box appears (see Figure 6-8).

5. **Type the Trigger SQL in the Text field.**

   Type in the SQL necessary to create your trigger. For more information about the SQL needed to create a trigger, see the next section.

6. **Check the syntax of your SQL by clicking the Check Syntax button.**

7. **Click the OK button to create the trigger.**

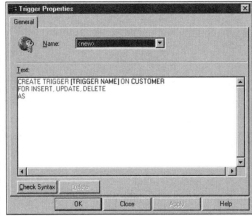

Figure 6-8:
The Trigger
Properties
dialog box,
showing an
automatic
text
template for
the trigger.

Creating triggers with SQL

You can use the SQL Server Query Analyzer to issue SQL statements directly to the server to create a trigger. Almost all SQL statements can be used within a trigger. The exceptions are any statements that affect database objects. The following list shows the SQL statements that are *not* allowed within a trigger:

ALTER DATABASE
ALTER PROCEDURE
ALTER TABLE
ALTER TRIGGER
ALTER VIEW
CREATE DATABASE
CREATE DEFAULT
CREATE INDEX
CREATE PROCEDURE

CREATE RULE

CREATE SCHEMA

CREATE TABLE

CREATE TRIGGER

CREATE VIEW

DENY

DISK INIT

DISK RESIZE

DROP DATABASE

DROP DEFAULT

DROP INDEX

DROP PROCEDURE

DROP RULE

DROP TABLE

DROP TRIGGER

DROP VIEW GRANT

LOAD DATABASE

LOAD LOG

RESTORE DATABASE

RESTORE LOG

REVOKE

RECONFIGURE

SELECT INTO

TRUNCATE TABLE

UPDATE STATISTICS

To issue the SQL statement to create a trigger, follow these steps:

1. **Start the SQL Server Query Analyzer by choosing Start⇨Programs⇨ Microsoft SQL Server 7⇨Query Analyzer.**

2. **Type the SQL needed to create the trigger.**

   Guess what statement you use to create a trigger. As you may expect, it's the CREATE TRIGGER statement. For more information about the CREATE TRIGGER statement, see Chapter 8.

Before you can construct your trigger, you need to break the trigger into logical questions, like these:

✔ What type of trigger will you use?

✔ What are the conditions of the trigger?

✔ What are the action(s) of the trigger?

✔ How will you execute the action(s) of the trigger?

Consider the scenario that I mention earlier: Suppose that you want to create a trigger to notify automatically the HR Manager when a salary entered for a new employee is greater than $100,000. Here's how you answer the preceding questions:

✔ I'll use an **INSERT** trigger.

✔ The condition of the trigger is for the **Salary** column in the **EMPLOYEES** table to exceed 100,000.

✔ The action of the trigger is to e-mail tmann@vbasic.com, the HR Manager.

✔ I'll execute the trigger action by using the **xp_sendmail** extended stored procedure.

Now, use the answers to the questions and apply the CREATE TRIGGER SQL statement.

```
 1: CREATE TRIGGER TRG_NotifySalary
 2: ON EMPLOYEES
 3: FOR INSERT,UPDATE
 4: AS
 5:
 6: declare @tempsalary money
 7: declare @tempemployee varchar(30)
 8: declare @tempstring varchar(50)
 9:
10: IF UPDATE (Salary)
11: BEGIN
12:     select @tempsalary = (select Salary FROM Inserted)
13:     if @tempsalary > 100000
14:     BEGIN
15:     select @tempemployee = (select name FROM Inserted)
16:     select @tempstring = "Salary for " + @tempemployee
            + " Exceeds $100,000"
17:     exec master.dbo.xp_sendmail
            'tmann@vbasic.com',@tempstring
18:     END
19: END
```

The preceding statement is quite complicated, so I'm going to explain what it does. This statement follows the CREATE TRIGGER syntax:

Line 1 names the trigger **TRG_NotifySalary**.

Line 2 indicates that the table in which the trigger is created is called **EMPLOYEES**.

Line 3 specifies that the trigger will fire when data is either inserted or updated.

Line 4 indicates that every statement after the one in Line 4 defines the actions of the trigger.

Lines 6, 7, and 8 declare variables that are used later in the trigger.

Line 10 is an **IF** structure that executes the code within the structure only if a value is inserted or updated into the **Salary** column.

Line 11 starts the code block for the condition of the **Salary** column being updated with a value.

Line 12 inserts a value into the **@tempsalary** variable. This value is based on a small query from the Inserted virtual table. SQL Server maintains this table automatically and holds the values that are inserted into the table. The **Salary** value that has been inserted (from the Inserted table) is assigned to the **@tempsalary** variable.

Line 13 tests to see whether the value inserted into the table is greater than 100,000. If it is, the code block between Lines 14 and 18 are executed.

Line 14 marks the beginning of this code block. Line 18 marks the end of this code block.

Line 15 assigns the name of the employee that is inserted to the **@tempemployee** variable. The reason for this variable is so that a string can be built in Line 16.

Line 16 builds a string and assigns it to the **@tempstring** variable. This string is then used in Line 17.

Line 17 executes an extended stored procedure that sends a mail message. Notice that in this line, the **xp_sendmail** command is preceded by **master.dbo**. This is because the **xp_sendmail** extended procedure exists in the **master** database, not the **Strategic Innovations Consulting** database. The mail message that is sent is the string that was built in Line 16. Line 19 marks the end of the first code block.

Every time a value is inserted or updated into the EMPLOYEES table, this trigger is automatically run. That's the *beauty* of triggers. You do nothing. Everything happens automatically.

Chapter 7

Fun with Stored Procedures

● ●

In This Chapter

▶ Taking advantage of system procedures

▶ Thinking outside the box with extended procedures

▶ Unleashing your creative side with user-defined procedures

● ●

*H*ave you ever created a function in a programming language? If you have, stored procedures are very similar. A *stored procedure* is a package of SQL code that is compiled and stored within SQL Server as a single module. This module can then be called up and executed easily. Once you create the stored procedure, you no longer have to worry about the SQL that made up the procedure, unless it needs modification.

Stored procedures are classified in three different ways, some of which you can create, and some you can't. The classifications are:

✔ System Procedures (Execute Only)

✔ Extended Procedures (Create and Execute)

✔ User-Defined Procedures (Create and Execute)

Throughout this chapter, I show you how to create and use stored procedures. Let the fun begin. . . .

System Procedures

A system procedure is a stored procedure that Microsoft created and included into Microsoft SQL Server 7 to provide administrative and informational tasks. To find out certain system information, you ordinarily need to know which tables Microsoft stores the data in. With a system procedure, you don't have to know the tables. You simply call the system procedure from the SQL Server Query Analyzer.

One convention to be aware of is that a system procedure always begins with the prefix **sp**, followed by an underscore character. Therefore, if you see a procedure named **sp_help**, you know that it's a system procedure provided by Microsoft and not a procedure your coworker created.

System procedures are automatically included when you install SQL Server. You don't have to purchase anything or install anything separately. What a deal!

Discovering available system procedures

In earlier versions of Microsoft SQL Server, you had to query system tables to find out what system procedures were available. Microsoft makes it easy to find this out in version 7.0. To know what system procedures are available, follow these steps:

1. **Choose Start⇨Programs⇨Microsoft SQL Server 7.0⇨Enterprise Manager to start the SQL Server Enterprise Manager.**

2. **Expand the tree so that you see the Stored Procedures entry within the desired database under the Databases entry.**

   For more information about expanding the tree, see Chapter 1.

3. **Select the Stored Procedures entry by clicking.**

   After selecting the Stored Procedures entry, notice the list of stored procedures on the right-hand part of the screen (see Figure 7-1). System procedures are always located in the master database.

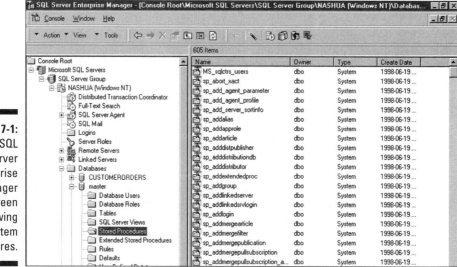

Figure 7-1: The SQL Server Enterprise Manager screen showing system procedures.

Viewing the SQL for a system procedure

All stored procedures, including system procedures, are made up of SQL. You may often like to view the SQL to understand or edit how a stored procedure works. For more information about SQL, see Chapter 8. To view the SQL for a system procedure, follow these few steps:

1. **Select the system procedure in the right-hand pane of the SQL Server Enterprise Manager.**

2. **Double-click the system procedure to view.**

   For example, double-click sp_addalias, which brings up the Stored Procedure Properties dialog box (see Figure 7-2). These properties not only show the SQL for the system procedure, but also allow you to click Permissions to view the security settings for the system procedure.

Figure 7-2:
The Stored Procedure Properties dialog box, showing the sp_addalias system procedure.

Executing a system procedure

Execute a system procedure as though you were executing any SQL command by using the SQL Server Query Analyzer (see Chapter 1). To execute a system procedure, follow these steps:

1. **Choose Start➪Programs➪Microsoft SQL Server 7.0➪Query Analyzer to start the SQL Server Query Analyzer.**

   You're then prompted to log into SQL Server. Type your ID and password in the Login Name and Password boxes.

2. Type your query.

A query can consist of multiple statements or a single statement containing the name of a system procedure. For example, type **sp_helpdb**. Choose the Query⇨Execute With Grid menu option to execute the query. This sp_helpdb is a system procedure that returns information about the database you specify. If you don't specify a database, information about all databases is returned (see Figure 7-3).

Extended Procedures

An extended procedure is similar to a system procedure or a user-defined stored procedure, except that the procedure is not stored in SQL Server, but rather in a DLL or some other external file or process. Extended procedures greatly expand the capabilities of SQL Server 7. An example of an extended procedure is an interface with SQL Server from your e-mail system.

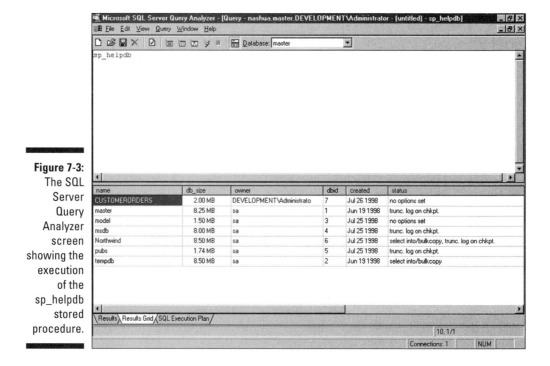

Figure 7-3:
The SQL Server Query Analyzer screen showing the execution of the sp_helpdb stored procedure.

A convention to be aware of is that an extended procedure usually begins with the prefix **xp**, followed by an underscore character. Therefore, if you see a procedure named xp_fileexist, you know this is an extended procedure. However, with every rule there are exceptions. Some extended procedures begin with the prefix **sp**, followed by an underscore character.

Unveiling available extended procedures

In earlier versions of Microsoft SQL Server, you had to query system tables to find out what extended procedures were available. Microsoft makes it easy to find this out in version 7.0. To find out what extended procedures are available, follow these steps:

1. **Choose Start⇨ Programs⇨Microsoft SQL Server 7.0⇨Enterprise Manager to start the SQL Server Enterprise Manager.**

2. **Expand the tree so that you see the Extended Stored Procedures entry within the master database under the Databases entry.**

   For more information about expanding the tree, see Chapter 1.

3. **Select the Extended Stored Procedures entry by clicking.**

   After selecting the Extended Stored Procedures entry, notice the list of stored procedures on the right-hand part of the screen (see Figure 7-4). Extended procedures are always located in the master database.

Figure 7-4: The SQL Server Enterprise Manager screen showing extended procedures.

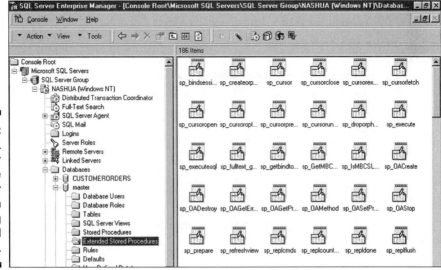

Viewing the properties for an extended procedure

All extended procedures have properties that list the procedure name and path of the library (DLL) when the procedure name is stored. *DLL* stands for Dynamically Linked Library. Windows is based on these types of libraries. Within these libraries, there are one or more functions that your extended stored procedures can call to achieve some purpose. Such a purpose could be something like logging someone off of your network (not mischievously, but for administrative reasons). This type of functionality is not built into SQL Server 7, so your extended procedures must call external functions in DLLs.

You probably want to view properties for extended stored procedures so that you can see what the path is for the DLL library. To view the properties for an extended procedure, follow these few steps:

1. **Select the extended procedure in the right-hand pane of the SQL Server Enterprise Manager.**

   See the section, "Unveiling available extended procedures," earlier in this chapter to see how to select the extended procedure.

2. **Double-click the extended procedure to view it.**

   For example, double-click xp_cmdshell, which brings up the Extended Stored Procedure Properties dialog box (see Figure 7-5). These properties not only show the properties for the extended procedure, but also enable you to click Permissions to view the security settings for the extended procedure.

Figure 7-5:
The
Extended
Stored
Procedure
Properties
dialog box,
showing the
xp_cmdshell
extended
procedure.

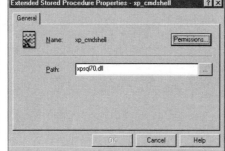

Executing an extended procedure

Execute an extended procedure as though you were executing any SQL command, by using the SQL Server Query Analyzer (see Chapter 1).

Many of the extended procedures installed with Microsoft SQL Server 7 run only on Windows NT, version 4.0 and higher — they can't run on Windows 95 or Windows 98.

To execute an extended procedure, follow these steps:

1. **Choose Start⇨Programs⇨Microsoft SQL Server 7.0⇨Query Analyzer to start the SQL Server Query Analyzer.**

   You're prompted to log into SQL Server. Type your ID and password in the Login Name and Password boxes.

2. **Type your query.**

   A query can consist of multiple statements or a single statement containing the name of an extended procedure. For example, type **xp_enumgroups**. Choose the Query⇨Execute With Grid menu option to execute the query. This xp_enumgroups is a system procedure that returns information about the database you specify. If you don't specify a database, information about all databases is returned (see Figure 7-6).

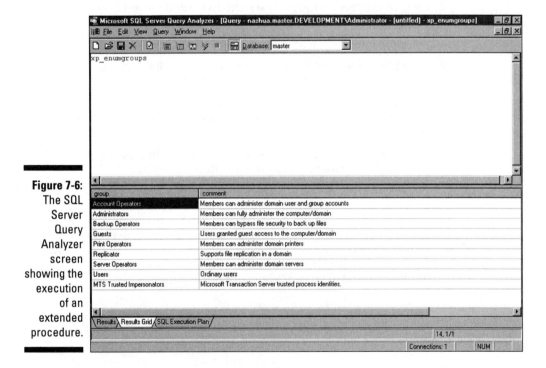

Figure 7-6: The SQL Server Query Analyzer screen showing the execution of an extended procedure.

Creating extended procedures

Creating an extended procedure isn't as glorious as it sounds. You must create and encapsulate some functionality into a DLL by using another language, such as Visual Basic, Visual C++, or Visual J++. Therefore, creating an extended procedure in SQL Server is not much more than instructing SQL Server about the name of one or more functions that you have placed inside a DLL as well as the location of the DLL.

Although it's beyond the scope of this book to illustrate how to create DLLs, you can refer to the following books for more information on a specific language:

- ✔ *Visual Basic 5 For Windows For Dummies* by Wally Wang (IDG Books Worldwide, Inc.)

- ✔ *Visual C++ 5 For Dummies* by Michael Hyman and Bob Arnson (IDG Books Worldwide, Inc.)

- ✔ *Visual J++ For Dummies* by Michael Hyman (IDG Books Worldwide, Inc.)

To create a new extended procedure in SQL Server, follow these steps:

1. **Choose Start⇨_Programs⇨Microsoft SQL Server 7.0⇨Enterprise Manager to start the SQL Server Enterprise Manager.**

2. **Expand the tree so that you see the Extended Stored Procedures entry within the master database under the Databases entry.**

   For more information about expanding the tree, see Chapter 1.

3. **Select the Extended Stored Procedures entry by clicking.**

   After selecting the Extended Stored Procedures entry, notice the list of stored procedures on the right-hand part of the screen (refer to Figure 7-4). Extended stored procedures are always located in the master database.

4. **Create a new Extended Stored Procedure by clicking the Action⇨New Extended Stored Procedure menu item.**

   Clicking the Action⇨New Extended Stored Procedure menu item brings up a dialog box containing properties for the extended procedure (see Figure 7-7). Again, remember that you aren't actually creating the extended procedure — you're only indicating to SQL Server where the procedure is that you've created in another language. Alternatively, you can right-click the Extended Stored Procedures tree entry and choose the New Extended Stored Procedure menu option.

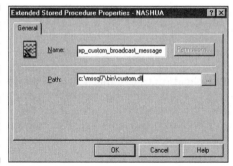

Figure 7-7:
The SQL
Server
Enterprise
Manager
screen
showing
extended
procedures.

5. **Type data in the Name and Path fields.**

   Type the name of the procedure that resides in the DLL and the path of
   the DLL. For example, if you write a DLL function that sends a broad-
   cast message to all users in the company 10 minutes before you take
   the server down, you can type **xp_custom_broadcast_message** in the
   Name field, and **c:\mssql7\bin\custom.dll** in the Path field.

   Of course, for the extended procedure to work, you have to create a
   DLL named custom.dll and place it in the c:\mssql7\bin directory. Also,
   it needs to contain the xp_custom_broadcast_message function. If not,
   you receive an error while trying to execute the extended procedure.

   You may want to differentiate your custom extended procedures from
   the ones that Microsoft provides when you install SQL Server 7 because
   that way you'll know where to turn if there are errors. You can't yell at
   Microsoft if the extended procedure is your own. I suggest you use the
   prefix **xp_custom_**. You can come up with your own convention, if you
   don't like mine. The main point is to differentiate your extended
   procedures from the Microsoft procedures.

6. **Click OK to save your changes.**

   After you click OK to save your changes, notice that the name of your
   new extended procedure is now listed in the Enterprise Manager.

If you want to change permissions on the extended procedure, you can't do
it at the same time that you create the extended procedure. You have to
save your changes and bring up the properties dialog box again, by double-
clicking the extended procedure you want in the Enterprise Manager. The
Extended Stored Procedure Properties dialog box returns, but this time the
Permissions button is enabled.

Creating User-Defined Stored Procedures

You can create your own user-defined stored procedures. Unlike system procedures, your own stored procedures can exist in any database. It's very common for a client/server application to use many stored procedures. Stored procedures are made up of SQL, utilizing control statements (such as IF, THEN, and ELSE) and variables. Stored procedures allow for the abstraction of SQL code whose purpose is to provide a specific function. For example, you can have a stored procedure that creates a customer record in all the appropriate tables in a client/server system. In this example, the person who is executing the stored procedure doesn't even have to know which tables are being populated with customer information. This concept is called *abstraction* because all the functionality that happens at a lower level is abstracted from the person who calls the procedure. All she knows is that a stored procedure is called, a few parameters are passed, and magically, the correct tables are populated with the correct data.

To create a user-defined stored procedure, follow these steps:

1. **Choose Start⇨ Programs⇨Microsoft SQL Server 7.0⇨Enterprise Manager to start the SQL Server Enterprise Manager.**

2. **Expand the tree so that you see the Stored Procedures entry within the desired database under the Databases entry.**

   For more information about expanding the tree, see Chapter 1.

3. **Select the Stored Procedures entry by clicking it.**

   After selecting the Stored Procedures entry, notice the list of stored procedures on the right-hand part of the screen.

4. **Create a new Stored Procedure by clicking the Action⇨New Stored Procedure menu item.**

   Clicking the Action⇨New Stored Procedure menu item brings up the Stored Procedures Properties dialog box, allowing you to create your stored procedure (see Figure 7-8). Alternatively, you can right-click the Stored Procedures tree entry and choose the New Stored Procedure menu option.

   Creating a stored procedure involves issuing the CREATE PROCEDURE SQL statement, which the Enterprise Manager does for you. What you type in next is totally up to you. Deciding what to type next is dependent on the functionality you desire from your stored procedure.

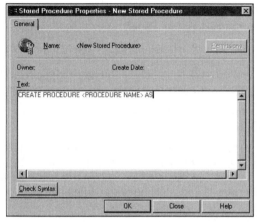

Figure 7-8:
The SQL
Server
Enterprise
Manager
screen
showing the
Stored
Procedure
Properties
dialog box.

5. Type the SQL that makes up your stored procedure.

Here I show you a specific example that you can use for a variety of
possibilities. Say you want to create a stored procedure called
sp_NewCustomer, a simple stored procedure that accepts five arguments. The arguments will be used to insert data into a table, called
Customer. The arguments are:

- Name

- Address

- City

- State

- Zip

The SQL syntax for creating a stored procedure is:

```
CREATE PROC[EDURE] procedure_name [;number]
        [({@parameter_name | parameter} data_type [
     VARYING] [= default]
        [OUTPUT])] [,...n]
        [WITH {RECOMPILE | ENCRYPTION ]
        [FOR REPLICATION]
        AS
        sql_statement [...n]
```

The following lists the arguments available for substitution in the
preceding statement:

- **procedure_name** is the name of your stored procedure, which is
the name you use when you execute your stored procedure.

- **;number** is an optional parameter that allows you to group
multiple stored procedures together.

- **@parameter_name** | **parameter** is an optional parameter that's the name of a parameter to be used as an argument in the stored procedure.

- **data_type** is the type of data that is represented by the parameter. The **data_type** must be a valid SQL Server 7 data type. You must specify this argument if you specify a @parameter_name.

- **VARYING** is an optional keyword that indicates that an output parameter's result set can vary.

- **default** is an optional keyword that can be specified for each @parameter_name. The default keyword is assigned to a value via an equal (=) sign. The default keyword indicates that when the stored procedure is called, this value will be used if the value for @parameter_name is not explicitly specified.

- **OUTPUT** is an optional keyword that indicates that the @parameter_name is used for output.

- **n** indicates that multiple parameters can be specified.

- **WITH RECOMPILE** is an optional set of keywords that instructs SQL Server to recompile the stored procedure every time it's run.

- **WITH ENCRYPTION** is an optional set of keywords that instructs SQL Server to encrypt the text of the stored procedure in the **syscomments** system table.

- **FOR REPLICATION** is an optional set of keywords that indicates that the stored procedure will be used for replication. For more information about replication, see Chapter 12.

- **sql_statement** is any valid SQL statement that you have permission to execute.

- **n** indicates that more than one sql_statement can be executed.

To understand how to use this syntax, see the following:

```
CREATE PROCEDURE sp_NewCustomer (
@name varchar(30),
@address varchar(30),
@city varchar(30),
@state char(2),
@zip char(5))

AS

INSERT INTO Customer (
cust_name,
```

```
cust_address,
cust_city,
cust_state,
cust_zip)

VALUES (
@name,
@address,
@city,
@state,
@zip)
```

Part III
Interface Design

"For further thoughts on that subject, I'm going to run a query on Leviticus and then perform an inner join on the Job tables. The result reads...".

In this part . . .

1 give you an overview into using Structured Query Language, or SQL. SQL is the "language" of databases. I also show you how to use SQL with Microsoft SQL Server 7 — with the tool provided by Microsoft, called the Query Analyzer. Also, for those of you who like the machine to do all the work, I show you how to let Microsoft SQL Server 7 create jobs, alerts, and tasks.

Chapter 8

Making Microsoft SQL Server 7 Work by Using SQL

· ·

In This Chapter
▶ Creating Database Objects with DDL
▶ Manipulating Data with DML
▶ SQL Constructs with DCL

· ·

*T*he term SQL stands for *Structured Query Language*. It is the language from which most databases, or database management systems (DBMS), allow manipulation of data and much more. SQL Server is no exception. A SQL statement is a bit of text containing clauses in a particular structure. I know this conjures up visions of Christmas time, but a *clause* is actually a part of a SQL statement that starts with a SQL keyword. I show you how to use clauses in your SQL statements throughout this chapter.

SQL-92 and you

A SQL statement is defined by the SQL standard, named SQL-92. This standard basically identifies the version of SQL to which a DBMS conforms. The standard defines things like syntax and keywords that are to be used. The main purpose for the standard is so that it can be used in databases other than Microsoft SQL Server (not that you would ever do that). Each database vendor develops its own extensions to the SQL-92 language to allow you to take advantage of specific database features. This is why Transact SQL, the SQL language used in Microsoft SQL Server 7.0, is a subset of the SQL-92 standard set. Transact SQL is proprietary to Microsoft SQL Server but must be used to get the full benefit of the specific database features.

The rest of this chapter is dedicated to showing you how to use SQL with SQL Server 7. However, bear in mind that I can't show in this chapter the full range of SQL supported in SQL Server 7. It is just too expansive. For more information about SQL as an entire topic, refer to *SQL For Dummies,* 2nd Edition, by Allen G. Taylor (from IDG Books Worldwide, Inc.). So why do I show you SQL at all in this chapter if you can refer to this book? Actually, because SQL is the basis of SQL Server (quite literally), the book would be incomplete if I didn't at least show you the basics.

You can execute any of the statements that I show you in this chapter using the SQL Server Query Analyzer or any other tool that allows the execution of SQL statements (see Chapter 9). The same functionality achieved by the SQL statements that I show you in this chapter can be achieved graphically by using the SQL Server Enterprise Manager (see Chapters 5 and 6). However, if you want to create a program that accesses Microsoft SQL Server and issues queries, you will not have the Enterprise Manager at your disposal. Therefore, you need this chapter to construct your queries. So buckle up and here we go.

The Categories of SQL

SQL is a language that is divided into a series of *categories.* It can be confusing because these categories are also called "languages," but they really are not. These categories are all part of the SQL language. The categories are:

- ✔ Data Definition Language (DDL)
- ✔ Data Manipulation Language (DML)
- ✔ Data Control Language (DCL)

In each one of these categories, the SQL statements are made up of a series of clauses, just as the English language is. To make a SQL statement readable, each clause is usually specified on a separate code line.

In this chapter, I show you how to use all these categories of SQL statements.

Using Data Definition Language (DDL) Statements

A *Data Definition Language,* or DDL, is a SQL statement that is designed to specifically manipulate database objects, such as databases, tables, indexes, views, defaults, rules, and triggers. (For more information about database objects, see Chapters 5 and 6.) This section shows you how to create a database, a table, and an index.

Creating a database: The mother of all containers

A database serves as a big container to hold other objects like tables, indexes, views, and even data. However, to contain these objects, you must create the database itself first with the CREATE DATABASE statement.

Suppose you want to create a database to hold all of your customer information, like contact information, orders, and invoices. To create a database named Customer, issue this SQL statement:

```
CREATE DATABASE Customer
```

Where do I put all my data?

After you create a database (see the preceding section), you can create one or more tables to stuff your data into. A *table* is a database object that logically looks like a spreadsheet, containing rows and columns. Each row is sometimes referred to as a *record* in the table. Each column is sometimes referred to as a *field* in the table.

A table is created inside a database, so the database must exist first. Because more than one database can be on the server, you must instruct SQL Server as to which database the table is to be created into. To indicate which database to use, you must "switch" to the desired database with the USE statement. To switch to the Customer database, use this statement:

```
USE Customer
```

After you have switched to the desired database, nothing is standing in your way of creating a table to store your data into. To create a table, you use the CREATE TABLE statement. Within the CREATE TABLE statement, you specify the name of your table, the columns your table is to contain, and the type of data each column represents.

If you wanted to create a table, named Contact (for customer contact information), you probably need to store things like ContactID, LastName, FirstName, Address, City, State, Zip, and Phone. You'll probably need more than that, but I want to keep it simple for now. Believe it or not, we've just identified the columns in the table. The only other thing we need to do is to define the types of data that each column represents. This is referred to as a *datatype*. (For more information about datatypes, see Chapter 4, or the Cheat Sheet at the front of this book.) I'll take the liberty of showing you the CREATE TABLE statement with datatypes:

```
CREATE TABLE Contact
(ContactID integer,
LastName varchar (30),
FirstName varchar (30),
Address varchar (30),
City varchar (30),
State char (2),
Zip varchar (10),
Phone char (10))
```

The ContactID field is defined as an integer because it will store number data. The LastName, FirstName, Address, and City fields are created with the Varchar datatype. This allows for variable character data. I defined each of these with a maximum length of 30. The State field allows for character data with a maximum length of 2. The Zip field is also a Varchar datatype, but the maximum length of 10. The length is decreased (from the other fields) because a United States zip code will never have more than 10 characters. The Phone field is defined as char with a maximum length of 10. The field is not defined as a varchar because the phone number will never be a variable length. It is always 10 characters, excluding dashes and parentheses.

If you don't want to issue the USE statement first before creating a table, you can explicitly identify the database name so that you are assured that the table is created where you expect it to be. To explicitly state where you want the table created, type the database name, followed by **.dbo.**, followed by your table name. For example, this statement creates the table Contact in the Customer database:

```
CREATE TABLE Customer.dbo.Contact
(ContactID integer,
LastName varchar (30),
FirstName varchar (30),
Address varchar (30),
City varchar (30),
State char (2),
Zip varchar (10),
Phone char (10))
```

Additionally, you can specify constraints for the table, at the same time as you create the table. A *constraint* is a limitation placed on a table, such as an index. If you want to indicate that the ContactID column in the Contact table is a primary key, use this statement:

```
CREATE TABLE Contact
(ContactID integer CONSTRAINT Primary1 PRIMARY KEY,
LastName varchar (30),
FirstName varchar (30),
Address varchar (30),
City varchar (30),
State char (2),
Zip varchar (10),
Phone char (10))
```

The preceding statement adds a constraint clause. This statement actually creates an index with the name Primary1 and defines it as a primary key for the Contact column. For more information about primary keys, see Chapter 4.

Okay, all this is well and good, but what if you want to force a user to type a last name and first name for a contact? How do you indicate this to SQL Server? You need to tell SQL Server that it shouldn't accept blank values (called *null* values). Do this with the NOT NULL keywords. Therefore, to create a Contact table that forces you to put data into the LastName and FirstName fields, issue this SQL statement:

```
CREATE TABLE Contact
(ContactID integer,
LastName varchar (30) NOT NULL,
FirstName varchar (30) NOT NULL,
Address varchar (30),
City varchar (30),
State char (2),
Zip varchar (10),
Phone char (10))
```

How do I speed up my queries?

An index is a way to instruct SQL Server how to speed up querying the database. Because an index is used to speed up queries, you must first know how your data will be accessed. For example, if your data will always be accessed by a Contact ID, you probably want to place an index on that column. If, on the other hand, your data will be looked up by Last Name, you probably want to place an index on that column. If your data will be accessed by using either column, you probably want to place an index on both columns.

You also need to decide on the type of index used. Your choices are clustered and nonclustered.

- ✔ A *clustered* index uses a binary tree search algorithm and indicates that SQL Server will physically order the records based in order of the values in a specific column or columns of data. Because SQL Server has to do more work by physically reordering data, INSERT and UPDATE statements can slow down data accessing, but retrieving data is faster. You can have only one clustered index on a single table. A clustered index is also usually associated with the primary key index.

- ✔ A *nonclustered* index also uses a binary tree search algorithm but does not physically order the records. Therefore, querying is usually faster than not using an index at all but not as fast as using a clustered index. A nonclustered index does not generally hurt performance when you use INSERT and UPDATE statements.

To create an index, you use the CREATE INDEX statement. If you want to create a clustered index on the Contact table, on the ContactID column you issue this statement:

```
CREATE CLUSTERED INDEX Index1 ON Contact (ContactID)
```

You can substitute the index name, Index1, with any name you choose. This name is used only as an identifier so that you can manipulate the index at a later time. This manipulation includes deleting or dropping the index, as well as altering it.

Clustered and nonclustered index considerations

People generally tend to make the clustered index the primary key, but this is not a requirement. A clustered index may be any field in the database. Use the clustered index to group data that will often be retrieved by a GROUP BY clause. When you want to use the clustered index on other than a primary key, you should not use the primary key constraint to create a primary key.

A nonclustered index can be affected by the fill factor used when creating the index. A fill factor leaves blank space in the index to be filled in by future additions to the data. If you do not use a fill factor, then when you do inserts of data, you make the index create extents to hold the data (extents are chained storage spaces). This can slow down inserts.

Likewise, you can create a nonclustered index on the same table and column by issuing this statement:

```
CREATE NONCLUSTERED INDEX Index1 ON Contact (ContactID)
```

A multiple key index is one whose specified fields are made up of more than one column in a table. If you want to create a multiple key index, simply specify the columns in the index. To ensure that the ContactID and LastName columns are part of an index, use this statement:

```
CREATE NONCLUSTERED INDEX Index1 ON Contact (ContactID,
        LastName)
```

It is important to know that SQL Server 7 does not allow you to create a multiple key index when you use the CREATE TABLE statement. You must first create the table and then use the CREATE INDEX statement to specify multiple keys. However, if you aren't trying to create multiple key indexes, you may find it useful to specify the index (constraint) within the CREATE TABLE statement.

Seeing things differently

If you want to hide columns from a table in a database, you can do that with a view. A *view* is a database object that allows you to define which columns, in one or more tables, are exposed to the view. Being exposed to a view means that you define the columns that you wish to be visible in the view. In other words, a view is a logical table.

To create a view, use the CREATE VIEW statement. Suppose you have a table named Employee with columns named Employee_ID, Last_Name, First_Name, and Salary. You probably don't want to show the Salary column to just anyone, so you can create a view on the Employee table, like this:

```
CREATE VIEW Dont_Show_Salary
AS
SELECT Employee_ID, Last_Name, First_Name
FROM Employee
```

With the preceding statement, you define a view with the name, Dont_Show_Salary. The columns exposed in the view are defined in the SELECT statement after the AS clause. For more information about the SELECT statement, see "Querying data" later in this chapter.

Then, to use the view, you can access it as if it were a table, like this:

```
SELECT *
FROM Dont_Show_Salary
```

Ruling the world

Okay, if not the world, at least your database! A rule defines what values are valid to be placed in a column. As you may have guessed, you use the CREATE RULE statement to suit this purpose. For example, suppose you want to create a rule to allow only the numbers 1 through 5, you use the CREATE RULE statement like this:

```
CREATE RULE Between_1_and_5
AS
@val >= 1 and @val <= 5
```

The rule is given a name, Between_1_and_5. Then it is defined using a variable name. I use @val. Then this value is tested to ensure that it is greater than or equal to 1 and less than or equal to 5.

Now that the rule is defined, it can be used, or *bound,* to any of the columns in the database in which the rule was created. To bind the rule to a column, you must use a system stored procedure, called **sp_bindrule**. For more information about system stored procedures, see Chapter 7. Use the sp_bindrule system stored procedure like this:

```
EXEC sp_bindrule 'Between_1_and_5', 'Employee.Employee_ID'
```

The system stored procedure binds the Between_1_and_5 rule to the Employee_ID column in the Employee table.

Whose default is it, anyway?

It's not my fault if you don't specify data for columns in your INSERT statement. However, I know how to fix the situation. You can specify a *default* value for any column of data that is left null when you insert data. This ensures that there is a value in the column. Defaults are especially important where they concern columns that do not allow null values.

Creating a default is done by issuing the CREATE DEFAULT statement, like this:

```
CREATE DEFAULT DEF_Level1
AS 'Level 1'
```

The preceding statement creates a default, named DEF_Level1, and assigns a constant value of Level1. This could be used for a situation where you specify a salary level for an employee. If you leave the salary level null, the value Level1 will automatically be inserted.

However, just like with a rule, a default must be bound to one or more columns. Do this using the system stored procedure, named sp_bindefault, like this:

```
sp_bindefault DEF_Level1,'Employee.Salary_Level'
```

This binds the DEF_Level1 default to the Salary_Level column of the Employee table.

Horsing around with triggers

Triggers are an important way to enforce referential integrity. *Referential integrity* is a concept that mandates data in one column of a table be related to the same data value in a field of another table. A trigger can help to enforce this integrity because a trigger runs based on certain events that you define. You can write SQL to enforce your referential integrity rules when these events run (or in other words, fired). The possible events are:

- ✔ Insert
- ✔ Update
- ✔ Delete

You create a trigger with the CREATE TRIGGER statement. In this statement, you define what will happen when data is inserted, updated, and/or deleted.

The best way to learn how to write a trigger, is to see one in action. Suppose you want to create a trigger that inserts a record in the Salary table when a record is inserted into the Employee table. The trigger goes on the Employee table. You do that like this:

```
CREATE TRIGGER TRG_Insert_Salary
ON Employee
FOR INSERT
AS
INSERT Salary (Employee_ID)
SELECT Employee_ID
FROM inserted
```

The trigger that I created is called TRG_Insert_Salary. It is created on the Employee table and fires when a record is inserted into the table. When a row is inserted into a table that contains a trigger, the value(s) that are inserted are duplicated into the *inserted* table. This way you can query the table to find out what was inserted.

Likewise, when a row is deleted from a table that contains a trigger, the value(s) that are deleted are stored in the *deleted* table.

With the preceding SQL Statement, every time a record is inserted into the Employee table, the value that is inserted for Employee_ID is also inserted into the Salary table.

Triggers can also be used for other purposes. Such a purpose includes executing a stored procedure to e-mail the purchase agent to order more stock if the inventory of a certain product falls below a specified level.

Using Data Manipulation Language (DML) Statements

A *Data Manipulation Language,* or DML, is a SQL statement that is designed to specifically manipulate data that lies within database tables. You'll be spending most of your time with statements in this section. For more information about tables, see Chapter 5. Okay, get going so you can be on your way trying out this stuff.

DML consists of four keywords. These keywords are also known as *clauses.* They are:

- INSERT — Adds new rows of data into one or more tables
- UPDATE — Updates existing rows of data into one or more tables
- DELETE — Deletes existing rows of data from one or more tables
- SELECT — Queries existing data from one or more tables

Getting data in

Getting data into a table is a snap. To put data into a table, use the INSERT statement. You have two ways to insert data: by either supplying "hard-coded" data or getting the data from another table.

Supplying "hard-coded" data

"Hard-coded" data indicates to SQL Server that you will specify values and insert one row of data at a time. You can insert a row of data (record) into the Contact table like this:

```
INSERT INTO Contact (ContactID, LastName, FirstName, Ad-
        dress, City, State, Zip, Phone)
VALUES (1012, 'Mann', 'Anthony', '4600 S. Ulster Street,
        Suite 240', 'Denver', 'CO', '80206',
        '3038463020')
```

The values indicated are not significant. I only want to show that when you supply "hard-coded" values, you need to use the VALUES clause to indicate to SQL Server that you will supply the actual values. In addition, I want to show that you need to respect the data types in all columns. This means that a character and date field needs to be surrounded by quotes. Numeric and money fields don't have quotes.

Getting data from another table

You can insert data into one table, based on data in another table. For example, suppose you have a temporary table named Temp_Contact. It has the same structure as the Contact table. You need to insert the data from Contact into Temp_Contact. This scenario would allow you to query data without affecting performance of the Contact table (are you getting all of this?). You insert all records from the Contact table into Temp_Contact like this:

```
INSERT Temp_Contact (ContactID, LastName, FirstName, Ad-
        dress, City, State, Zip, Phone)
SELECT ContactID, LastName, FirstName, Address, City,
        State, Zip, Phone
FROM Contact
```

This statement inserts all data in each column from the Orders table and inserts it into Temp_Contact in the same columns because the statement specifies the column order. Getting the column order correct is important because, as long as the data types are compatible, the SQL statement will succeed. Therefore, it's your responsibility to make sure the columns specified are in the correct order.

If you want to limit the number of rows, specify a WHERE clause. If you want to limit the insertion shown above to all contacts in Colorado, you can create this statement:

```
INSERT Temp_Contact (ContactID, LastName, FirstName, Ad-
            dress, City, State, Zip, Phone)
SELECT ContactID, LastName, FirstName, Address, City,
            State, Zip, Phone
FROM Contact
WHERE State = 'CO'
```

It's your prerogative to change your data

What if you already have data in a table and you want to change it? This, too, is a piece of cake. Do this with the UPDATE statement.

You use the UPDATE statement to substitute the current value of one or more columns of data with a different value. Using the UPDATE statement works only with existing data; it will not insert new data. To insert new data, you must use the INSERT statement, as shown earlier in this chapter.

Suppose a customer moves and you want to update her address. For this example, assume there is a Customer table with the following columns:

Cust_ID – number (integer)

Cust_Name – varchar (30)

Address_1 – varchar (30)

Address_2 – varchar (30)

City – varchar (30)

State – char (2)

Zip – varchar (10)

Phone – char (10)

Fax – char (10)

Email – varchar (30)

I'll take you through a couple of different scenarios to understand the UPDATE statement. The first scenario is that the customer's zip code changed. The key to being able to update this record is that you know the

Cust_ID and that every customer has a different Cust_ID. That way you know exactly which record to update. In this scenario, you can update the zip code for the customer from whatever it currently is to 80111. The SQL statement to perform the update looks like this:

```
UPDATE Customer
SET Zip = '80111'
WHERE Cust_ID = '2345'
```

If it was possible to have more than one Cust_ID with the value of 2345, all rows containing this value would be updated. That's why you have to be very careful when using the UPDATE statement.

You can join statements in the WHERE clause to further qualify the update. For example, suppose you want to additionally qualify the update to specify that the record(s) will be updated also only when the Zip column contains a value of 80241. This statement looks like this:

```
UPDATE Customer
SET Zip = '80111'
WHERE Cust_ID = '2345'
AND Zip = '80241'
```

For the second scenario, suppose you want to update more than one field. This is how you would update a customer's entire address record:

```
UPDATE Customer
SET Address_1 = '123 Main Street',
Address_2 = 'Suite A',
City = 'DENVER',
State = 'CO',
Zip = '80111',
Phone = '3031111111',
Fax = '3032222222',
Email = 'someone@anywhere.com'
WHERE Cust_ID = '2345'
```

Notice that every field that gets updated is separated by a comma. The WHERE clause applies to all fields in the statement only if the Cust_ID is 2345.

You can even update data in one table, based on the data in another table by using the concepts I show in the "Querying data" section later in this chapter.

Getting data out

Well, through all of these tests, you now have a bunch of junk data in your database. You can delete this junk data by using the DELETE statement.

With the DELETE statement, either all data can be deleted or data can be targeted so that only specific rows of data are deleted. But realize that the DELETE statement deletes all columns of data in an entire row! It does not delete specific columns of data within a row. If you want to delete specific columns of data, use the UPDATE statement (see "It's your prerogative to change your data" earlier in this chapter).

To delete all rows of data in a Customer table, use this statement:

```
DELETE FROM Customer
```

To delete only row(s) in the Customer table for the customer with a Cust_ID of 1001, you construct the statement like this:

```
DELETE FROM Customer
WHERE Cust_ID = 1001
```

You can even delete data in one table, based on the data in another table by using the concepts I show in the "Querying data" section in this chapter.

Querying data

What good is your data if you can't query it? *Querying* data means running a report, based on criteria that you specify. Querying data is done by using the SELECT statement. The SELECT statement is the most common of all SQL statements. Because it is so common, there are lots of ways to use it, and I'm going to cruise you through the important ones.

If you are unsure of what rows an UPDATE statement will affect, transform the UPDATE statement into a SELECT statement using the same WHERE clause. This procedure shows you the rows that will be updated if you issue the UPDATE statement instead.

Simple selects

A *simple select* is a query that looks up data only in one table. The main parts of the SELECT statement could be thought of like this:

```
SELECT what
FROM location
WHERE limitations
```

The SELECT, FROM, and WHERE keywords are all considered to be *clauses*.

If you want to query the database to find all customers who live in Colorado, you could issue this statement:

```
SELECT Cust_ID, Cust_Name
FROM Customer
WHERE State = 'CO'
```

This statement returns only the Cust_ID and Cust_Name for all customers who live in Colorado. If you want to retrieve all columns of data for every customer in Colorado, you can either specify every column in the Customer table by name, separated by a comma, or use the * wildcard. The * wildcard indicates that you want all possible columns. You use the * wildcard like this:

```
SELECT *
FROM Customer
WHERE State = 'CO'
```

Compound selects

A *compound select* is a query that looks up data in more than one table. To look up data in more than one table, you must perform what is called a join in the WHERE clause of the SQL statement. A *join* is just like the name suggests. It specifies the columns that are to be joined between tables. In addition, you must specify all the tables used in the query in the FROM clause. If you specify only the criteria you desire in the SELECT statement without specifying join information, you won't achieve the desired results — or the statement will result in error. For example, consider this statement:

```
SELECT Cust_Name
FROM Customer,Orders
WHERE State = 'CO'
AND Order_Date = '12/1/98'
```

The Cust_Name and State fields exist in the Customer table. The Order_Date exists in the Orders table. However, nothing is in the statement to indicate how to join the two tables together.

With these two tables, the "glue" to link the tables is the Cust_ID field. It exists in both tables and allows you to look up fields in one table based on the values in another. The following statement is the correct statement to link the two tables together:

```
SELECT Cust_Name
FROM Customer,Orders
WHERE State = 'CO'
AND Order_Date = '12/1/98'
AND Customer.Cust_ID = Orders.Cust_ID
```

The reason for the syntax in the last line of the statement that specifies the table name is that SQL Server needs to know the specific table if one or more tables contain the same column name. If the table names are not specified, this is known as an *ambiguous join.*

The data will be returned in no specific order, unless you add an ORDER BY clause to the end of the statement. If you want all customer's names to be ordered alphabetically, add this clause:

```
ORDER BY Cust_Name
```

I hope I don't confuse you on this one, but I think I should show you another way to construct joins. Some people recommend creating joins in the FROM clause. A join is performed in the FROM clause with the JOIN and ON keywords. Look at this statement:

```
SELECT Customer.Cust_Name
FROM Customer JOIN Orders ON Customer.Cust_ID =
          Orders.Cust_ID
WHERE Customer.State = 'CO'
AND Orders.Order_Date = '12/1/98'
```

The JOIN keyword indicates that the Orders table is joined with the Customer table. The ON keyword indicates the columns in the respective tables to be joined. Therefore the Cust_ID column of the Orders table (noted on the right-hand side of the equals sign) is joined with the Cust_ID column of the Customer.

Inner joins

In the preceding section, I show you how to perform a join. This join is implicitly called an *inner join.* However, using an inner join may not return the results you expect.

TECHNICAL STUFF

Using an alias

Want to see something really cool? Suppose you didn't want to repeat your table names, such as **Customer** or **Orders** all the time. You can use a reference to a table name with fewer characters than the full table name, known as an *alias*. An alias is specified with the AS keyword in the FROM clause. Consider this SQL statement used for a compound select statement:

```
SELECT C.Cust_Name
FROM Customer AS C JOIN Orders AS O ON C.Cust_ID = O.Cust_ID
WHERE C.State = 'CO'
AND O.Order_Date = '12/1/98'
```

Any series of characters directly after the AS keyword is the alias used in the entire SQL statement. **Customer** is aliased as **C** and **Orders** is aliased as **O**. Instead of specifying the entire table names, you can use the defined aliases.

An inner join matches values on columns between tables. If there is no match, then no record is returned, from either table. However, you may want to know that there is a missing (or null) value in one of the tables. Suppose you have two tables (with the column names listed in parentheses):

- ✔ Customer (Cust_ID, Cust_Name)
- ✔ Orders (Cust_ID, Order_Date)

Because a customer does not have to place an order, there can be a record in the Customer table, but not the Orders table. Therefore, if you perform a query joining the Cust_ID columns between the two tables, the only customers that will be shown are those with orders. This will not list *all* of the customers, along with their order dates.

To illustrate my point, refer to Table 8-1 for the Customer table and Table 8-2 for the Orders table.

Table 8-1	Sample Customer Table
Cust_ID	*Cust_Name*
1001	John Smith
1002	Fred Jones
1003	Mary Smith

Table 8-2	Sample Orders Table
Cust_ID	*Order_Date*
1001	10/24/96
1001	1/1/97
1003	5/4/95

If you want to retrieve all Order_Dates for all customers and order them by Cust_Name, you may think that you issue one of these statements:

```
SELECT Cust_Name, Order_Date
FROM Customer JOIN Orders ON Customer.Cust_ID =
          Orders.Cust_ID
ORDER BY Cust_Name
```

. . . or this statement:

```
SELECT Cust_Name, Order_Date
FROM Orders, Customer
WHERE Orders.Cust_ID = Customer.Cust_ID
ORDER BY Cust_Name
```

You'd be right, except you may not get back the data you expect. (Don't you just hate when that happens?) The data returned is shown in Table 8-3.

Table 8-3	Sample Results of Inner Join
Cust_ID	*Order_Date*
John Smith	10/24/96
John Smith	1/1/97
Mary Smith	5/4/95

Notice that Fred Jones does not appear in the result at all because the join used in the WHERE clause in the preceding statement is an inner join. To view all the records, even if it doesn't find a match in the join table, you need to construct an outer join. I talk about outer joins in the next section. Take a deep breath, we're going deep!

Outer joins

An *outer join* is a join that returns all records, even if there are no corresponding records in any of the join tables. If you want to return all customers and their corresponding orders (if they have any), using the data shown in Tables 8-1 and 8-2, you must issue a SELECT statement with an outer join, like this:

```
SELECT Cust_Name, Order_Date
FROM Customer LEFT OUTER JOIN Orders ON Customer.Cust_ID =
          Orders.Cust_ID
ORDER BY Cust_Name
```

The preceding statement returns the following results, shown in Table 8-4.

Table 8-4	Sample Results of Outer Join
Cust_Name	*Order_Date*
Fred Jones	NULL
John Smith	10/24/96
John Smith	1/1/97
Mary Smith	5/4/95

There are three types of outer joins. One is a *left outer join,* or sometimes referred to as a left join. The second type is a *right outer join,* or sometimes referred to as a right join. The last type is a *full outer join*, or sometimes referred to as a full join. Determining which type of join to use depends on how you construct the SQL statement.

A left join specifies that all rows in the table on the left part of the SQL statement will return every row of data, even if there is no data that matches in the table on the right part of the SQL statement. A right join is exactly the opposite of a left join. The table on the right part of the SQL statement will return every row of data, regardless of a match in the table on the left part of the SQL statement. A full join is actually a combination of the two joins. All data from both tables are returned, regardless of matching values in the opposite table.

Here's how it works. The SQL statement that I show you at the beginning of this section is equivalent to this statement:

```
SELECT Cust_Name, Order_Date
FROM Orders RIGHT OUTER JOIN Customer ON Orders.Cust_ID =
          Customer.Cust_ID
ORDER BY Cust_Name
```

In either type of outer join statement, the join is not performed in the WHERE clause. It is actually performed in the FROM clause. The FROM clause specifies not only the tables to be joined but the columns to be joined, as well. You specify columns directly after the ON keyword, and you specify the tables directly after the FROM keyword.

If you want all records to be returned in both tables, use this statement:

```
SELECT Cust_Name, Order_Date
FROM Orders FULL OUTER JOIN Customer ON Orders.Cust_ID =
          Customer.Cust_ID
ORDER BY Cust_Name
```

I know you're probably new at all of this — but this is important stuff. So I'm going to help you. If you don't know which type of join to construct, or in what order, you can follow these rules:

✔ If the table that can contain missing data is specified directly after the FROM keyword, use the RIGHT OUTER JOIN keywords, followed by the table that cannot contain missing data.

✔ If the table that can't contain missing data is specified directly after the FROM keyword, use the LEFT OUTER JOIN keywords, followed by the table that can contain missing data.

✔ If you need to return each and every row of data regardless of matching values in the tables, use the FULL OUTER JOIN keywords.

Using Data Control Language (DCL) Statements

A *Data Control Language,* or DCL, is a SQL statement that allows you to control how your statements are executed. DCL statements are centered around the concept of a transaction. A *transaction* is one or more SQL statements that manipulate data in a database that are treated as a complete unit. If any error occurs, the entire set of statements isn't executed. If errors do not occur, the entire set of statements is executed, thereby affecting the database.

DCL consists of three sets of statements. They are:

✔ BEGIN TRANSACTION — Starts a transaction

✔ COMMIT TRANSACTION — Accepts all changes made to the database since the last BEGIN TRANSACTION statement

✔ ROLLBACK TRANSACTION — Discards all changes made to the database since the last BEGIN TRANSACTION statement

These statements are very easy to use because they require no parameters or optional arguments. What you see is what you get!

To show how transactions are used, refer to these statements:

```
BEGIN TRANSACTION

INSERT Orders (Order_ID,Cust_ID,Order_Date,Order_Total)
VALUES (1234,3225,'05/22/98',344.68)

INSERT Orders (Order_ID,Cust_ID,Order_Date,Order_Total)
VALUES (5678,3225,'04/1/97',500.00)

IF @@error = 0
            COMMIT TRANSACTION
ELSE
            ROLLBACK TRANSACTION
```

In this example, I insert two rows of data into the Orders table within a transaction. If any error occurs, the transaction is rolled back. If no errors occur, the transaction is committed. This ensures that either both or no rows of data are inserted.

That's all there is to transactions. Aren't they as easy as I said they were? Transactions really do give you a great way to control your SQL statements in case of failure.

Chapter 9

Now That I Have a Structure, How Do I Use It?

*C*hapters 1 through 8 walk you through the process of creating your database structure in Microsoft SQL Server 7. In this chapter, I provide a step-by-step trek to another exciting destination — actual use of your structure! If you need a quick refresher on SQL before you take the next leap, check out Chapter 8 — you can be up to speed in no time.

Using SQL Server Query Analyzer

The SQL Server Query Analyzer is a wonderful, user-friendly tool from Microsoft that enables you to issue SQL statements and view the results of SQL queries. In addition, I want to let you know that as you get more proficient with SQL Server 7.0, you can use the Query Analyzer to view the query plan chosen by the SQL Server. A *query plan* is how SQL Server 7.0 decides to optimize your query. Because this is an advanced topic, I don't discuss query plans in the book.

To use the SQL Server Query Analyzer, follow these steps:

1. **To start the SQL Server Query, choose Start➪Programs➪Microsoft SQL Server 7➪Query Analyzer.**

2. **Log on to the SQL Server by filling in the following fields in the Connect to SQL Server dialog box (see Figure 9-1), and then click OK.**

Figure 9-1:
The
Connect to
SQL Server
dialog box.

- **SQL Server:** You can select the desired SQL Server from the drop-down list of registered SQL Servers. By default, the registered SQL Server on the current computer is presented. My SQL Server is called Nashua.

- **Use Windows NT authentication:** This option uses Windows NT authentication. This means that you are authorized to use the SQL Server Query Analyzer if SQL Server validates the login you gave when you logged into Windows NT (with your login name and password).

- **Use SQL Server authentication:** This option uses SQL Server to validate your login when you attempt to connect to SQL Server. When this option is chosen, the Login Name and Password text boxes become enabled. You must supply the Login Name and Password into the text boxes.

After you log in to a SQL Server, you see the SQL Server Query Analyzer, as shown in Figure 9-2.

3. **In the SQL Server Query Analyzer, choose your database from the Database drop-down list, which contains all the databases on the server that you logged in to.**

Alternatively, you can use SQL to change the database — just type the USE keyword, followed by the name of the database, and then execute your query. For example, this statement changes the active database to the pubs database:

```
USE pubs
```

4. **Type in your SQL.**

You can type in any valid SQL. What's a valid SQL statement, you ask? These are valid SQL Statements:

- **Stored Procedures** (see Chapter 7)

- **Extended Procedures** (see Chapter 7)

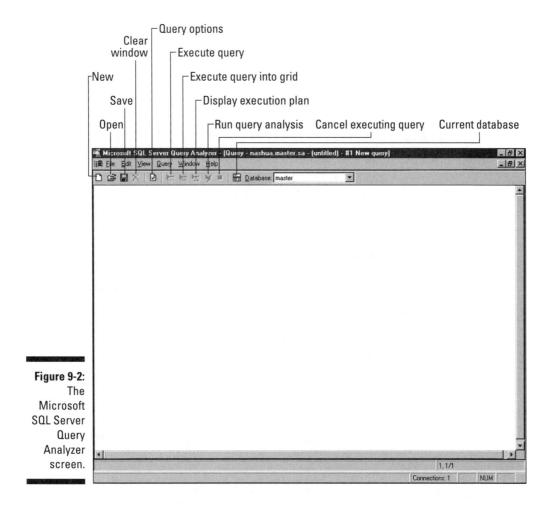

Query options

Clear window

Execute query

New

Execute query into grid

Save

Display execution plan

Open

Run query analysis   Cancel executing query   Current database

Figure 9-2:
The
Microsoft
SQL Server
Query
Analyzer
screen.

- **Dynamic Data Language, or DDL** (see Chapter 8)

- **Data Manipulation Language, or DML** (see Chapter 8)

- **Data Control Language, or DCL** (see Chapter 8)

Here's an example of a valid SQL statement:

```
SELECT *
FROM authors
ORDER BY au_lname
```

You can even place SQL commands in a batch. A *batch* is a process that contains multiple commands that are executed as a unit. Individual commands must contain the GO keyword between them so that SQL Server can execute the command just prior to every GO keyword.

For example, this is a valid batch statement:

```
USE pubs
GO
SELECT *
FROM authors
ORDER BY au_lname
GO
```

5. **Click the Query options icon, and then click one of the following:**

   • **Execute:** Executes your query and displays the results in the Results tab at the bottom of the screen.

   • **Execute with Grid:** Executes your query and displays the results in the Results Grid tab at the bottom of the screen.

   • **Display Execution Plan:** Executes your query and displays the results in the Plan tab at the bottom of the screen.

The Execute option (see Figure 9-3) displays the results in text form, but without placing the columns of text in a separate column. Instead, to simulate columns, text is supplemented with spaces so that all the beginning text in each column lines up nicely.

The Execute with Grid option (see Figure 9-4) shows the results in columnar form, meaning that every column of data is actually displayed in a grid column. Every row is also displayed in its own row in the grid.

The Display Execution Plan option (see Figure 9-5) does not display the results of a query, but the plan of execution instead. This plan of execution shows how the SQL Server optimizer will execute the query. The optimizer is a part of the server technology that determines the most efficient way to run a query.

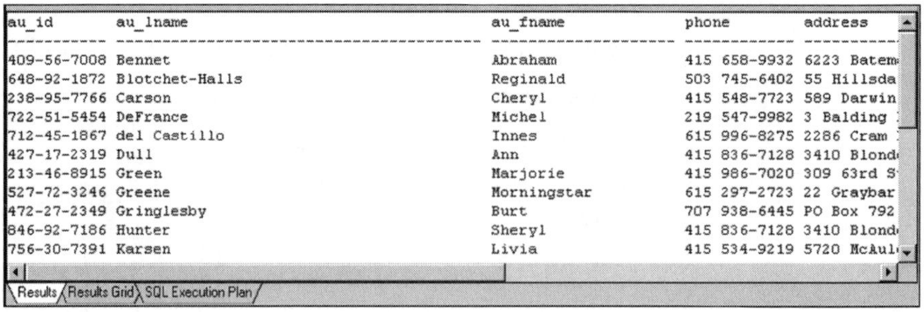

Figure 9-3:
The
Microsoft
SQL Server
Query
Analyzer
screen,
showing
results in
the Results
tab.

Figure 9-4:
The
Microsoft
SQL Server
Query
Analyzer
screen,
showing
results in
the Results
Grid tab.

au_id	au_lname	au_fname	phone	address	city
409-56-7008	Bennet	Abraham	415 658-9932	6223 Bateman St.	Berkeley
648-92-1872	Blotchet-Halls	Reginald	503 745-6402	55 Hillsdale Bl.	Corvallis
238-95-7766	Carson	Cheryl	415 548-7723	589 Darwin Ln.	Berkeley
722-51-5454	DeFrance	Michel	219 547-9982	3 Balding Pl.	Gary
712-45-1867	del Castillo	Innes	615 996-8275	2286 Cram Pl. #86	Ann Arbor
427-17-2319	Dull	Ann	415 836-7128	3410 Blonde St.	Palo Alto
213-46-8915	Green	Marjorie	415 986-7020	309 63rd St. #411	Oakland
527-72-3246	Greene	Morningstar	615 297-2723	22 Graybar House Rd.	Nashville
472-27-2349	Gringlesby	Burt	707 938-6445	PO Box 792	Covelo
846-92-7186	Hunter	Sheryl	415 836-7128	3410 Blonde St.	Palo Alto
756-30-7391	Karsen	Livia	415 534-9219	5720 McAuley St.	Oakland

Results \ Results Grid \ SQL Execution Plan

Figure 9-5:
The
Microsoft
SQL Server
Query
Analyzer
screen,
showing the
Plan tab.

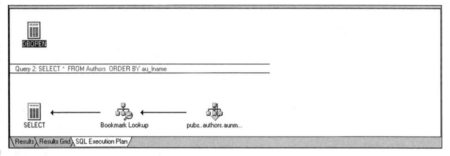

Although optimizer theory is outside the scope of this book, it's
important to know that you can obtain details about every specific
element of the plan by clicking the element. You then see a yellow box,
indicating the details about the selected element (shown in Figure 9-6).

Figure 9-6:
The
Microsoft
SQL Server
Query
Analyzer
screen,
showing
details in
the Plan
tab.

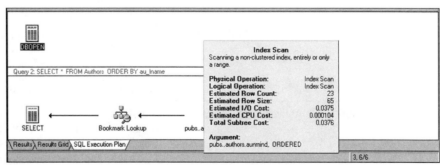

Connecting to SQL Server 7

You can connect to a database via several different methods, each of which refers to a separate technology that boasts its own benefits and involves individual costs. Because Microsoft comes out with new technologies and continues to support the old ones, these connection issues can cause confusion. Rather than suggest that this potential puzzle is a bad thing, I just call it the nature of the beast. In Table 9-1, I outline various ways to connect to SQL Server 7 and the technical terms that relate to those connections.

Table 9-1	SQL Server 7 Connectivity Technical Talk	
Term	*Stands For*	*Definition*
COM	Common Object Model	The Microsoft architecture for components talking to each other on the Desktop.
DCOM	Distributed Common Object Model	The Microsoft architecture for components talking to each other from multiple (distributed) computers.
ODBC	Open Database Connectivity	An underlying database communication technology. Microsoft recommends using ODBC for application development outside the COM environment. However, ODBC remains the most common, but not the fastest, way to connect to a database, even within the COM environment.
DAO	Data Access Objects	Set of programmable objects, originally used within Microsoft Visual Basic for the connection and manipulation of Microsoft Access objects. DAO is now supported by multiple environments, like Visual Basic, Visual C++, and Microsoft Access. Using DAO to request data from a client applica tion to SQL Server can be slow.
RDO	Remote Data Objects	Set of programmable objects, used to request data from a client application to SQL Server. This connection is quite fast. RDO is now supported by multiple environments, like Visual Basic and Visual C++.
ADO	ActiveX Data Objects	Set of programmable objects, also used to request data from a client application to SQL Server. This connection is very fast. Microsoft recommends using ADO for developing your business applications.

Term	Stands For	Definition
SQL-DMO	Structured Query Language-Distributed Management Objects	SQL-DMO is a set of objects that enable you to administer and manage SQL Server 7 through standard SQL queries.
OLE DB	Object Linking and Embedding for Databases	An underlying communication technology. Microsoft recommends using OLE DB when you develop low-level applications within the COM environment. This is typically how different SQL Server components talk to each other. You can also use the OLE DB technology through ODBC. This is done through a concept called a provider. This provider defines the communication between two objects. Therefore, you can use the OLE DB provider for ODBC.
Net-Library		The network protocol that's used between the client application and the server. The network protocol can be either Named Pipes, TCP/IP (using Windows sockets), NetBEUI, Novell SPX/IPX, Banyan Vines, Shared Memory, Multiprotocol, or AppleTalk.
DB-Library		The library (DLL) that's used for the client request to talk to a specific database. The client application makes a request through the DB-Library and transmits that request to the server through the Net-Library.

Navigating with Cursors

A cursor is more than a blinking blip on your monitor. In database terms, the cursor is a way to manipulate your result sets. A *result set* is a set of data that matches your query request. It can contain any number of rows of data. A *cursor* is a user-definable subset of the entire result set. A cursor can be one row or a set of rows.

One advantage of using a cursor is the efficiency of working with a small set of data, rather than the large record set. However, it does take some overhead to create the cursor. *Overhead* is a term that describes the extra time or resources (memory or disk space) a process requires.

In order for SQL Server to know how and when to create the cursor, the cursor must first be declared in one of two ways:

- ✔ By using Database API cursor-specific functions
- ✔ By using Transact-SQL statements

Transact-SQL statements are the most common way to access cursors, which you can discover in the next section, "Transact-SQL statements for Cursors." For more information about database API cursor functions, refer to the specific documentation for the API you're using. Cursor-specific functions are available in the following database APIs:

- ✔ ODBC
- ✔ OLE DB
- ✔ DB-Library

There are four different types of cursors, each of which is outlined in Table 9-2, along with its pros and cons.

Table 9-2	Cursor Types	
Cursor Type	*Pros*	*Cons*
Static	Requires few resources	Does not detect if data changes are made
	Cursor can be scrolled	Cursor is read-only
Dynamic	Detects if data changes are made	Requires more resources
	Cursor can be scrolled	
	Cursor is read-write	
Forward-only	Detects if data is changed in rows that have not been fetched	Does not detect if data changes are made in rows that have been fetched
		Cursor can't be scrolled backwards
Keyset-driven	Data changes to keyset columns are available through a SQL Server variable	Does not detect if data changes are made to nonkeyset columns

Cursor Transact-SQL statements are executed just like any other Transact-SQL — through a client program or through the SQL Server Query Analyzer. The following list shows the types of functionality each cursor statement performs:

✔ Declaring the cursor

✔ Opening the cursor

✔ Using the cursor

✔ Closing the cursor

✔ Deleting the cursor

Declaring the cursor

Where does it all start, you may wonder. The answer: with the DECLARE CURSOR statement. If you don't declare the cursor, no other operations can be performed on it. The DECLARE CURSOR statement follows this general syntax:

```
DECLARE cursor_name [INSENSITIVE] [SCROLL] CURSOR
          FOR select_statement
          FOR {READ ONLY | UPDATE [OF column_list]}]
```

The preceding statement is made up of these parts:

cursor_name is the name of your cursor.

INSENSITIVE is an optional keyword. If it is supplied, cursor data is temporarily copied to a table in the tempdb database.

SCROLL is an optional keyword. If it is supplied, the cursor can be scrolled in all directions (First, Previous, Next, and Last).

select_statement is the SELECT statement that generates the record set.

FOR READ ONLY is an optional set of keywords. If it is supplied, the cursor will not be updateable. This can't be used with the FOR UPDATE keywords.

FOR UPDATE is an optional set of keywords. If it is supplied, the cursor will be updateable. This can't be used with the FOR READ ONLY keywords.

OF column_list is an optional list of columns that can be updated, if the FOR UPDATE keywords are specified.

Here is an example of the DECLARE CURSOR statement:

```
DECLARE CUR_Temp SCROLL CURSOR
FOR SELECT * FROM Authors
FOR UPDATE
```

This example declares an updateable, scrollable cursor, called CUR_Temp. The cursor is comprised of all records and columns in the Authors tables.

Opening the cursor

Opening the cursor is how the cursor generates a record set. When the cursor is opened, the record set (as defined in the DECLARE statement) is populated. The keyword for opening a cursor is OPEN (imagine that?), and it follows this general syntax:

```
OPEN { { [GLOBAL] cursor_name } | cursor_variable_name}
```

The preceding statement is made up of these parts:

GLOBAL is an optional keyword. If supplied, this indicates that the global cursor is to be opened. This is only useful when there is a global and local cursor with the same name.

cursor_name is the name of the already declared cursor. This can't be used with a *cursor_variable_name*.

cursor_variable_name is the name of the already declared cursor variable. This can't be used with a *cursor_name*.

An example of an OPEN statement is:

OPEN CUR_Temp

Using the cursor

You can use the cursor after it's declared and opened. Remember, a cursor is simply a result set (or a subset of a result set). Either way, it contains specific rows of data. Using the cursor means accessing those rows of data to manipulate them. To use the cursor, the FETCH keyword is used. It follows this general syntax:

```
FETCH
    [ [NEXT | PRIOR | FIRST | LAST
    | ABSOLUTE {n | @nvar} | RELATIVE {n | @nvar}]
    FROM ] { { [GLOBAL] cursor_name } |
        cursor_variable_name}
    [INTO @variable_name[,...n] ]
```

The preceding statement is made up of these parts:

NEXT is an optional keyword. If it's supplied, the very next row in the cursor is retrieved. This can't be used with the PRIOR, FIRST, LAST, ABSOLUTE, or RELATIVE keywords.

PRIOR is an optional keyword. If it's supplied, the row just prior to the current row in the cursor is retrieved. This can't be used with the NEXT, FIRST, LAST, ABSOLUTE, or RELATIVE keywords.

FIRST is an optional keyword. If it's supplied, the very first row in the cursor is retrieved. This can't be used with the NEXT, PRIOR, LAST, ABSOLUTE, or RELATIVE keywords.

LAST is an optional keyword. If it's supplied, the very last row in the cursor is retrieved. This can't be used with the NEXT, PRIOR, FIRST, ABSOLUTE, or RELATIVE keywords.

ABSOLUTE is an optional keyword. If it's supplied, the keyword moves the current row in the cursor *n* number of rows from the beginning of the cursor (if *n* is positive) or *n* number of rows from the end of the cursor (if *n* is negative). Instead of specifying a value for *n* in the SQL statement, a variable, @*nvar* can be used. This can't be used with the NEXT, PRIOR, FIRST, LAST, or RELATIVE keywords.

RELATIVE is an optional keyword. If it's supplied, the keyword moves the current row in the cursor *n* number of rows from the current position. If *n* is positive, the cursor rows are advanced. If *n* is negative, the cursor rows are reversed. Instead of specifying a value for *n* in the SQL statement, a variable, @*nvar* can be used. This can't be used with the NEXT, PRIOR, FIRST, LAST, or ABSOLUTE keywords.

GLOBAL is an optional keyword. If supplied, this indicates that the FETCH is to apply to the global cursor. This is only useful when there is a global and local cursor with the same name.

cursor_name is the name of your cursor.

INTO is an optional keyword. If supplied, @*variable_name* is the name of the variable that is to contain the result set of the FETCH. If you use the INTO keyword, you must specify enough variables (separated by commas) to contain every column returned by the fetch.

An example of the FETCH statement is:

```
FETCH
FIRST
FROM CUR_Temp
```

This statement simply fetches the first record from the cursor and displays it. Suppose you declare a cursor to select all records from the Authors table in the Pubs database. Figure 9-7 shows the results of the first fetch in the SQL Server Query Analyzer.

Use the NEXT keyword to move to the next record. Here's how:

```
FETCH
NEXT
FROM CUR_Temp
```

SQL Server 7 has a system variable that stores the FETCH status; it's called @@FETCH_STATUS. You can use this variable in your procedures to perform specific actions when the variable contains certain values. These are the possible values of @@FETCH_STATUS:

- 0 - Fetch is successful.
- -1 - Fetch failed or the row was beyond the result set.
- -2 - Row fetched is missing.

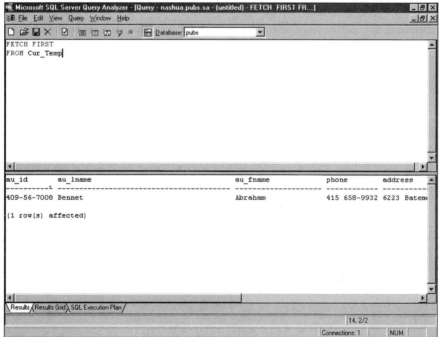

Figure 9-7:
The SQL
Server
Query
Analyzer,
showing
FETCH first
results.

The @@FETCH_STATUS variable is commonly used to loop through rows in a cursor until there are no more rows. You can issue a statement similar to this:

```
WHILE @@FETCH_STATUS = 0
BEGIN
        FETCH NEXT
        FROM CUR_Temp
END
```

This code enters a loop (with the WHILE statement) and loops as long as @@FETCH_STATUS returns zero. If it doesn't return zero, there are no more rows in the cursor.

Closing the cursor

Closing the cursor releases the record set from memory and frees any locks that the cursor is holding. Note that closing the cursor does not delete it. The keyword for closing a cursor is the CLOSE keyword. It follows this general syntax:

```
CLOSE { { [GLOBAL] cursor_name } | cursor_variable_name}
```

The preceding statement is made up of these parts:

GLOBAL is an optional keyword. If supplied, this indicates that the global cursor is to be closed. This is only useful when there is a global and local cursor with the same name.

cursor_name is the name of the already declared cursor. This can't be used with a *cursor_variable_name*.

cursor_variable_name is the name of the already declared cursor variable. This can't be used with a *cursor_name*.

An example of the CLOSE statement is:

```
CLOSE CUR_Temp
```

Deleting the cursor

Deleting the cursor is known as *deallocating* the cursor, primarily because any variable assigned with the DECLARE keyword needs to be removed from memory. Therefore, as you may expect, the keyword for removing a variable from memory is DEALLOCATE. It follows this general syntax:

```
DEALLOCATE { { [GLOBAL] cursor_name } |
          cursor_variable_name}
```

The preceding statement is made up of these parts:

GLOBAL is an optional keyword. If supplied, the keyword indicates that the global cursor is to be deallocated. This is only useful when there is a global and local cursor with the same name.

cursor_name is the name of the already declared cursor. This can't be used with a *cursor_variable_name*.

cursor_variable_name is the name of the already declared cursor variable. This can't be used with a *cursor_name*.

An example of the DEALLOCATE statement is:

```
DEALLOCATE CUR_Temp
```

Examining SQL Server and Visual Basic

Okay, now you have a SQL Server database. What if you want to write a program that accesses your SQL Server database? Lots of companies want you to write an application that uses the data in SQL Server. This is the type of application that my consulting company (Strategic Innovations Consulting) faces all the time. One of the most common computer languages is Microsoft Visual Basic, which can be used to write such an application.

Although this book is not about Visual Basic, I thought I'd show you how to communicate with SQL Server from Visual Basic, known as VB. As of the time of this writing, VB5 was the current version and VB6 was on its way shortly. The examples I show you in this section are based on VB5. This, of course, assumes you have VB5 installed on your machine. For this example, I assume that you already know something about Visual Basic and this is your first attempt to use SQL Server with Visual Basic.

This section isn't designed to equip you with a full understanding of VB5; rather, I offer just enough information to help you build a basic understanding of how you can use the programming language. If you want to pick up the details of Visual Basic 5, you can refer to *Visual Basic 5 For Dummies* by Wallace Wang (from IDG Books Worldwide, Inc.). You can also refer to another book I wrote (from SAMS), *Visual Basic 5 Developer's Guide.*

This example shows how to use Remote Data Objects (RDO). RDO libraries are located on your computer only if you have the Enterprise Edition of VB5.

To use VB5, follow these steps:

1. **Choose Start⇨Programs⇨Microsoft Visual Basic 5⇨Visual Basic 5 to start VB5 (as shown in Figure 9-8).**

2. **Open a new Standard EXE project.**

   Depending on your VB5 configuration, you may be presented with a dialog box when running VB5. This dialog box prompts for the type of project to create. Click Standard EXE.

   If this dialog box does not come up, VB5 starts with the Standard EXE option already selected. This is just perfect for my example.

3. **Choose Project⇨References, and then click the check box to the left of the Microsoft Remote Data Object 2.0 entry to set a reference to the Remote Data Object (RDO) Library (see Figure 9-9).**

   When you see a check mark in the box, click the OK button to close the dialog box and set the reference.

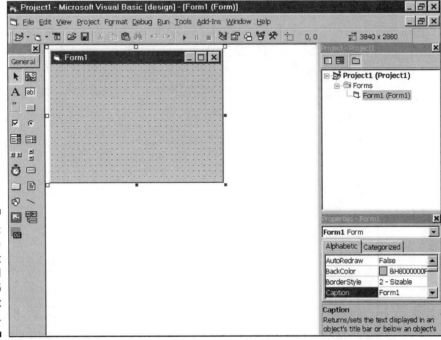

Figure 9-8:
The
Microsoft
Visual
Basic 5
Development
Environment.

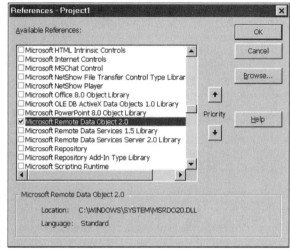

Figure 9-9:
The Visual
Basic 5
References
dialog box.

4. **Add a ListBox to your form by double-clicking the listbox control in the toolbox and resize it as desired.**

5. **Double-click anywhere on the Form that's highlighted by default to open the Form_Load code window (shown in Figure 9-10).**

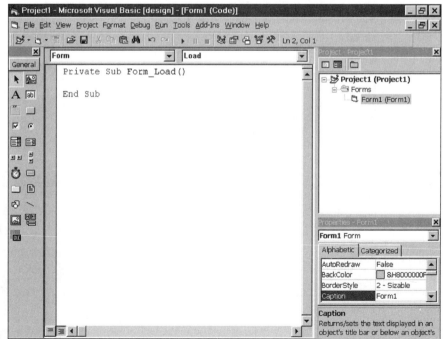

Figure 9-10:
The Visual
Basic 5
Form_Load
code
window.

6. Type in the VB code to access SQL Server.

Although you can find hundreds of possible ways to verse your code, here's one option:

```
'declare variables
Dim objConnection As rdoConnection
Dim objEnvironment As rdoEnvironment
Dim objResult As rdoResultset
Dim sSQL As String

'set environment
Set objEnvironment = rdoEnvironments(0)

'set username and password so login dialog isn't
        presented
objEnvironment.UserName = "sa"
objEnvironment.Password = ""

'establish the connection to SQL Server
Set objConnection =
        objEnvironment.OpenConnection("SQLServer7")

'create SQL to send to SQL Server
sSQL = "USE pubs" & Chr$(13)
sSQL = sSQL & "SELECT au_lname FROM Authors"

'create the resultset
Set objResult = objConnection.OpenResultset(sSQL)

'fill the text box with all data from result set
Do While Not objResult.EOF
    'add data from first column of result set to list
        box
    List1.AddItem objResult.rdoColumns(0)

    'move to the next record
    objResult.MoveNext
Loop
```

 The suggested statement only works if you have an ODBC data source already set up with the name of **SQLServer7**. If you don't, use the name of your own SQL Server data source.

7. Choose Run⇨Start to run the VB code.

This code selects all of the authors' last names in the pubs table and places them into a Visual Basic list box (see Figure 9-11). Again, this code is for the benefit of Visual Basic programmers who are trying to use SQL Server in conjunction with VB for the first time.

Figure 9-11:
Visual
Basic 5
example
showing
authors in a
list box.

English is spoken here

I want you to know that Microsoft SQL Server 7.0 comes with English Query, which is a program that allows you to issue commands to a database by specifying English phrases instead of SQL. However, you must know that Microsoft SQL Server 7.0 doesn't understand English, so the English Query translates English phrases into SQL so that the server can understand what you mean.

To do this translation, you must give English Query a lot of information about how to determine what phrases are associated with which SQL actions. I hate to keep you on the edge of your seat, but because of space limitations, I don't show you how to use English Query in this book. I just want you to know that it exists. See SQL Server's Books Online for more information on using English Query.

Chapter 10

Using Jobs and Alerts to Make SQL Server Work for You

. . . .

In This Chapter

▶ Creating Jobs

▶ Using Operators

▶ Alerting yourself

. . . .

*H*ave you ever wondered how to get your job done without actually having to do it? Well, with SQL Server jobs, that's exactly what happens. A job is a task that can be done automatically. As a matter of fact, prior to version 7.0, jobs were called tasks.

Think of a *job* as a series of steps that are executed in a sequence at specified times that you determine. These jobs are treated as a whole and can notify you or someone else about the status of the job. A whole job is one that either completes entirely, or not at all. In other words, a job is not partially successful. The status of the job is knowing whether or not the job has completed successfully.

Think of an *alert* as a response to an error condition. An error condition is when SQL Server generates an error. An error can be caused by lots of things, like poor SQL statement syntax. You can specify which error conditions your alert is to respond to. If you were not able to specify the error conditions for an alert, the alert would respond more often than you would like. For example, if you want to know when a backup failed, you need to specify this error condition only in an alert.

The way an alert works is that an operator is notified when the error condition that you specify occurs. An *operator* is a person who is in charge of jobs and is notified about alerts. In this chapter, I show how to create jobs, operators, and alerts. Also, I show how all these concepts relate together to make SQL Server work for you!

Creating a Job

To create a job, follow these steps:

1. **Choose Start⇨Programs⇨Microsoft SQL Server 7.0⇨Enterprise Manager to start the SQL Server Enterprise Manager.**

2. **Expand the tree so that you see the SQL Server Agent entry.**

   Refer to Chapter 1 to check out how to expand the tree.

3. **Bring up the New Job Properties dialog box by choosing Action⇨New⇨Job.**

    Alternatively, you can use the mouse to right-click the Jobs icon and select the New Job menu. Another way to create a new job is to click the New Job icon on the toolbar.

   Whichever method you choose to create a new job, each brings up a dialog box consisting of four tabs (General, Steps, Schedules, and Notifications), to allow you to bring up the parameters and data relating to the new job (see Figure 10-1). The General tab appears by default.

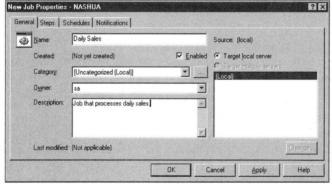

Figure 10-1: The General tab of the New Job Properties dialog box.

Entering general data

Enter general data that describes the job as a whole in the General tab. Describing the job involves giving it a name and description, and assigning the owners of the job. An *owner* is one who creates the job or is responsible for maintaining the job. To enter general data, make sure that the General tab is selected. A selected folder appears in the foreground and looks like a folder in a filing cabinet.

Fill in the following fields to enter general data in the General tab.

- ✔ **Name:** Give your job a name, such as **Daily Sales**, so that you can identify the job later.

- ✔ **Category:** Choose from the drop-down list of categories. A category is used to list jobs according to their type of function. A job doesn't need to be categorized. By default, [Uncategorized (Local)] is shown. This is fine, unless you want to change it. An example of when you may want to change the category is if you are creating many jobs relating to backing up. In this case, you should choose the category that closely matches the job function you are trying to achieve, such as Database Maintenance. To see what categories are available, click the arrow to expose the drop-down list of categories.

- ✔ **Owner:** Select the owner from the drop-down list of owners. An owner is one who is responsible for maintaining the job. By default, the currently logged in user is shown. If you want to select a different owner, you can do so now.

- ✔ **Description:** Give your job some type of description so that you know what it does, in case you forget it! Type in something like **Job that processes daily sales**.

Creating the sequence of steps

The Steps tab (shown in Figure 10-2) is used to review, edit, add, and delete steps in the sequence of steps that make up the job. From here, you can create a new step.

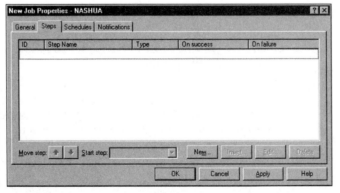

Figure 10-2:
Create or change job steps in the Steps tab.

1. To create a brand new step, click the New button.

Clicking the New button enters a new step field within the Steps tab. It then immediately brings up a new dialog box, called the New Job Step dialog box, shown in Figure 10-3. This dialog box contains two more tabs, the General tab and the Advanced tab, which allow you to specify attributes of the new step. Many Microsoft programs work this way. It may seem awkward to have tabs within tabs, but it really does make sense to organize the dialog box this way! (I know tabs within tabs can be confusing, but bear with me and you'll get through it.)

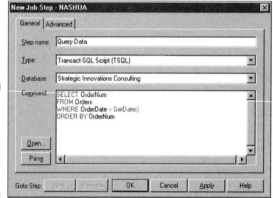

Figure 10-3: The General tab of the New Job Step dialog box.

If your machine is slow, this note is for you. After you click the New button, the new step entry within the Steps tab shows up immediately, but the dialog box may not show up right away.

2. Type general information about the new job step in the General tab of the New Job Step dialog box.

- **Step Name:** Give your new job step a name (such as **Query Data**) so that you can identify the job step later.

- **Type:** Choose the type of step you want to designate from the drop-down list of types. The step type indicates the specific function of the job step. TSQL is chosen by default because most of the time you create jobs that issue TSQL statements. *TSQL*, or Transact-SQL, is one or more SQL statements that is executed to produce some result.

- **Database:** Choose the database you want to use from the list of databases registered on the server. By default, master is shown. I chose Strategic Innovations Consulting, which is the database used in my query. You choose a database that contains the tables used in your query. If you choose the wrong database, your query can't run.

- **Command:** Type in the command that you want to use to process the new step that you just defined. The Type you selected dictates what command is valid for you to use. For example, if you select TSQL, you must type a valid SQL statement in the Command text box. If you select ActiveScripting, you must type in a valid script.

Because my TSQL command is based on an Orders table within my Strategic Innovations Consulting database, my Command looks like this:

```
SELECT OrderNum
FROM Orders
WHERE OrderDate = GetDate()
ORDER BY OrderNum
```

My Orders table contains the columns OrderNum (an automatically generated reference number) and OrderDate (the date the order was placed). For more information about SQL, see Chapter 8. It provides a great overview into the use of SQL.

If you have a command already stored in a file, you can insert the contents of that file by clicking on the Open button and selecting the file.

If you want to verify the format of the Command, simply click the Parse button. Doing so results in a message box appearing, letting you know whether there are any problems with your Command or whether the parse succeeded. If the parse succeeded, there are no errors.

3. **Click the Advanced tab at the top of the New Job Step dialog box and type advanced information about the new job step (see Figure 10-4).**

   Use the Advanced tab on the New Job Step dialog box to define additional, or more advanced information about the new step, such as additional options and what to do upon success or failure of the Command entered in Step 2.

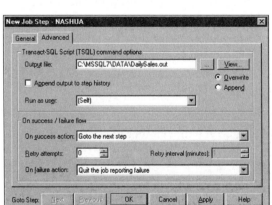

Figure 10-4: The Advanced tab of the New Job Step dialog box.

- **Output file:** Type in a file name that stores the results of the Command entered in Step 2. I use a file called DailySales.out in the C:\MSSQL7\DATA directory.

- **Run as user:** Choose Run as user from the drop-down list of database users. Because different users have different permission levels, SQL Server needs to know the user under which the TSQL statement(s) will run. By default, (Self) is shown. Self indicates that the job is run as the user you are logged into at the time the job is created. In other words, whoever you are logged into right now!

It's important to know that the top part of the Advanced tab dialog box, labeled **Transact-SQL Script (TSQL) command options**, presents different options if you choose anything other than **Transact-SQL Script (TSQL)** as a Type in the preceding Step 2. Table 10-1 shows the fields you need to fill out if you choose any of the other **Type** options.

Table 10-1	Advanced Tab Options Available for the General Tab Types
Type	*Options Available*
Active Script	None
Operating System Command (CmdExec)	Output file
Replication Distributor	None
Replication Transaction-Log Reader	None
Replication Merge	None
Replication Snapshot	None
Transact-SQL Script (TSQL)	Output file and Run as user

- **On success action:** Choose On success action from the drop-down list of possible actions. By default, **Goto the next step** is shown. The possible actions are:

  Quit the job reporting success — Stops processing the current job that reports a step completed successfully.

  Quit the job reporting failure — Stops processing the current job that reports a step failed.

  Goto the next step — Continues to the next step in the current job.

- **Retry attempts:** Type the number of attempts a failed action should retry. By default, **0** is shown. You may want to enter a number of retry attempts if you believe your Command entered in

Step 2 relies on the timing of another process. If this is the case, a number of retries may prove successful. However, in most cases, if a Command fails, retrying the Command only results in a delay in the job completion (with a failure status).

- **Retry interval (minutes):** If you enter a number other than zero in the Retry attempts field, the Retry interval field becomes enabled, allowing you to specify the number of minutes of elapsed time before attempting a retry of executing the Command entered in the preceding Step 2.

- **On failure action:** Choose On failure action from the drop-down list of possible actions. By default, **Quit the job reporting failure** is shown. The possible actions are:

  Quit the job reporting success — Stops processing the current job that reports a step completed successfully.

  Quit the job reporting failure — Stops processing the current job that reports a step failed.

  Goto the next step — Continues to the next step in the current job.

4. **Click OK.**

   The OK button applies all changes and closes the dialog box. You are returned to the Steps tab within the New Job Properties dialog box. Additionally, you see the new job step that you just created listed within this tab.

After you click OK for the job, the last step's success action is changed from the **Goto the next step** option to the **Quit the job reporting success** option.

Scheduling the frequency of the job

You use the Schedules tab to review, edit, add, and delete the scheduled frequencies at which the job runs. Any of these frequencies encompasses the entire job, not separate steps. Because I use an example about reporting on daily sales, the frequency of the job is to run only once daily.

Click the Schedules tab located at the top of the New Job Properties dialog box to bring up the Schedules tab, shown in Figure 10-5.

It's a good idea to schedule a query to run in the middle of the night so that it does not affect server performance during the day. This way, network traffic stays at a minimum level when more people need to be accessing the network.

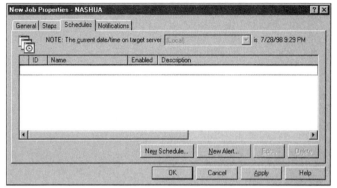

Figure 10-5:
Use the
Schedules
tab to
create or
change job
schedules.

1. **To create a brand new schedule, click the New Schedule button.**

   Clicking the New Schedule button enters a new schedule field within the Schedules tab and then immediately brings up the New Job Schedule dialog box, allowing you to specify attributes of the new schedule. (See Figure 10-6.)

2. **Type in information about the new job schedule.**

   • **Name:** Give your schedule a name, such as **Daily Sales Schedule**, so that you can identify the schedule later.

   • **Enabled:** Choose whether or not the schedule is enabled, or active. By default, you see a check mark in the box indicating that the schedule is active. You may want to have some schedules that are only run once in a while, or that you use for testing. If you are following my example, ensure that the box is checked.

   • **Schedule Type:** Select the type of schedule you wish to create. You can choose from one of four options:

   Start automatically when SQL Server Agent starts — Starts the job when the SQL Server Agent starts (either automatically or manually). This allows you to specify a boot-up schedule.

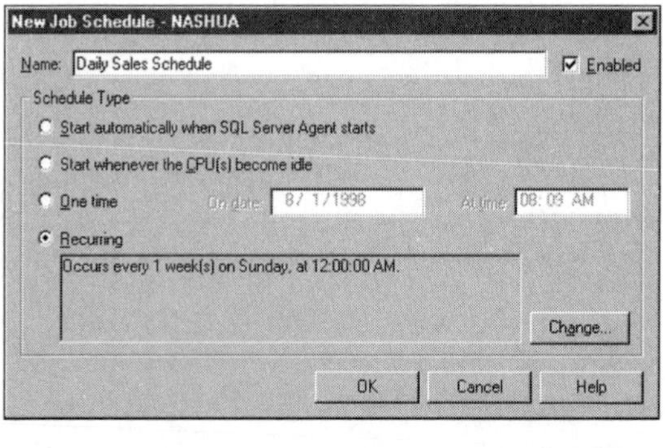

Figure 10-6:
The New
Job
Schedule
dialog box
awaits your
scheduling
wisdom.

Start whenever the CPU(s) become idle — Starts the job whenever the system processor(s) is not busy. If a very calculation-intensive query is running, there is no time for the job to run. This option enables you to perform periodic system processing without sacrificing CPU cycles for a user's query.

One time — Runs the job once, at a specified date and time. Choosing this option enables the **On date** and **At time** fields, allowing you to specify the date and time, respectively.

Recurring — Runs the job on a recurring basis, at intervals that you specify. Because this is the most popular option for a job, it is selected by default. Also by default, the schedule runs once a week, on the current day, at midnight. To change the Recurring option, continue with the next step.

3. **Click the Change button.**

   Clicking the Change button allows you to change, or edit, the recurring schedule shown within the Recurring option field. Doing so brings up the Edit Recurring Job Schedule dialog box (see Figure 10-7).

4. **Click the Daily option.**

   This option is located within the **Occurs** section. Other choices are Weekly and Monthly.

5. **Click the Occurs once at option.**

   This option is located within the **Daily frequency** section. You need to check this option because the schedule needs to run only once a day. The other option is the **Occurs every** option. It is used to specify a period of time within the time option chosen in the **Occurs** section to schedule the job.

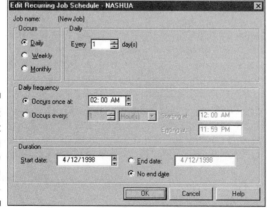

Figure 10-7:
The Edit
Recurring
Job
Schedule
dialog box.

6. **Type in the time of day you want the job to run.**

   A time in the middle of the night is best for computing intensive daily queries. Type **02:00 AM**.

7. **Type in a Duration.**

   In the Duration section, a **S̲tart Date** of today is entered by default, and the **No end d̲ate** option is checked by default. If you want to specify an end date, click the **E̲nd date** option and type an end date in the box provided.

8. **Click the OK button on the Edit Recurring Job Schedule dialog box.**

   The OK button saves all changes to the Edit Recurring Job Schedule dialog box and closes it. The New Job Schedule dialog box reappears.

9. **Click the OK button on the New Job Schedule dialog box.**

   The OK button applies all changes to the New Job Schedule dialog box and closes it. You are returned to the Schedules tab within the New Job Properties dialog box. Additionally, you see the new schedule that you just created listed within this tab.

10. **Click the OK button on the New Job Properties dialog box.**

    The OK button applies all changes to the New Job Properties dialog box and closes it.

What do I do when the job completes?

The Notifications tab is used to indicate what actions need to be performed when the job completes. A job can complete with one of two statuses: successful or unsuccessful (failure). You use either of these statuses to specify actions to take when the job completes. You actually need not do anything when the job completes — that is, if you don't care about the status of the job completion. However, if you do care about the status of the job completion and wish for someone or something to be notified, read on!

To bring up the Notifications tab, click the Notifications tab located at the top of the New Job Properties dialog box (see Figure 10-8).

Either an individual or SQL Server can be notified about the status of a job. The individual is defined as the operator. This means that if you wish to have a user notified about a job status, the user must first be setup as an operator. Notifying SQL Server can be specified without setting up an operator.

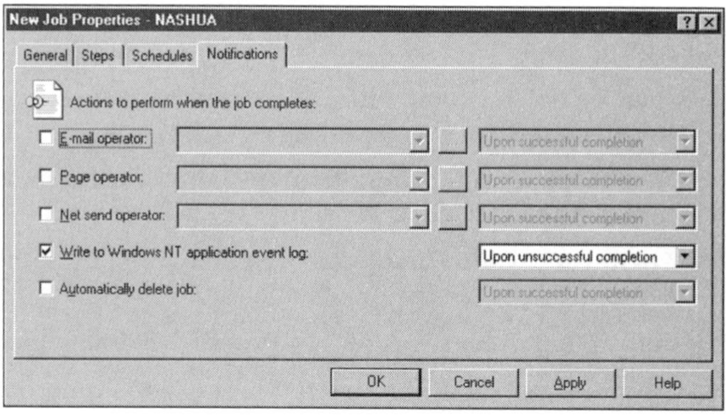

Figure 10-8:
Indicate
actions
to be
performed
upon job
completion
in the
Notifications
tab.

New Job Properties - NASHUA   ? ×

General | Steps | Schedules | Notifications |

Actions to perform when the job completes:

☐ E-mail operator: [▼] [ ] [Upon successful completion ▼]

☐ Page operator: [▼] [ ] [Upon successful completion ▼]

☐ Net send operator: [▼] [ ] [Upon successful completion ▼]

☑ Write to Windows NT application event log: [Upon unsuccessful completion ▼]

☐ Automatically delete job: [Upon successful completion ▼]

                    [OK] [Cancel] [Apply] [Help]

1. Specify action(s).

You can specify one or more actions to take by clicking on the check box next to the action listed on the dialog box in the Notifications tab (refer to Figure 10-8):

- **E-Mail operator:** Notifies an operator by e-mail.

- **Page operator:** Notifies an operator by paging.

- **Net send operator:** Notifies an operator by sending a pop-up message over the network. This is available only on Windows NT 4.0 and later, not Windows 95 or later.

- **Write to Windows NT application event log:** Writes the status of the job to the application event log under Windows NT.

- **Automatically delete job:** Deletes the job when complete. This is useful for a one-time only job.

2. Specify the operator(s).

If you choose **E-mail operator**, **Page operator**, or **Net send operator**, you need to specify the name of the operator. To do so, select from the drop-down list for each type of operator that you checked for notification. By default, the name of the operator assigned to the currently logged in user is shown.

I choose E-mail operator, so that I am notified when a job fails.

To specify a new operator, refer to the section, "Hello . . . Operator?" later in this chapter.

3. Specify condition(s).

If you choose **E-mail operator**, **Page operator**, or **Net send operator**, you need to specify the condition under which the operator will be notified. By default, the **Upon successful completion** option is shown.

You can choose a different option, if desired. The following are the options available:

- **Upon successful completion** — Operator will be notified only if the job completes successfully.

- **Upon unsuccessful completion** — Operator will be notified only if the job completes unsuccessfully (failure).

- **Whenever the job completes** — Operator will be notified regardless of the status of the job completion.

4. **Click the OK button on the New Job Properties dialog box.**

   The OK button applies all changes to the New Job Properties dialog box and closes it.

Hello . . . Operator?

An *operator* is an individual who is notified of the status of a job. The operator receives a specific type of notification within the time period as defined by the job. If you wish to be set up for notification upon the completion of a job, you must be added as an operator. SQL Server 7 provides the ability to add new operators. To set up a new operator, follow these steps:

1. **Expand the tree so that you see the SQL Server Agent entry.**

   Refer to Chapter 1 to check out how to expand the tree.

2. **Bring up the New Operator Properties dialog box by choosing Action➪New➪Operator.**

   Alternatively, you can use the mouse to right-click the Operators icon and select the New Operator menu.

   Any method you choose to create a new operator brings up a dialog box consisting of two tabs, the General tab and the Notifications tab, to allow you to type the parameters and data relating to the new operator. The General tab comes up first by default. (See Figure 10-9.)

Entering general data . . . one more time

Type general data about the operator in the General tab, such as name, contact information (e-mail address, pager name, net send address), and duty schedule. A *duty schedule* is the hours that the specified operator is available to be notified.

✔ **Name:** Give your operator a name. I enter my name as **Anthony T. Mann**. Entering the full name allows for quick reference to an operator.

✔ **E-mail name:** Type the name of the person to e-mail, as it appears in your address book. I enter my e-mail as **tmann**. If you wish to choose from the address book on your system, click the **...** button. After you enter an E-mail name, you can test the e-mail by clicking the Test button.

✔ **Pager e-mail name:** Type the name of the person to page, as it appears in your address book. I enter my name as **tmann**. If you wish to choose from the address book on your system, click the **...** button. After you enter a Pager e-mail name, you can test the pager by clicking the Test button.

✔ **Net send address:** Type the address of the machine to notify using the network. After you enter a Net send address, you can test the net send address by clicking the Test button. Clicking the Test button sends a pop-up message to the user that is logged into the network with the address (Login ID) you have entered in this field.

✔ **Pager on duty schedule:** Check the days and type the times the operator is available to be notified. An operator is considered to be available 24 hours if this person is available Monday through Thursday. For Friday, Saturday, or Sunday, you must type the times that the operator is available to be notified. By default, these times are between 8:00 AM and 6:00 PM.

Click the OK button to apply all changes and close the dialog box.

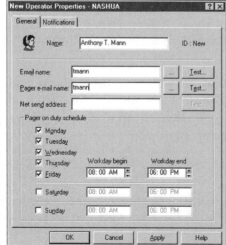

Figure 10-9:
The General tab of the New Operator Properties dialog box.

Viewing an operator's notifications

The Notifications tab shows an operator's capability to receive notifications. (See Figure 10-10.) You're unable to enter information in this dialog box — notifications are specified when you create a job (see the section, "Creating a Job" earlier in this chapter). This dialog box exists to enable you to view in one place all the notifications assigned to the currently selected (or added) operator.

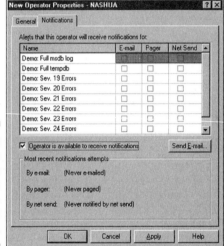

Figure 10-10: The Notifications tab lets you view the assigned notifications.

This dialog box is read-only, with the exception of the check box: Operator is available to receive notifications. This check box lets you to specify whether the operator will receive any notifications. The dialog box shows the following fields:

- ✔ **Alerts that this operator will receive notifications for:** Shows the name, E-mail name, and pager name specified for the operator.

- ✔ **Operator is available to receive notifications:** This check box can be used to indicate that an operator will not receive any notifications. To specify this, simply uncheck this box. By default, the box is checked, indicating that the operator will receive the notifications listed at the top of the dialog box.

- ✔ **Most recent notification attempts:** Shows the most recent notifications by e-mail, pager, or net send. For a new operator, all fields indicate that notification has never been made.

Click the OK button to apply all changes and close the dialog box.

Using Alerts

An *alert* is an event that responds to criteria you specify. For example, an alert can notify you when a specific error occurs.

Although SQL Server 7 now runs on Windows 95 or higher, alerts are available only on Windows NT 4.0 and higher. If you are running Windows 95 or higher, the icon for Alerts will not even show up. For an alert to work, you must have the SQL Server Agent service running. To do this, bring up the control panel by selecting Start⇨Settings⇨Control Panel. Then double-click the Services icon to bring up the dialog box shown in Figure 10-11. Ensure that the SQLServerAgent service is started.

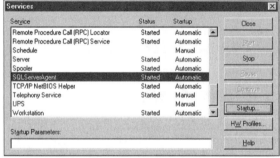

Figure 10-11:
The
Windows NT
Services
dialog box.

The SQL Server Agent is notified of the job status when the criteria you specify is satisfied, thereby generating the alert, also known as *raising an alert*.

To create a new alert, follow these steps:

1. **Start the SQL Server Enterprise Manager.**

   Select Start⇨Programs⇨Microsoft SQL Server 7.0⇨Enterprise Manager.

2. **Expand the tree so that you see the SQL Server Agent entry.**

   Refer to Chapter 1 to check out how to expand the tree.

3. **Bring up the New Alert Properties dialog box by choosing Action⇨New⇨Alert.**

   Alternatively, you can use the mouse to right-click the Alerts icon and select the New Alert menu.

   Any method you choose to create a new alert brings up a dialog box consisting of two tabs, the General tab and the Response tab, to allow you to type the definition and response to the new alert. The General tab appears first by default. (See Figure 10-12.)

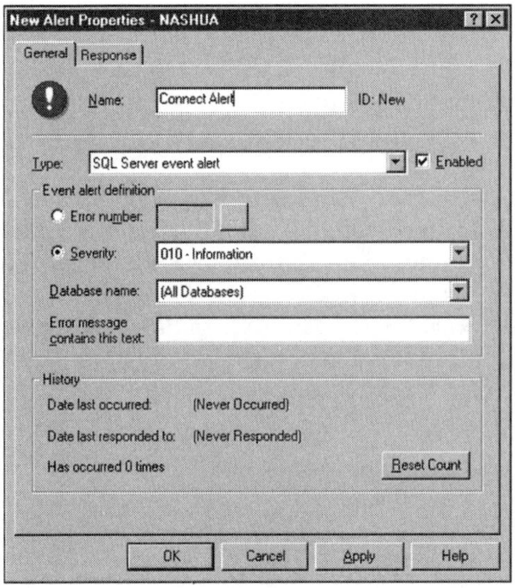

Figure 10-12:
The General tab of the New Alert Properties dialog box.

Defining alert conditions

You can use the General tab to define alert conditions. This tab is where you specify the criteria for which an alert is raised. First, you determine whether you want the alert to be raised if a specific error occurs, a certain severity of error occurs, or even if the text of the error contains specific characters.

To define alert conditions, type the following information in the General tab:

- ✔ **Name:** Give your alert a name (such as **Connect Alert**), so that you can identify the alert later.

- ✔ **Type:** At this time, only one type of alert is available, the SQL Server event alert, which is selected by default and cannot be unselected.

- ✔ **Enabled:** Indicates that this alert will be enabled if the check box is checked. If unchecked, this alert will not be enabled. This field is checked by default.

- ✔ **Error Number:** Click this option button if you want to raise the alert when a specific error number occurs. Once clicked, the text box becomes enabled, allowing you to type the specific error number. Alternatively, you can click the ... button, which shows you a dialog box containing the possible error numbers to choose from.

- ✔ **Severity:** Click this option button if you want to raise the alert when a specific severity of error occurs. The *severity* indicates how critical the error is. An error could simply be informational, or it could be critical to the point that processing can't continue. Once clicked, the drop-down list of possible errors becomes enabled. This option is selected by default, and the drop-down list shows 010-Information. This indicates that the alert will be generated only for errors that are only informational, not critical.

✔ **Database name:** Select the database name used by SQL Server to determine when to raise the alert. You can choose from any registered database, or all databases. **All Databases** is chosen by default.

✔ **Error message contains this text:** If you wish to further qualify the conditions of the alert, in addition to the other criteria shown above, you can type the text that the alert must contain to match the criteria. For example, if you want the alert to respond when there is a connection error, you might type **connect** in this box.

Click the OK button to apply all changes and close the dialog box. Alternatively, you can click the Apply button to apply changes and leave the dialog box open. This allows you to move to the next section.

Defining alert responses

Enter information in the Response tab to define which operator(s) receive responses to the alert criteria specified in the General tab. For more information about operators, refer to the section, "Hello...Operator?" earlier in this chapter. Click the Response tab located at the top of the New Alert Properties dialog box. (See Figure 10-13.)

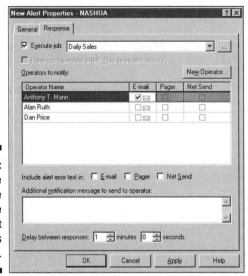

Figure 10-13:
The Response tab of the New Alert Properties dialog box.

To define which operator(s) receive a response to the alert criteria, enter the following information:

- ✔ **Execute Job:** If you want one of the responses to the alert to be to execute a job, check this field. If the field is checked, you can select the name of the job from the drop-down list of jobs.

- ✔ **Raise corresponding SNMP Trap when alert occurs:** If you are using SNMP, this check box is enabled. If you are not, it is disabled, as is the case in Figure 10-13. For more information about SNMP, refer to *Microsoft Windows NT 4 For Dummies* by Andy Rathbone and Sharon Crawford (published by IDG Books Worldwide, Inc.).

- ✔ **Operators to notify:** In addition to executing a job, you can have specific operators notified about the alert being raised. This field is a grid containing four columns. The first is the name of the operator. The second is a check box for notifying the operator by e-mail. The third is a check box for notifying the operator by pager. The fourth is a check box for notifying the operator by net send. To use this grid, simply check the types of notification (e-mail, pager, or net send) next to the adjacent operator's name. Doing so notifies any operator with a check mark in the appropriate column when the alert is raised. If you want to specify a new operator, click the New Operator button.

- ✔ **Include alert error text in:** This field is a series of three check boxes. You can choose to include the actual text message of the error by clicking any or all of the choices. The choices are **E-mail**, **Pager**, and **Net Send**.

- ✔ **Additional notification message to send to operator:** If you want additional text (other than the error text) to be sent to the operator, type that text in here. For example, you could type the name of the alert, such as **Connect Alert**.

- ✔ **Delay between responses for a recurring alert:** This field allows you to specify, in minutes and seconds, how much of a delay you want between recurring alerts of the same type. This delay makes it possible not to be notified many times about the same alert. Often an error can appear many times within a short time span. If the error occurs 10 times a minute, you don't want to receive 10 e-mails! Therefore, you may want to leave this value at the default of 1 minute and 0 seconds.

Click the OK button to apply all changes and close the dialog box. Alternatively, you can click the Apply button to apply changes and leave the dialog box open.

Chapter 11

Maintaining Flexibility by Importing and Exporting Data

In This Chapter

▶ Reusing your existing data through importing

▶ Sharing data with other applications by exporting

*W*hen it comes to data, you must maintain flexibility. Flexibility refers to the ability to use data in multiple locations. If there were no provision to use data from some other location into SQL Server (Importing) or from SQL Server to some other location (Exporting), many companies would never use SQL Server. The lack of flexibility is too limiting. Companies need to be able to use data from other databases or locations. In this chapter, I show you how to import and export using SQL Server 7.

I have seen many times that some people confuse the terms importing and exporting. The confusion seems to come not when thinking of a single system importing or exporting, but when thinking of one system importing and another exporting to complete some process. It's the same type of confusion that sets in when discussing debits and credits in accounting. Therefore, look at it this way. Suppose you owe a friend $100. This person is going to import (deposit) the money you give into an account. However, for your friend to import the money, you need to export it (withdrawal). The side of the transaction you are looking at dictates whether you have an import or an export. Keep this in mind as you read this chapter.

Because different types of data are formatted differently, you may need to reformat your files so that the database you're importing to accepts the files. Of course, realize that the screens that I show in this chapter will change based on the options you choose — different data-source options need different types of data specified. Therefore, the screen automatically adjusts itself to allow you to fill in the data necessary for the data source that you choose. For example, if your data source is Microsoft Access, you need to specify the file name (database) that contains the data. If you specify a different data source, you don't have to specify the file name, but you specify other information, as determined by the data source. You can see what I mean as you read the rest of this chapter!

To help you follow the flow of the wizards that I show you in this chapter, see the flowcharts in Appendix A.

Importing Data to a SQL Server Database

Knowing how to construct your database and insert data is one thing (see Chapters 5 and 8). But what if you need to use *legacy data,* data that's stored in another database system? In this section, I show you how to import legacy data located in another system into Microsoft SQL Server 7.

The Import Wizard, sometimes referred to as the DTS Import Wizard, guides you through the process of importing your data. A series of steps prompts you for information.

To import your data using the Import Wizard, follow these steps:

1. **Choose Start⇨Programs⇨Microsoft SQL Server 7.0⇨SQL Server Enterprise Manager to start the SQL Server Enterprise Manager.**

   You then see the tree of folders on the left-hand side of the screen.

2. **Expand the tree so that you see the Databases entry.**

   Refer to Chapter 1 to check out how to expand the tree to find the database you need.

3. **Select a database you want to import into SQL Server 7 by clicking on it.**

   Expand the database under the Databases entry in the tree so that you view all the databases. Select the database you want to import data into.

4. **Choose Action⇨Task⇨Import into SQL... to begin the Import Wizard.**

   Alternatively, you can use the mouse to right-click the specific desired database listed under the Databases entry and select the Task⇨Import into SQL... menu option.

   Any method you choose brings up a wizard, allowing you to specify information about the import (see Figure 11-1).

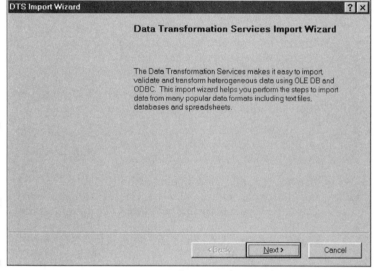

Figure 11-1:
The Data
Transformation
Services
Import
Wizard
welcomes
you!

5. **After you read the introduction screen, click Next.**

   The Choose a Data Source dialog box appears (see Figure 11-2).

6. **Choose a Data Source relating to the source data. Then click Next.**

   A data source indicates the format of data used for your import.

   To perform this example, you must have Microsoft Visual Basic installed on your computer, along with the sample databases.

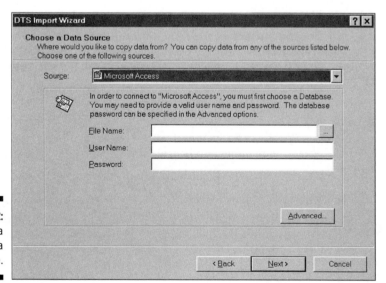

Figure 11-2:
Choose a
data
source.

The fields in this dialog box that you need to provide information for are:

- **Source:** *Source data* is the data that you are importing into SQL Server. All fields on this screen relate to the source data. Select the system that provides the data you're importing.

  I use a specific example in this section. Note that different data sources require that you provide different information.

  Choose **Microsoft Access** as the source. (I will show you how to import the data from the Microsoft Access Biblio database into the SQL Server 7 pubs database.)

- **File Name:** Click the ellipsis button (…) to choose the file name of the Microsoft Access database you want to import data from. If you have Visual Basic installed on your computer, the Microsoft Access database Biblio.mdb is also installed. I use this in my example. If you used all of the default locations when you installed Microsoft Visual Basic, the path to the Biblio database is `C:\Program Files\DevStudio\VB\Biblio.mdb`.

- **User Name:** If your database uses security, you need to type in a user name (and **Password**). If you are following my example, the Biblio database does not use security, so you can leave this field blank.

- **Password:** If your database uses security, you need to type in a Password (and **User Name**). If you are following my example, the Biblio database does not use security, so just leave this field blank.

7. **From the Choose a Destination dialog box (see Figure 11-3), choose a destination for the import. Then click Next.**

   This dialog box prompts you to specify where to import the data into.

   - **Destination:** Select the format for the data with the Destination drop-down list. For my example, choose **Microsoft SQL Server 7.0 Only (OLE DB Provider)**, which is also the default option.

   - **Server:** Enter or select the server that contains the database you will import into. By default, **(local)** is selected, indicating that the computer which is running the Import Wizard will be used.

   - **Use Windows NT authentication:** Use this option if you want the user's logon name and password to be used for authentication.

   - **Use SQL Server NT authentication:** This option is used if you want to indicate in the **User Name** and **Password** fields the data for SQL Server to authenticate. This is the default option. Once this option is chosen, the User Name and Password fields become enabled. Enter the desired name and password. I use **sa** as my login with no password.

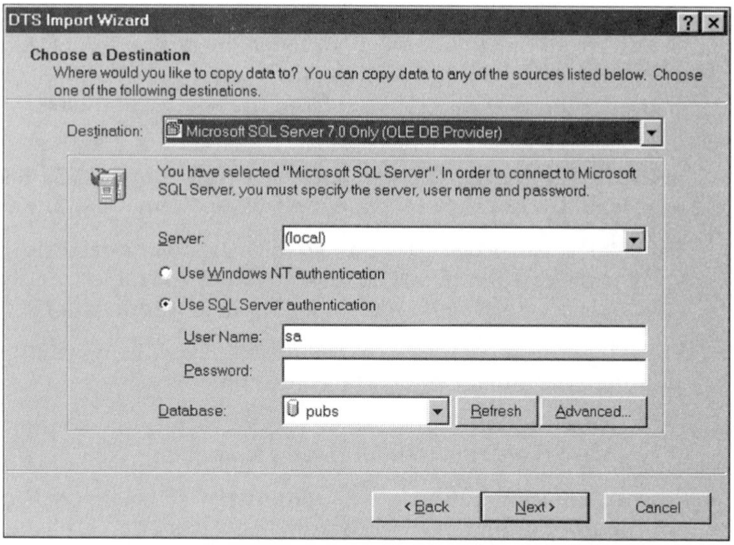

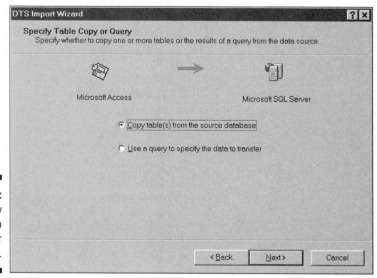

Figure 11-3:
Choose a
destination
for your
import.

- **Database:** Select from the drop-down list of databases the database that contains the table you will use to import data into. For my example, choose the **pubs** database. If you don't see your desired table in the database, click the Refresh button.

8. **In the Specify Table Copy or Query dialog box (see Figure 11-4), specify whether to copy one or more tables or the results of a query from the data source. Then click Next.**

Figure 11-4:
Specify
tables to
copy or
query.

This dialog box prompts you to specify whether you want to copy all records from the source table, or use a query that limits the records to a specific subset of data. Choose the appropriate option. For my example, choose **Copy table(s) from the source database**, which is also the default option.

9. **In the Select Source Tables dialog box (see Figure 11-5), select the source tables in the Select Source Tables dialog box. Then click Next.**

This dialog box prompts you to specify the source tables to assign to specific destination tables. A *source table* is the table where data is coming from. A *destination* table is the table where data is going to.

The tables are presented in a grid format, allowing for multiple rows and three columns of data. The three columns are:

- **Source Table:** Check the check box next to the source table name to use that table to import data from.

- **Destination Table:** If the source table is checked, you can specify a destination table. By default, the destination table name is the same as the source table name, only it's in the destination database. If the destination table already exists, SQL Server automatically appends data to the end of the table. If the destination table doesn't exist, SQL Server creates a new table.

- **Transform:** This option specifies additional information about the import. For example, you can specify the data types for the different columns of data. To access the transform screens, click the ellipsis button (...). Because the transform option is an advanced topic, it is outside the scope of this book, and I don't cover it here. Consult the online help for SQL Server 7 for more information.

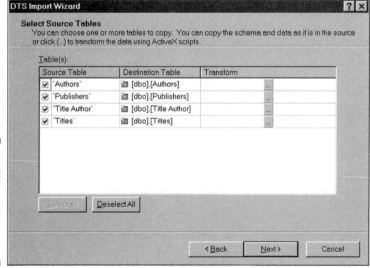

Figure 11-5:
Select source tables for your destination tables.

10. **In the Save, Schedule, and Replicate Package dialog box (see Figure 11-6), select the save, schedule, and replicate option that you want. Then click Next.**

This dialog box prompts you to specify whether or not you want to save the DTS package. A *DTS package* is the entire set of instructions you configured. If you save the package, you can run it again at a later time. If you don't save it, the information you specified is lost after this import.

- Uncheck the **Save Package on SQL Server** option if this is a one-time import.

- Check the **Save Package on SQL Server** option if you plan to use the specified import information again.

If you choose the save option, you can also specify that you want to execute the import at a later time by clicking the **Schedule DTS package for later execution** check box. (This check box is only enabled when you choose the save option.) Clicking on the ellipses button (...) creates a new job. For more information about creating jobs, see Chapter 10.

11. **In the Completing the DTS Import Wizard dialog box (see Figure 11-7), review your choices. Then click Finish.**

This dialog box prompts you to review your choices. After you review your choices, you can click the <u>B</u>ack button to change any information that you typed earlier, or click the Finish button to begin the import.

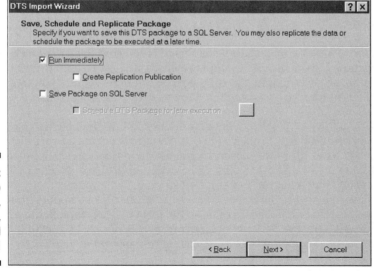

Figure 11-6:
Get ready to save, schedule, and replicate!

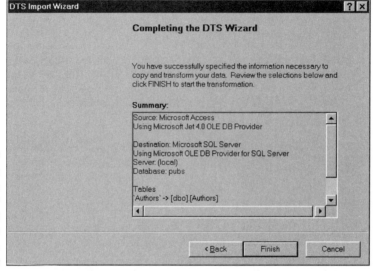

Figure 11-7:
Here you
review your
choices
before
finishing.

Exporting Data from a SQL Server 7 Database to Another Database

Use the Export Wizard when you need to export data from a database in SQL Server 7 to another database. In this section, I show how the Export Wizard, also referred to as the DTS Export Wizard, guides you through a series of steps to perform the exporting process, prompting you for data at each step.

The data that you wish to be exported is referred to as the *export*. In this section, I use a specific example to illustrate how to export files to another database server. Note that different destinations require you to provide different information than that shown in the following steps.

Although your files may contain graphics, tables, and elements other than text, often an export goes from SQL Server to a common text file, as opposed to a proprietary format, such as Microsoft Access, because — at a minimum — most other servers have an import from a common text file. It's unlikely that a payroll system, for example, can import directly from a Microsoft Access database. However, it probably can import from a text file because that is the most common file format. Therefore, in the example I present here, I show how to export from SQL Server to a text file because it is the most common type of exporting that occurs.

The Export Wizard also asks you to specify whether you want to copy all records from one source table, or use a query that limits the records to a specific subset of data.

I show you how to export the data from the SQL Server 7 pubs database into a text file. The pubs database is one that is installed automatically when you setup SQL Server 7. It's a sample database that includes book, author, and publisher information for some books. I can't believe I'm not in the database!

To export your data using the Export Wizard, follow these steps:

1. **Choose Start⇨Programs⇨Microsoft SQL Server 7.0⇨SQL Server Enterprise Manager.**

2. **Expand the tree in the All Folders pane to view the Databases folder.**

   Refer to Chapter 1 to see how to expand the tree.

3. **Click the database you want to export data from.**

4. **Choose Action⇨Task⇨Export from SQL... to bring up the Export Wizard (see Figure 11-8).**

   You can also right-click the database and then choose the Task⇨Export from SQL... Enterprise Manager menu option. The Welcome screen of the Export Wizard appears.

5. **After you have read the Welcome screen, click the Next button to continue.**

6. **In the Choose a Data Source dialog box (see Figure 11-9), choose the source data for the export. Then click Next.**

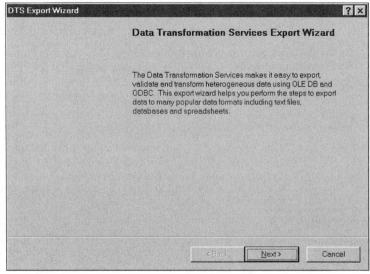

Figure 11-8:
The Data Transformation Services Export Wizard greets you warmly.

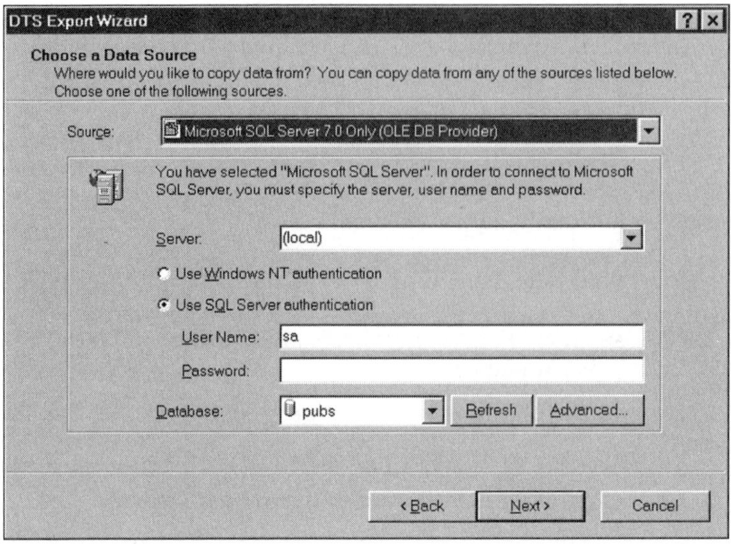

Figure 11-9:
Choose a
data source
for export.

This dialog box prompts you to specify from where the data is coming for the export. The fields in this dialog box that you need to provide information for are:

- **Source:** Select the format for the data with the **Source** drop-down list provided. For my example, choose **Microsoft SQL Server 7.0 Only (OLE DB Provider)**, which is also the default option.

- **Server:** Enter or select the server that contains the database you will export from. By default, **(local)** is selected, indicating that the computer running the Export Wizard will be used.

- **Use Windows NT authentication:** Use this option if you want the user's logon name and password to be used for authentication.

- **Use SQL Server NT authentication:** This option is if you want to indicate in the **User Name** and **Password** fields the data for SQL Server to authenticate. This is the default option. After you choose this option, the User Name and Password fields become enabled. Enter the desired name and password. I use **sa** as my logon with no password.

- **Database:** Select from the drop-down list of databases the database that contains the table you will use to import data into. For my example, choose the **pubs** database. If you don't see your desired table in the database, click the Refresh button.

7. **In the Choose a Destination dialog box (see Figure 11-10), select the system, or destination, that accepts the data you're exporting. Then click Next.**

   • **Destination:** Click Text File from the drop-down list. This step brings up a sub-screen in the dialog box that enables you to provide more information on the destination.

   • **File Name:** Type the name of the text file you want to create, or choose an existing text file by clicking the ellipsis button (...). Type **C:\Authors.txt** for this example.

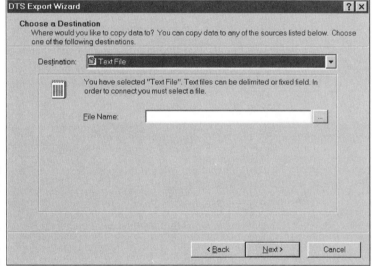

Figure 11-10:
Choose a
Destination
for your
data.

8. **In the Specify Table Copy or Query dialog box (see Figure 11-11), click Copy table(s) from the source database (which is also the default option). Then click Next.**

9. **In the Select Destination File Format dialog box (see Figure 11-12), select the destination file format of the text file you want to export. Then click Next.**

   This dialog box prompts you to specify the file format of the text file you are using to export data from. The fields you need to provide information for are:

   • **Source:** Choose the table from the available source tables used for the export. The data from this table is exported in the format you select in this dialog box. Choose the table **pubs.dbo.[authors]**.

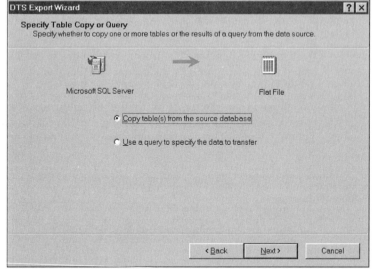

Figure 11-11:
Specify
table(s) to
copy or
query.

Figure 11-12:
Select the
destination
file format of
the text file
you export.

Note that the format **database.dbo.[table]** is a more precise
specification of the table. You can use the table name alone, but
doing so indicates that the table you're exporting is in the current
database (the one you are logged in to). If your table is in the
current database, you then need to specify that database in the
table name. The **dbo** between the database and the table name
stands for *database owner*. A database owner is one who creates a
database. You need to include **dbo** to indicate permissions
necessary to access the table.

- **Delimited:** Click this option when you want every field in your text file to be separated by a character that you specify. Often, a record is made up of variable-length fields, separated (or delimited) by commas. However, problems can occur if your data contains commas. This step enables you to specify the delimiters in your text file. Click Delimited for this example.

- **Fixed Field:** Click this option when you want every field in your text file to be the same width (number of characters).

- **File Type:** Choose the type of file, ANSI or Unicode, that you want your file to be, from the drop-down list. ANSI is a standard by which you can only use the characters chosen in the current character set. Unicode is a standard by which you can use characters defined by a much larger standard that may cross character sets. Using Unicode uses twice as much storage space as using ANSI.

- **Row Delimiter:** Choose from the drop-down list of choices how you want to indicate that there are no more fields (columns) in a record. The default is {CR}{LF}, which is a carriage return and a line feed. {CR}{LF} is typically used in a text file export or import.

- **Column Delimiter:** Choose how you want to separate column data from the drop-down list. (This field is enabled only if you choose the **Delimited** option.) The default is **Comma**, which is typically used in a delimited text file export or import.

- **Text Qualifier:** Choose how you want to indicate that a field is a text field, rather than a numeric field, from the drop-down list. The default is **Double Quote** (" "), and is typically used in a text file export or import. You want to qualify text fields because some systems don't accept what appears to be a numeric field in a text file into a character field. For example, **93843** appears to be a numeric field. If a system attempts to import it into a character field, the import may fail. This field should appear as **"93843"** to import into a character field.

- **First row has column names:** Check this check box when you want the first row of data to contain the actual names of the fields in the table from which it came, which makes the text file easier to read. This doesn't affect how the computer reads the data. That is, unless you know the system that will import your exported file requires the column names in the first row, don't check this box. This option is not selected by default.

- **Transform:** This button allows you to specify additional information about the export. For example, you can specify the data types for the different columns of data. To access the transform screens, click this button. Because the transform option is an advanced topic, it is outside the scope of this book, and I don't cover it here. Consult the online help for SQL Server 7 for more information.

10. **In the Save, Schedule and Replicate Package dialog box (see Figure 11-13), choose the save, schedule, and replicate package option you want. Then click Next.**

This dialog box prompts you to specify whether you want to save the *DTS package,* the entire set of instructions you configured. If you save the package, you can run it again at a later time. If you don't save it, the information you configured is lost after this export.

- Uncheck the **Save Package on SQL Server** option if this is a one-time export.

- Check the **Save Package on SQL Server** option if you plan to use the specified export information again.

If you choose the save option, you can also specify that you want to execute the export at a later time by clicking the **Schedule DTS package for later execution** check box. (This check box is only enabled when you choose the save option.) Clicking on the ellipsis button (...) creates a new job. For more information about creating jobs, see Chapter 10.

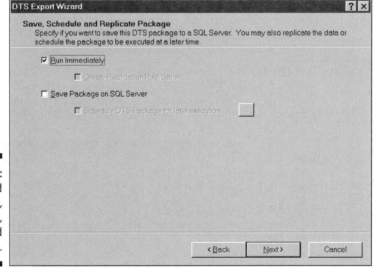

Figure 11-13:
Go ahead
and save,
schedule,
and
replicate.

11. **In the Completing the DTS Export Wizard dialog box (see Figure 11-14), review your choices. Then click Finish.**

    This dialog box prompts you to review your choices. After you review your choices, you can click the <u>B</u>ack button to change any information that you typed earlier, or click the Finish button to begin the export.

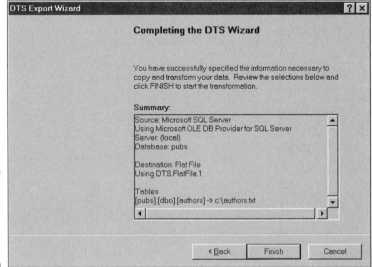

Figure 11-14:
Review your
choices and
accept the
consequences!

Part IV
Enterprise Issues

The 5th Wave   By Rich Tennant

NERD MOMS

Okay, young man, it's time to wash your hands, brush your teeth and back up your data.

Awwww, Mom.

In this part . . .

Enterprise issues are the hot topic *du jour*. Because it is unlikely that you will personally use SQL Server in your home, you'll probably encounter it at work. Therefore, you'll want to know all about enterprise issues. The "enterprise" represents your entire company, with all of its data. I show you about data warehousing techniques and how to create data warehouses with Microsoft SQL Server. Another very important topic in the enterprise is security. Security is the act of making your data safe, which is always a good thing. I show you all about views and users.

The icing on the cake is the last topic: the Web. Everyone is now scrambling to get on the Web. You can be ahead of the pack with the information I give you in this chapter about publishing your data to the Web.

Chapter 12

Building the Best Little Warehouse in Texas

*O*ne of the hottest topics today in the enterprise is Data Warehousing. As lots of companies expand and have the need for more servers in lots of locations, these companies need to consider data warehousing. In this chapter I tell you all of the ins and outs of the features that Microsoft provides for you to build the ultimate data warehouse.

For a more in-depth coverage of creating a data warehouse (not just with Microsoft SQL Server 7.0), see *Data Warehousing For Dummies* by Alan R. Simon (from IDG Books Worldwide, Inc.).

Understanding Data Warehousing Concepts

In some ways, data warehouses can be considered hidden treasures, resources that many people say they've never tapped. How can this be? Truth is, most of the people who tell me they've never created or encountered a data warehouse have actually used one without knowing it.

A data warehouse is more conceptual than tangible. *Data warehouse* is a phrase that describes storing (or warehousing) data in such a way that it can be efficiently used for querying and reporting. A data warehouse does not follow traditional normalizing techniques. Typically, your table(s) in the data warehouse is (are) denormalized. *Denormalizing* your data promotes repeating data, using only a few tables because every join in a normalized table results in a performance hit. A *performance hit* refers to performance degradation caused by a specific database operation. For more information on normalization, see Chapter 4.

A data warehouse is sometimes called a Decision Support System, or DSS. A DSS is a database that allows companies to run lots of reports and make corporate decisions based on those reports. The reason that a company needs a data warehouse is because if a company ran these reports on their regular database, it would bring the system to its knees (metaphorically speaking). Therefore, you create a data warehouse, which is separate from the regular database, to run your reports from.

A data warehouse is updated according to a certain schedule rather than on real-time basis. This schedule is normally automated so that at a certain time, data is updated in the warehouse. An example of this would be updating the warehouse at 2:00 a.m. This process of updating the data warehouse is known as *publishing,* the same term used to describe placing data on the Internet.

To a client application, a data warehouse looks like any other database. The only difference is that the tables usually have been denormalized (see Figure 12-1). Denormalized tables are tables that include repeating data for the strict purpose of eliminating most joins between tables, which can increase efficiency when performing queries against large amounts of data.

Now, don't take what I just mentioned as being gospel. There are many ways to construct a data warehouse, but denormalizing is one of them (and probably the most common). What I'm saying is that there is no one generic way of creating a data warehouse. All data warehouses are constructed to fit the business needs of a company.

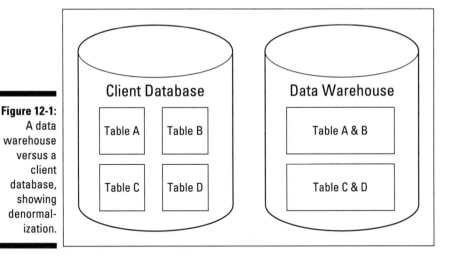

Figure 12-1:
A data
warehouse
versus a
client
database,
showing
denormal-
ization.

Sizing Up the Fit between Microsoft SQL Server 7 and Data Warehousing

Microsoft SQL Server 7 supports data warehousing through a concept called replication. *Replication* enables SQL Server 7 to employ distributed architecture to duplicate data in one or more tables and databases, which helps keep data current in multiple sites. The frequency at which the data is replicated is configurable. *Distributed architecture* is a concept whereby a company has multiple servers in different locations. This allows the processing to be "distributed" across multiple servers and ensures that you don't have one server doing all the work. Next time you feel you are doing all of the work in your company, tell your boss that you need to be distributed. See what your boss says.

Just because I talk about replication in this chapter doesn't mean that it is only used for data warehousing. It is a key component of distributed computing.

SQL Server 7 supports the following three types of replication:

- ✔ **Snapshot:** This is the replication used if a subscriber's data does not need to be kept up-to-date; for example, a sales engineer in the field who only needs last month's data on his or her notebook computer. You can also use snapshot replication for periodic data backups.

- ✔ **Transactional:** This replication is updated by the publisher only and maintains transactional integrity, such as the case of an order-taking system. *Transactional integrity* ensures that if there is a problem during the database transaction, the entire transaction is either written to the database (committed), or not written to the database (rolled back). This ensures that if you place an order for 3 items, the database does not process only 2 of them. It processes all 3 items or none.

- ✔ **Merge:** This form of replication can be updated by either the publisher or the subscriber. The replication engine then merges the data together so that both databases reflect changes. For example: a sales engineer in the field who needs current data, but who also plans to make changes at a client's site.

Replication is provided through publishers and subscribers. A *publisher* is a database that makes its data, called *articles*, available to subscribers — fairly like what IDG Books is doing for this book. A *subscriber* is one who attempts to read the publication. You, for example, are a subscriber to my publication, *Microsoft SQL Server 7 For Dummies*. A subscription is the act of accepting a publication as a whole. You can't just subscribe to Chapters 5 and 6. You must subscribe to the whole book (borrowing it from a friend not withstanding) because the publication is considered to be the entire book and all its chapters, or articles.

Within the subscription arena, you can find two types of subscriptions. They are push and pull.

- ✔ A *push* subscription is one that is automatically forced by the publisher to the subscriber (almost like junk mail). A push subscription is an automated way for the subscriber to receive regular updates to a subscription from the publisher.

- ✔ A *pull* subscription is one that must be manually requested from the publisher by the subscriber.

Additionally, replication relies on a distributor to coordinate between publishers and subscribers. The *distributor,* which can be any SQL Server, handles all aspects of making data available to subscribers.

Using Microsoft SQL Server 7 Wizards to Aid in Replication

Microsoft SQL Server 7 provides five wizards to help you replicate your databases. These wizards are:

- ✔ Configure Publishing and Distribution Wizard
- ✔ Create Publication Wizard
- ✔ Pull Subscription Wizard
- ✔ Push Subscription Wizard
- ✔ Uninstall Publishing and Distribution Wizard

Throughout the rest of this chapter, I describe how you can use these wizards to replicate your databases. In all my examples, the name of my Windows NT 4 Server is Nashua.

Configure Publishing and Distribution Wizard

If you want to configure the current server, or any other server, as a distributor, you can seek out the magic of the Configure Publishing and Distribution Wizard. This wizard also enables you to change properties that relate to the replication. To use the Configure Publishing and Distribution Wizard, follow these steps:

1. **Choose Start**➪**Programs**➪**Microsoft SQL Server 7.0**➪**Enterprise Manager to start the SQL Server Enterprise Manager (see Figure 12-2).**

Figure 12-2:
The SQL Server Enterprise Manager, as it appears when you bring up the screen.

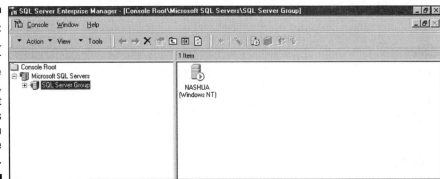

2. **Expand the tree until you see the name of your server and then click the name of your server.**

   For more information about expanding the tree, see Chapter 1. You click the name of your server to highlight because the Configure Publishing and Distribution Wizard needs a server context that will be used with the wizard.

3. **Choose Tools⇨Wizards to bring up the Select Wizard dialog box.**

4. **Click the Configure Publishing and Distribution Wizard item (under the Replication category) and then click the OK button.**

   A welcome dialog box appears; click Next when you're ready to continue.

5. **In the Choose Distributor dialog box, click one of the following options buttons to choose a distributor and then click Next (see Figure 12-3).**

   - **Yes, use *servername* as the distributor:** *Servername* is the name of the server that launched the wizard. This option, chosen by default, specifies that the current server is designated as the distributor of your replication.

   - **No, use another server:** Click this option if you want to designate another server as the distributor of your replication. When you click this option, you're presented a list of registered servers. Click the desired server to use. If you see no servers listed, then you have not configured any server to be a distributor. You must register a server. To register a server, click the Register Server button. (When you choose the No option, the Register Server button becomes enabled, allowing you to register a new server.)

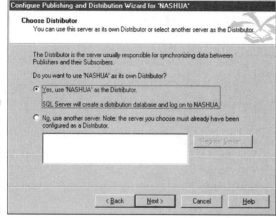

Figure 12-3: Choose the server that you want to use as your distributor.

6. **Click one of the following option buttons to choose whether you want to accept all the default settings for your replication (and then click <u>N</u>ext).**

   - **<u>Y</u>es, let me customize the settings:** Click this option button if you want to customize your settings differently than the default settings. I suggest you choose this option because it gives you more control. When you click the customize option, you need to complete a few more steps. (Don't despair — only a few fill-ins and you're home free!)

   - **<u>N</u>o, use the following default settings:** This option is chosen by default and enables these settings:

     The server chosen in Step 5 is used as a distributor.

     The same server used for publication will be used for subscription.

     The distribution database, named Distribution, will be stored in the DATA subdirectory of wherever you installed Microsoft SQL Server 7.

     The server chosen in Step 5 is used as a distributor when it is configured as a publisher.

7. **Fill in the following distribution database information fields and then click <u>N</u>ext.**

   - **<u>D</u>istribution database name:** Type the name of the database that you want to configure for distribution. By default, this name is Distribution, which works just fine. You'll need to change the name if you already have a distribution database, named Distribution.

   - **<u>F</u>older for the distribution database file:** Type the name of the folder in which you want to store the distribution database. By default, this is the DATA subdirectory of wherever you installed Microsoft SQL Server 7. You can browse for a folder by clicking the B<u>r</u>owse button.

   - **F<u>o</u>lder for the distribution log file:** Type the name of the folder in which you want to store the distribution log. By default, this is the DATA subdirectory of wherever you installed Microsoft SQL Server 7. You can browse for a folder by clicking the Bro<u>w</u>se button.

8. **From the Registered servers list of the Enable Publishers dialog box, place a check mark to the left of those publishers that you want to use the server specified in Step 5. Click the <u>N</u>ext button when you are finished.**

   You see only a list of registered servers (as shown in Figure 12-4). If you have a server that does not appear in the list, click the Register <u>S</u>erver button to register that server. (If you click the Register <u>S</u>erver button, a dialog box will be presented of the servers for you to register.)

If you want to select all servers in the list, click the <u>E</u>nable All button. If you prefer to select none of the servers in the list, click the Enable N<u>o</u>ne button. If you opt to use none of the servers in this list, no server will use the distributor, even though it is set up.

Just because you choose to use a particular server as a distributor does not mean that it's configured as a publisher. A server specified on this dialog box is used as a distributor only when it's configured as a publisher.

Figure 12-4:
A server
must be
configured
as a
publisher to
be used
as a
distributor.

Configure Publishing and Distribution Wizard for 'NASHUA'

Enable Publishers
You can enable servers to use this Distributor after they are configured as Publishers.

To set the login information and working folder for a server, select it, and then click the build button (...).

<u>R</u>egistered servers:

Publishers	Distributor DB	
✔ NASHUA	distribution	...

<u>E</u>nable All

Enable N<u>o</u>ne

Register <u>S</u>erver...

Click Register Server to register a server in SQL Server Enterprise Manager before enabling it as a Publisher.

< <u>B</u>ack   <u>N</u>ext >   Cancel   <u>H</u>elp

9. **In the Enable Publication Databases dialog box, click to place a check mark in the appropriate columns to indicate whether you want Transactional or Merge replication (as shown in Figure 12-5); then click <u>N</u>ext.**

   If you want to enable Transactional replication for all databases, click the <u>E</u>nable All button in the Transactional section. If you want to enable Transactional replication for none of the databases, click the Enable N<u>o</u>ne button in the Transactional section. If you want to enable Merge replication for all databases, click the Enable <u>A</u>ll button in the Merge section. If you want to enable Merge replication for none of the databases, click the Enab<u>l</u>e None button in the Merge section.

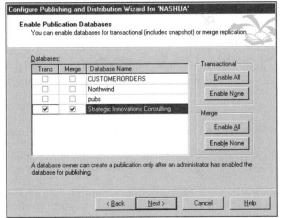

Figure 12-5:
Check your
choice of
replication
types.

10. **Click your choice of server(s) for subscribing to publications available from the distribution database. When you're ready to proceed, click Next.**

    If you have a server that does not appear in the list, click the Register Server button to register that server.

    If you want to select all servers in the list, click the Enable All button. If you want to select none of the servers in the list, click the Enable None button.

11. **Review your choices in the Completing the Configure Publishing and Distribution Wizard dialog box.**

    If you want to change any of the criteria that you specified in an earlier step, click the Back button until you reach the appropriate dialog box. If you like what you see in the list of selected options, click the Finish button.

Create Publication Wizard

What could be better than a wizard that steps you through creating a publication? That's exactly what this wizard does. Hold onto your hat ... I'm going to show you how to use the wizard.

The Create Publication Wizard helps you publish data to the distributor. (You can find its flowchart in Appendix A, by the way.) To use this wizard, follow these steps:

1. **Choose Start⇨Programs⇨Microsoft SQL Server 7.0⇨Enterprise Manager to start the SQL Server Enterprise Manager.**

2. **Expand the tree until you can click the name of the database that you want to publish and then click the name of your server.**

   For more information about expanding the tree, see Chapter 1. The reason that you click the name of your server is because the Create Publication Wizard needs a database context.

3. **Choose Tools⇨Wizards to bring up the Select Wizard dialog box.**

4. **Click Create Publication Wizard (under the Replication category), click the OK button, and then click Next when you're ready to begin.**

5. **In the Choose Publication Type dialog box, click one of the following option buttons for your preferred publication type (as shown in Figure 12-6) and then click Next:**

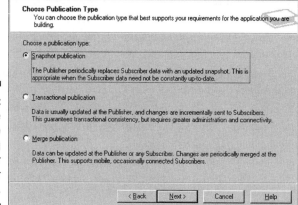

Figure 12-6: Choose one of three updating plans for your publication.

- **Snapshot publication:** This option, chosen by default, is appropriate if a subscriber's data doesn't require constant updating. For example, a sales engineer in the field may need only last month's data on his or her notebook computer. You can use snapshot publication for periodic backups of your data. To continue with this example, choose this option.

- **Transactional publication:** A transactional publication is updated by the publisher only, ensuring transactional integrity. An order-taking system is an example of this publication type.

- **Merge publication:** A merge publication can be updated by the publisher or the subscriber. The replication engine merges data from two databases so that both reflect changes. For example, a sales engineer in the field not only needs current data, but also makes changes at a client's site.

6. **Click one of the following two option buttons to indicate the type of subscribers for the publication and then click Next:**

   - **All Subscribers will be SQL Servers:** Use this option if all of the data to be published is stored in Microsoft SQL Server. If at all possible, I encourage the use of this option because it is the fastest way to access your data.

   - **One or more Subscribers will not be SQL Servers:** Use this option if at least one of the sources of data that is published comes from a data source other than Microsoft SQL Server. Such a data source could be Oracle. This is slightly slower than your data being stored completely within Microsoft SQL Server.

7. **Specify articles to be published by clicking check boxes in the Specify Articles dialog box (shown in Figure 12-7); click Next when you're finished.**

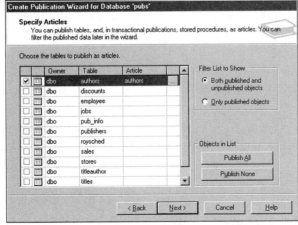

Figure 12-7: Publications are made up of articles, which are tables.

- **Specify Articles:** This field is a grid of data that shows all available articles for publication. The articles consist of tables owned by the database that you highlighted when you entered the wizard. To select an article for publication, click the left-hand column in the grid. As you click the column, SQL Server automatically adds the name of the table in the database to the Article Name column. Additionally, stored procedures can be available for publication if you made this publication a Transactional publication in Step 5.

- **Both published and unpublished objects:** Choosing this option shows all objects in the grid.

- **Only published objects:** Choosing this option shows in the grid only the objects that have been enabled for publication.

When you enable an article in the grid, notice the **...** button. This button is used to configure options for the article. These configure options are presented in a series of tabs, each of which is equipped to make this journey through the Create Publication Wizard even more exciting and eventful.

If, by chance, you're currently not up to the challenge of meeting these tabs one-by-one, feel free to jump ahead several pages to Step 8 (I won't take it personally). The next few pages of tab exploration await your return — when you're ready.

Entering general data

The General tab offers fields for entering data that identifies the article as a whole, such as name and description (see Figure 12-8). The General tab is available when you select either Snapshot, Transactional, or Merge Replication.

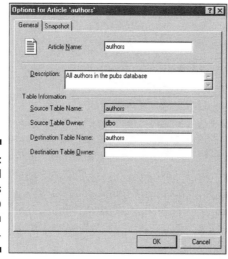

Figure 12-8:
The General tab enables you to describe an article.

Fill in the following fields to enter data in the General tab:

- **Article Name:** Give the article a name. By default, the name proposed is the name of the table or stored procedure.

- **Description:** Enter a description for your article. A detailed description is always a good idea. In this field, you could type something like **Authors table** or **All authors in the pubs database**.

- **Source Table Name:** This is a read-only field that mimics the table name chosen.

- **Source Table Owner:** This, too, is a read-only field that mimics who owns the table. Most likely, this will show dbo, indicating the database owner.

- **Destination Table Name:** Give your published table a name. By default, this is the same name as the source table. This option is only available for Snapshot or Transactional replication.

- **Destination Table Owner:** List the owner for the published table. I advise that you leave this field blank. This specifies that no single individual owns the table. This option is only available for Snapshot or Transactional replication.

- **Consider changes made to the same row as a conflict:** This option indicates to SQL Server that if both the subscriber and the publisher make changes to the same row of data, a conflict will occur. This option is available only to Merge replication; it's not visible for Snapshot and Transactional replication.

- **Consider changes made to the same column as a conflict:** This option indicates to SQL Server that if both the subscriber and the publisher make changes to the same column of data, a conflict will occur. Only available to Merge replication, this option is not visible for Snapshot and Transactional replication.

Commands

When performing Transactional replication, you can override some commands with other commands, enabling you to avoid the default behavior. The Commands tab allows you to override the standard functionality (see Figure 12-9). The Commands tab is only available when you select Transactional Replication.

Please note that this tab is for advanced users. I don't recommend changing anything on this tab if you are a first-time user. Remember, I'm a trained professional. Don't try this at home.

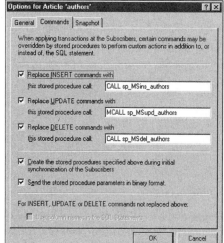

Fill in the following fields on the Commands tab:

- **Replace INSERT commands with this stored procedure call:**
Click this check box if you want to override the standard INSERT
statement used during Transactional replication with a stored
procedure of your own. When you choose this check box, you're
presented with a text box that enables you to enter a stored
procedure.

- **Replace UPDATE commands with this stored procedure call:**
Click this check box if you want to override the standard UPDATE
statement used during Transactional replication with a stored
procedure of your own. Choosing this check box enables you to
enter a stored procedure in the accompanying text box.

- **Replace DELETE commands with this stored procedure call:**
Click this check box if you want to override the standard DELETE
statement used during Transactional replication with a stored
procedure of your own. When you choose this check box, you
enable a text box in which you can specify a stored procedure.

- **Create the stored procedures specified above during initial
synchronization of the Subscribers:** Click this check box if you
want the specified stored procedures to be created the first time a
subscriber attempts to synchronize the data. This option is
checked by default.

- **Send the stored procedure parameters in binary format:** Click this check box if you want the parameters of the stored procedures to be sent in binary format. You want this option to be clicked if security is of a concern to you. As a matter of fact, Microsoft thinks this is important enough to check it for you by default.

- **Use column names in the SQL Statements:** If any of the above check boxes (the ones with INSERT, UPDATE, and DELETE) are not checked, this option becomes enabled. If there is a check mark in this box, column names will be used in the SQL statements.

Entering snapshot options

Snapshot options address ways to handle name conflicts and manage index copies (as shown in Figure 12-10). The Snapshot tab enables you to configure these options if you select either Snapshot, Transactional, or Merge publication.

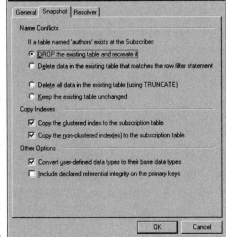

Figure 12-10: The Snapshot tab gives you name conflict and copy index options.

Fill in the following fields on the Snapshot tab:

- **DROP the existing table and recreate it:** Click this option button, which is chosen by default, if you want to delete or recreate a table that already exists at the subscriber location.

- **Delete data in the existing table that matches the row filter statement:** Click this option button if you want to delete only the data that matches the WHERE clause in the Row Filter statement.

- **Delete all data in the existing table:** Click this option button if you want to delete the data itself (using the TRUNCATE statement), allowing the structure of the table to remain the same.

- **Keep the existing table unchanged:** Click this option button if you do not want to make any changes to the existing table and data.

- **Copy the clustered index to the subscription table:** Click this check box, which is chosen by default, if you want to copy your clustered index to the subscription table. For more information about indexes, see Chapter 4.

- **Copy the non-clustered index(es) to the subscription table:** Click this check box if you want to copy your non-clustered indexes to the subscription table. For more information on indexes, see Chapter 4.

- **Convert user-defined data types to their base data types:** Click this check box, which is chosen by default, if you want to convert your user-defined data into the types that make up the user-defined type. For more information on user-defined types, see Chapter 4.

- **Include declared referential integrity on the primary keys:** Click this check box if you want to maintain any declared referential integrity (DRI) on the primary keys of your subscription database. For more information about DRI, see Chapter 4.

Resolving issues

Conflicts can arise during a records merge if both the publisher and the subscriber make changes to the same record. If you choose Merge replication, you can specify how these conflicts are resolved. The Resolver tab enables you to specify the module that handles the conflicts.

Fill in the following fields on the Resolver tab:

- **Use the default resolver:** Click this option if you want the SQL Server internal resolver to handle the conflicts that can arise when the publisher and subscriber both make changes to the same record in a table. When you install SQL Server 7, only the default resolver is available. This option is chosen by default; I recommend always using it.

- **Use this custom resolver:** Click this option if you want to use a custom resolver that has already been registered with the distributor.

You may now exhale (for those of you who accepted the mission to make it all the way through my discussion of Create Publication Wizard tabs)! If you decided to forego the pleasure until another time (or if you're just now joining this process in progress), don't hesitate to check out each tab's replication power and purpose — you may be surprised at all the available options!

8. **Enter a publication name and description in the following fields; click <u>N</u>ext when you're finished.**

   - **<u>P</u>ublication name:** Type the name of your publication. By default, the name appears as the database that was highlighted when you entered the wizard.

   - **Publication <u>d</u>escription:** Type the description of your publication. By default, the description is the replication model that you chose, followed by the database and server name relating to the article(s).

9. **Click the appropriate option button to specify whether you want to use the default options; then click <u>N</u>ext.**

   You may want to allow anonymous subscriptions if it's not possible to maintain every user in your database. You can choose from these fields:

   - **<u>Y</u>es, I will define data filters, enable anonymous subscribers, or customize other properties:** Click this option if you do not want to use all of the default values and you want to specify options for yourself. Such options include those listed in the option itself; defining data filters, anonymous subscribers, and configuring other properties.

   - **<u>N</u>o, create a publication without data filters and with the following properties:** Click this option if you want to use all of these default settings.

     The publication is not filtered. This means that all data that resides in the table(s) or stored procedure(s) you chose will be published. Also, the publication will be updated only once. It is updated at 11:30 p.m. on the day that you run the wizard. One final thing: The default publication access list will control who can access the published data.

   If you wish to change any of these default options, you must click the **<u>Y</u>es, I will define data filters, enable anonymous subscribers, or customize other properties** option button and change the parameters. To help you change the parameters, see the flow diagram in Appendix A.

10. **Confirm your choices in the wizard's review text box. Click Finish when you're satisfied with the options shown.**

   If you want to alter any of the criteria that you specified in an earlier step, click the <u>B</u>ack button until you reach the desired step — then, you can change the options you want changed and click the <u>N</u>ext button until you're at the end. That's all there is to it.

Pull Subscription Wizard

What's a pull subscription? A *pull subscription* is where the user's computer, not the server, requests, or pulls, data from the server. This way the user's computer, or *client,* controls the action. Most information services are pull subscriptions. The data is delivered when the user requests it.

You don't have to manually request the data. Your computer can be put on a schedule so that a request is made on a regular schedule. The main point is that the client computer requests information from the server.

With the Pull Subscription Wizard, you can retrieve data from a publisher on demand. (Consult its flowchart in Appendix A.) To use this wizard, follow these steps:

1. **Choose Start⇨<u>P</u>rograms⇨Microsoft SQL Server 7.0⇨Enterprise Manager to start the SQL Server Enterprise Manager.**

2. **Expand the tree until you can click the name of the server that you want to pull a subscription from.**

   For more information about expanding the tree, see Chapter 1. The reason that you need to click the name of your server to highlight it is because the Pull Subscription Wizard needs a server context to use with the wizard.

3. **Choose Tools⇨<u>W</u>izards to bring up the Select Wizard dialog box.**

4. **Click Pull Subscription Wizard (under the Replication category), and then click the OK button to start the Pull Subscription Wizard; click <u>N</u>ext when you're ready to begin.**

5. **Click the publication from which you want to pull a subscription, then click <u>N</u>ext (see Figure 12-11).**

   You can choose a publication that's available on any server on which a subscriber has registered articles.

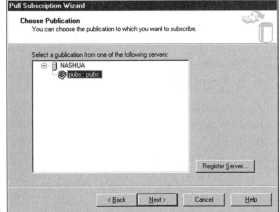

Figure 12-11:
You can find
a list of
publications
on a
server here.

6. **Click one of the following options buttons to indicate whether you want to initialize the subscription and then click Next:**

   • **Yes, start the initialization process immediately so I can start using the subscription as soon as possible:** This option is available if the publication was created so that it isn't published on a schedule. If you choose this option, the subscription is initialized immediately.

   • **Yes, start the initialization process as scheduled:** This option is available if the publication was created using a schedule. If you choose this option, which is the default, the subscription is initialized using that schedule.

7. **In the Set Distribution Agent Schedule dialog box, click one of the following option buttons to indicate how the subscription should be updated (see Figure 12-12), and then click Next:**

   • **Continuously:** Click this option if you want the subscription to be updated all the time. This option guarantees that the publication data will be always up to date.

   • **Using the following schedule:** By default, the subscription is updated every 5 minutes of every day. If you want to change this schedule, click the Change button and enter the desired schedule frequency.

   • **No schedule; synchronize on demand only:** Click this option if you want to manually indicate when your subscription is updated.

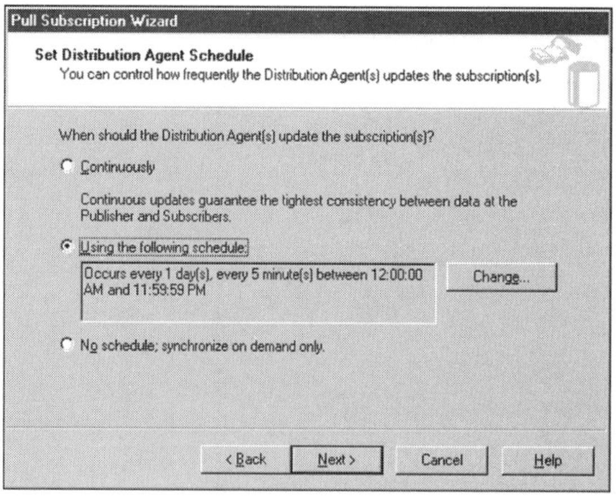

Figure 12-12:
You can
establish
subscription
update
schedules
in this
dialog box.

8. **Confirm that all required services are checked for the replication model you chose; click Next when you're finished.**

   Any service that is not started already and has a check mark in the left-most column will be started when you exit the wizard. Make sure that all services are selected so that you don't run into problems with your subscriptions.

9. **Review your choices in the text box, make any changes by clicking the Back button until you reach the step that you want to change, and then click Finish to, well, finish.**

Push Subscription Wizard

Okay, if you know what a pull subscription is, a push subscription is just the opposite. A *push subscription* is where the server sends, or pushes, data to a user's computer. This way the user does not have to request it. An example of a push subscription is stock quotes. The data for these quotes is sent by the server to a stock ticker on your computer.

The Push Subscription Wizard (whose flowchart appears in Appendix A) enables you to push data to a subscriber by following these steps:

1. **Choose Start⇨Programs⇨Microsoft SQL Server 7.0⇨Enterprise Manager to start the SQL Server Enterprise Manager.**

2. **Expand the tree so that you see the name of your server that you want to push a subscription from.**

   For more information about expanding the tree, see Chapter 1. You click the name of your server so that the Push Subscription Wizard has a server context to work with.

3. **Choose Tools⇨Wizards to bring up the Select Wizard dialog box.**

4. **Click the Push Subscription Wizard entry from the pull-down menu (under the Replication category) and then click OK.**

5. **In the Publish and Push Subscriptions dialog box that appears, expand the tree so that you can click the publication that you want to push (see Figure 12-13) before clicking the Push New Subscription button to launch the wizard.**

   The Wizard welcome dialog box appears; click Next when you're ready to roll on.

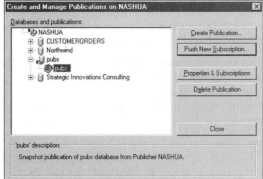

Figure 12-13:
Select a
publication
to be
pushed.

6. **Expand the tree and choose one or more subscribers by highlighting the desired subscriber, as shown in Figure 12-14, and then click Next.**

Figure 12-14:
Choose a
subscriber
for the push
subscription.

7. In the Choose a Destination Database dialog box, type the destination database into the text box (the name of the database of the sub-scriber); click Next.

If you want to browse the databases, click the Browse Databases button.

8. Click the option button that corresponds to the subscription update schedule that you prefer and then click Next.

By default, the schedule for SQL Server to push the subscription to the distributor is shown to be every hour of every day (similar to the Pull Subscription schedule — refer to Figure 12-12). If you want to change the schedule, click the Change button and change the schedule frequency as desired.

9. Click one of the following option buttons to indicate whether you want to initialize the subscription and then click Next:

- **Yes, start the initialization process immediately so I can start using the subscription as soon as possible:** This option is available if the publication was created so that it isn't published on a schedule. If you choose this option, the subscription is initialized immediately.

- **Yes, start the initialization process as scheduled:** This option is available if the publication was created using a schedule. If you choose this option, which is the default, the subscription is initialized using that schedule.

10. Review the left-most column to confirm that all services appear with a check mark next to them; click Next when you know everything's in order.

Certain services are required for every replication model chosen for the publication. Any service that is not started already and has a check mark in the left-most column will be started when you exit the wizard. By making sure that all your checks are in a row, you skip possible problems with your subscriptions.

11. Click Finish when you're comfortable with all your choices, as shown on the Completing the Push Subscription Wizard dialog box.

If you want to change any of the criteria that you specified in an earlier step, just click the Back button until you reach the step that requires attention.

Uninstall Publishing and Distribution Wizard

If you have taken your valuable time to read through my description of all of the wizards in this chapter, you now have one or more publications and distribution on your server. What if you don't want them anymore? That's simple . . . read on.

With the Uninstall Publishing and Distribution Wizard, you can remove publications or distribution on the current server. (You can find its flow-chart in Appendix A.) To use the Uninstall Publishing and Distribution Wizard, follow these steps:

1. **Choose Start⇨Programs⇨Microsoft SQL Server 7.0⇨Enterprise Manager to start the SQL Server Enterprise Manager.**

2. **Expand the tree to locate the name of the server that contains the publication you wish to uninstall, and then highlight it by clicking it.**

   For more information about expanding the tree, see Chapter 1.

3. **Choose Tools⇨Wizards to bring up the Select Wizard dialog box.**

4. **Click the Uninstall Publishing and Distribution Wizard entry from the pull-down menu (under the Replication category) and then click OK.**

   The Uninstall Publishing and Distribution Wizard welcomes you with an opening dialog box; click Next when you're ready to see what's in store for you.

5. **Click the option button that specifies whether you want to disable distribution and then click Next.**

   This step does not appear if there is no server acting as a distributor.

   You can choose from these fields:

   - **Yes, disable distribution (and publishing) on *ServerName*:** *ServerName* is the name of the server that currently enables distribution. Click this option if you want the discontinue distribution of the current server. This option will also discontinue publishing.

   - **No, continue to use *ServerName* as a Distributor:** *ServerName* is the name of the server that currently enables distribution. Click this option if you want to continue distributing of the current server. This option is chosen by default.

6. Click whether you want to disable publishing and then click <u>N</u>ext.

This step is available only if you indicate in Step 5 that you want to continue using the server as a distributor. You can choose from these fields:

- **<u>Y</u>es, disable publishing on *ServerName*:** *ServerName* is the name of the server that currently enables publishing. Click this option if you want to discontinue publishing on the current server.

- **N<u>o</u>, continue using *ServerName* as a publisher:** *ServerName* is the name of the server that currently enables publishing. Click this option, which is chosen by default, if you want to continue publishing on the current server.

7. Confirm the publications and subscriptions that you want to drop by viewing the publications that are to be dropped in the tree and then click <u>N</u>ext.

This dialog box shows the actual publications that will drop if you continue with the wizard (see Figure 12-15). Look closely at the list: An unintentional drop may creep up on you if you're not careful! There is nothing to select in the list. The tree is presented just for you to navigate and drill-down for confirmation.

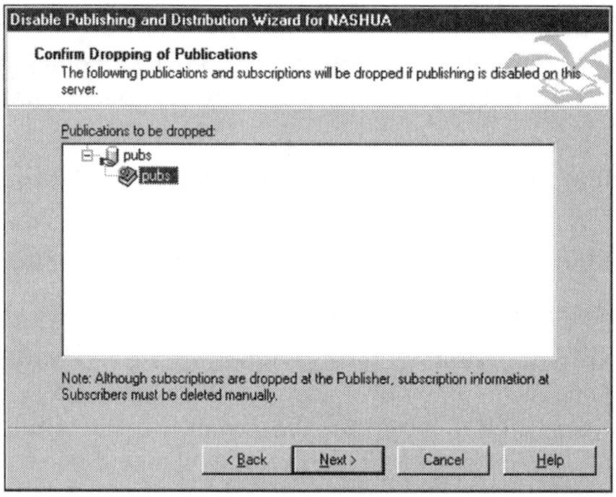

Figure 12-15:
Check the publications to be dropped carefully in this dialog box.

Disable Publishing and Distribution Wizard for NASHUA

Confirm Dropping of Publications
The following publications and subscriptions will be dropped if publishing is disabled on this server.

Publications to be dropped:
- pubs
  - pubs

Note: Although subscriptions are dropped at the Publisher, subscription information at Subscribers must be deleted manually.

< <u>B</u>ack   <u>N</u>ext >   Cancel   <u>H</u>elp

8. Confirm your Uninstall Publishing and Distribution Wizard choices in the text box provided.

If you want to revisit any previous Steps, click the <u>B</u>ack button until you reach the desired step that you want to change. When you're ready to sign off your selections, click the Finish button and rest assured that your publication(s) is(are) dropped!

A Quick Note About OLAP

Microsoft SQL Server 7 comes with OLAP (Online Analytical Processing) Services that enable a company to view multidimensional data in a data warehouse. Multidimensional data is data that is reported in such a way that allows you to configure each axis of the report and drill-down on any level of that data. An example of multidimensional data is a report that allows you to see data by time, by organization, by product. This is a three-dimensional report.

OLAP data is made up of data cubes. These data cubes are made up of dimensions and measures. I mentioned, just before, an example of what makes up a dimension. A measure is an actual value that can be associated with a dimension, like gross sales, inventory, and expenses.

Guess what? You can have OLAP set up a hierarchy of levels that allow you to drill down on any dimension. The reason that OLAP can provide all of this functionality and still be fast: If any calculations have to be done on your data, it is done in advance. That way, you don't have to sit there and wait forever while the server crunches through the numbers. Data is collected by OLAP services at the most detailed level. That way, OLAP can manipulate the data by summarizing it as necessary. For example, if data is collected for every day and you need to summarize by hour, you can't do it. If the data is stored for each day, you can't know anything about the data at an hourly level. On the other hand, if data is collected hourly, you can display data hourly, daily, weekly, or any other time period that is greater than an hour. In this case, if you want to report on daily sales, you do not have to store sales at the daily and hourly level — only the hourly level. OLAP will calculate the sales at the daily level, based on the hourly figures. The lowest level of data is referred to as *fine granularity*.

OLAP cubes can be created within the Microsoft Management Console (MMC). However, OLAP cubes can only be created on Microsoft Windows NT 4.0 or later. OLAP services cannot work on Microsoft Windows 95 or 98. Also note that before you can use any OLAP services, provided by Microsoft Decision Support Services (DSS), you must make sure that DSS is installed and the **DSS Analysis server** service is started.

Generally, to create a data warehouse using OLAP, you follow these steps:

1. **Use Microsoft Data Transfer Services (DTS) to transfer data to a star schema from your database.**

   A *star schema* is a way to organize your data warehouse so that there is one table in the center of the schema that contains the main subject of the warehouse — like sales. This table is called the *fact* table. Then, branching out in all directions, like a star, are many other tables that describe the data contained in the fact table. These other tables, called *dimension* tables, are denormalized so that data can be accessed quickly without having to join many tables together. Joining many tables would be detrimental to performance.

2. **Using OLAP Server, which comes with Microsoft SQL Server 7.0, create your data cubes.**

   Large cubes of data are left on the server for use while connected. Smaller cubes of data are created that are actually sent to clients to use, even while disconnected.

3. **Write your client application or use the sample application to manipulate the data cubes.**

   Check out the sample application that comes with Decision Support Services. For more information about installing Decision Support Services, see Chapter 2.

Chapter 13

Security: Protecting Against Peeping Toms!

*N*ot that you shouldn't trust your fellow coworkers, but sometimes you need to consider security as an issue. SQL Server 7.0 has lots of features that help you to secure your data. If you don't secure your data, anyone can get access to it. Do you want someone to know the salaries of every employee in the company? If not, read on. . . .

Adding a New User

For security purposes, anyone connecting to SQL Server must have a login ID and password. This ID and password combination is referred to as a *user*. The database administrator (DBA) is usually the person who sets up users in SQL Server.

Like most things in SQL Server, setting up users is quite simple. Enterprise Manager enables you to use a graphical program to set up users easily instead of going through the process of issuing SQL statements. If you're a SQL Server "old-timer," you may opt to use SQL statements, which are still available (but not the subject of this chapter).

Here's how you can add a new user with Enterprise Manager:

1. **Start the SQL Server Enterprise Manager by choosing Start▷Programs▷Microsoft SQL Server 7.0▷Enterprise Manager.**

2. **Expand the tree so that you see the Logins folder; then select the Logins folder by clicking it.**

   For more information about expanding the tree, see Chapter 1.

3. **Choose Action⇨New Login.**

   Alternatively, you can right-click the Logins folder, and then click New Login.

   Both methods bring up a dialog box, consisting of three tabs (General, Server Roles, and Database Access), to enable you to type and select the parameters and data relating to the new login (see Figure 13-1). The General tab appears by default.

4. **After you type or select the appropriate data, as discussed in the next three sections, click OK to save changes and close the dialog box.**

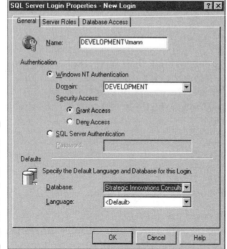

Figure 13-1:
The General
tab of the
SQL Server
Login
Properties
dialog box.

Entering general data for the login

In the General tab, you enter data that describes the login as a whole. General data includes information like the new user's name and security information. Fill in the following fields to enter data in the General tab:

✔ **Name:** Give the new user's login a name, which is usually referred to as the login ID or user ID. It's a good idea to use some type of convention when assigning names, such as the combination of first initial and last name — for example, **tmann**. Also consider how you want to use capitalization. All lowercase or all uppercase are frequently used.

✔ **Windows NT Authentication:** Choose this option if you want a Windows NT Server acting as a domain controller to verify the user name and password. This is useful in an Enterprise situation when all authentication occurs from one server. Choosing this option enables the **Domain** drop-down list and **Security Access** options.

Choose a domain name from the drop-down list or type the domain name that you want to authenticate the user's login ID. Then click the option button corresponding to the desired Security Access. Choosing the **Grant Access** option grants access to SQL Server for this user, if authenticated. Clicking the **Deny Access** option denies access to SQL Server for this user, if authenticated.

✔ **SQL Server Authentication:** Click this option if you want a SQL Server to verify the user name and password. This is useful when you want a system to be stand-alone. Choosing this option enables the Password text box, where you can type the desired password.

✔ **Database:** Choose from the drop-down list of available databases to indicate your preferred default database. A user has access to any database that he or she has permissions for. However, if the user never specifies a database, the default database chosen here is used.

✔ **Language:** Choose from the drop-down list of available languages to indicate the desired default language. A user has access to any language within SQL Server. However, if you never specify a language, the default language chosen here is used. The default language is chosen when you install SQL Server 7.0.

Selecting server roles

You can select server roles by using the Server Roles tab, as shown in Figure 13-2. When you click the Server Roles tab, the dialog box pops into view like a file folder in the foreground.

A *server role* is a permission that you can give to a user for specific authority to perform actions in SQL Server. It's important to know that roles affect SQL Server as a system, not as a specific database. A user can have limited privileges in a database — but have the ability to add new users. Although you probably won't encounter this situation often, just know that it's possible.

The server roles are presented in a list. You can scroll down to see all the available roles that you can assign to a user. You can assign all, none, or anywhere in between. To select a role, click the check box to the left of the role listed. A role is selected if you see a check mark in the check box.

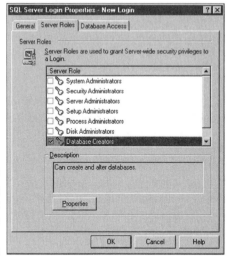

Figure 13-2:
Select
server roles
here.

You can add new roles, but not using this dialog box. For more information about adding new roles, see the "Adding New Roles" section later in this chapter.

The following roles are available when you install SQL Server 7:

- ✔ **System Administrators** enables a user to act as a system administrator
- ✔ **Security Administrators** enables a user to manage user logins
- ✔ **Server Administrators** enables a user to manage SQL Server 7 settings
- ✔ **Setup Administrators** enables a user to install replication and manage extended procedures (see Chapter 7 for a discussion of stored procedures)
- ✔ **Process Administrators** enables a user to manage SQL Server processes
- ✔ **Disk Administrators** enables a user to manage disk files
- ✔ **Database Creators** enables a user to manage databases

By default, no role is selected. You can choose to leave each check box unchecked.

If you want to view any of the actual commands or permissions available to a role, click the Properties button to bring up a dialog box that displays read-only commands and permissions.

Selecting database access

You can control a user's database access by using the Database Access tab (see Figure 13-3). The tab is used to assign the databases and the privileges that a user has access to within those databases. Click the tab to bring it forward, and then fill in the following fields to indicate general database access preferences:

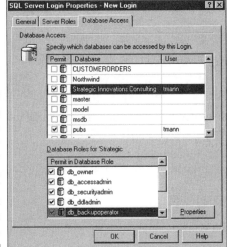

Figure 13-3:
The
Database
Access tab
of the SQL
Server
Login
Properties
dialog box.

✔ **Specify which databases can be accessed by this Login:** All databases for the currently selected SQL Server are presented in a list box. Give a user access to a specific database by scrolling down the list of databases and then clicking the Permit column check box that corresponds to the chosen database. The database is selected when you see a check mark in the Permit column check box.

✔ **Database roles for x:** *X* is not actually presented on the dialog box. *X* indicates the name of the database, as chosen in the Login section. Specify which databases can be accessed by this Login section above. When a database is selected with a check mark in the Permit column, possible database roles are listed. You can then choose from the list of available database roles. Note that these roles are not the same as SQL Server roles. Database roles can be given to a user within a specific database; SQL Server roles are system-wide. The possible roles are:

• **public** enables the user to have the same access as any other public user.

• **db_owner** enables the user to act as the owner of the database and has all permissions.

- **db_accessadmin** enables the user to act as the database administrator, allowing the user to add or remove Login IDs.

- **db_securityadmin** enables the user to act as the security administrator. This allows a user to manage all permissions, object ownerships, roles, and role memberships.

- **db_ddladmin** enables the user to issue Data Definition Language (DDL) statements. However, the user cannot issue GRANT, REVOKE, or DENY statements.

- **db_dumpoperator** enables the user to perform data dumps. This allows a user to issue DBCC, CHECKPOINT, and BACKUP statements.

- **db_datareader** enables the user to read data by granting SELECT permissions on any object.

- **db_datawriter** enables the user to write data. The user can GRANT INSERT, UPDATE, and DELETE permissions on any object.

- **db_denydatareader** disallows the user from reading data by denying or revoking SELECT permissions.

- **db_denydatawriter** disallows the user from writing data by denying or revoking INSERT, UPDATE, and DELETE permissions.

Adding New Roles

A role is a way to group together permissions for multiple users, which simplifies administering SQL Server because you can assign permissions to a role and then assign users to the role. Every time you add a new user, you just assign the user to the role. You don't have to specify permissions.

The easiest way to set up roles is through the Enterprise Manager because you can use a graphical program instead of issuing SQL statements. SQL Server veterans may prefer to use SQL statements — the option's still available, but I don't address the subject in this section.

Prior versions of SQL Server enabled users to be assigned to groups. In SQL Server 7, roles are more powerful than those former groups.

To add a new role, follow these steps:

1. **To start the SQL Server Enterprise Manager, choose Start⇨ Programs⇨Microsoft SQL Server 7.0⇨Enterprise Manager.**

2. **Find Databases on the expanded tree.**

   For more information about expanding the tree, see Chapter 1.

3. **Highlight the specific database in which you want to create the role by clicking the specific database.**

4. **Choose Action➪New➪Database Role to create a new role.**

   Alternatively, you can right-click the desired database under the Databases folder and choose the New➪Database Role menu option.

   Any method you choose to create a login brings up a dialog box, consisting of only one tab. This tab enables you to type or select the parameters and data relating to the new role, as shown in Figure 13-4.

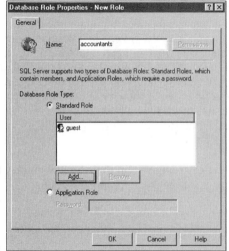

Figure 13-4:
Select your
database
roles here.

To enter data in the General tab, fill in the following fields:

- **Name:** You may want to relate the new role's name to the users and permissions that you expect to grant. Say, for example, the role will affect all people in the accounting department. Give the role an easy-to-remember name — Accounting!

- **Standard Role:** Click this option button if you want to assign specific users to this role. When the option is chosen, you have the opportunity to assign users by clicking the Add button. This option is chosen by default.

- **Application Role:** Instead of assigning specific users to this role, you can click this option to have users enter a password. When you choose this option, the Password text box becomes enabled. Type your password into this text box.

5. **Click the OK button to save changes and close the dialog box.**

Creating a New View

A *view* is an important concept in SQL Server. You can use a view to show a user, or a group of users, only the data that you want him or her to see. For example, you may want a Human Resources manager to have access to data in every column of an employee table, including salary and benefit information. On the other hand, you don't want one employee to see salary and benefit information for another employee. Employee addresses and phone numbers may not be considered confidential, making it perfectly acceptable for an employee to view someone else's personal information, but not salary information. In other words, a view is an alternative "look" at one or more tables.

To SQL, a view looks like any other table. A view is a database object for which you grant permissions. You construct SQL statements to query the view. Because a view is made up of one or more tables, your SQL statement works with views. A view is basically a logical table. In fact, you can do inserts, updates, and deletes on views if they meet certain conditions. Such conditions are that a view must not have calculated fields and the view must include all keys and not null fields for the underlying tables. For more information about SQL, see Chapter 8.

You can create a view in a variety of ways. On the next few pages, I show you all the ways to create a view. Strap yourself in and get going....

Consider the example that you have a table, named **Employees**, with the following columns:

EmployeeID
Name
Address
City
State
Zip
Phone
SSN
Hire Date
Terminate Date
Salary

You probably don't want everyone in your organization to know an employee's social security number (SSN), salary, address, and phone number. You can't just leave them out of the table because they must exist for the corporate records. You also don't want to create another table just to store the data in the few columns that everyone in the organization can see. If you did create another table, you are storing the same data in multiple places.

Therefore, you could construct a view, called **Emp_View**, that hides these columns. The Emp_View view then contains these columns:

EmployeeID
Name
Hire Date
Terminate Date

The view references the Employees table so data is not stored in multiple places, but it also doesn't force you to return data that everyone can see. Therefore, the term View is used to describe a way to look at the Employees table in a different way.

After a view is created, you access it just like you access a table. You can construct queries against it. You can also insert and update data into a view. For all intents and purposes, a view *looks* just like a table.

You can create a view in one of three ways. You can use the Create View Wizard, SQL Server Enterprise Manager, or you can use SQL. The next few pages outline how to use all three methods.

Creating a view with the Create View Wizard

The Create View Wizard, one of many wizards included with SQL Server 7, guides you through a series of steps, prompting you for input along the way (see Appendix A for a flowchart of the steps). To create a view by using the Create View Wizard, follow these steps:

1. **Choose Start⇨Programs⇨Microsoft SQL Server 7.0⇨Enterprise Manager to start the SQL Server Enterprise Manager. (See Figure 13-5.)**

2. **Expand the tree so that you see the name of your server.**

   For more information about expanding the tree, see Chapter 1.

3. **Bring up the Select Wizard dialog box by choosing Tools⇨Wizards.**

   The Select Wizard dialog box appears (see Figure 13-6).

4. **Select the Create View Wizard item (under the Database category) with the left mouse button and click OK.**

   The Create View Wizard prompts you to create your database by asking you a series of questions. These questions are presented in steps. The first step is an introduction dialog box letting you know what the wizard will do for you. Click the Next button when you are ready to begin.

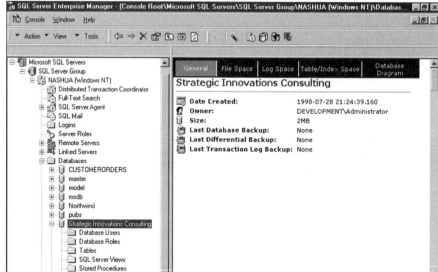

Figure 13-5:
The SQL
Server
Enterprise
Manager
screen.

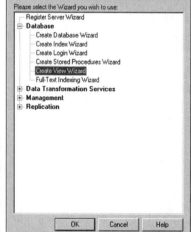

Figure 13-6:
The Select
Wizard lets
you select
your wizard.

5. **For the Select a Database step that appears, specify the name of the database and click Next.**

   Select from the drop-down list of existing databases for the **Database name** field. This database is used to store the view and to provide tables for the view.

6. **In the Select Tables dialog box that appears (shown in Figure 13-7), specify the table(s) to be used in the view, and then click Next.**

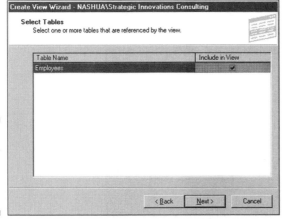

Figure 13-7:
Select your
tables to be
referenced
by the view.

Click the row in the grid shown in the **Include in View** column for each table to be included in the view. For the example I gave at the beginning of this section, I click **Employees**.

7. **In the Select Columns dialog box (shown in Figure 13-8), specify the column(s) to be used in the view. Then click _N_ext.**

Figure 13-8:
Tell SQL
Server
which
columns
you want to
view to
display.

Click the row in the grid shown in the **Select Column** column for each column in the tables chosen in the prior step that are to be included in the view. For the example I gave at the beginning of this section, I click **EmployeeID**, **Name**, **Hire Date**, and **Terminate Date**.

8. **In the Define Restriction dialog box (shown in Figure 13-9), specify additional criteria for the view. (However, for your first view, leave this step blank and click _N_ext to continue.)**

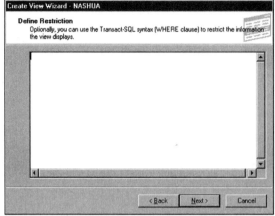

Figure 13-9:
Here you can define information you want restricted.

Additional criteria, also known as a *restriction,* can be specified to limit the number of records that are returned in the view. This field is optional. This limit is any valid WHERE clause (including the WHERE keyword). For more information about SQL or a WHERE clause, see Chapter 8. If you want all records to be returned, leave this step blank.

The criteria that you specify in this step can also be used to join columns in tables. For example, if you wanted to join the **EMPLOYEES** table with the **ORDERS** table, based on the **EmployeeID** column in each table, you would enter:

```
WHERE EMPLOYEES.EmployeeID = ORDERS.EmployeeID
```

9. **In the Name the View dialog box, name the view and then click Next.**

   Because all SQL Server objects need a name, this step is used to specify that name. By default, you are presented a name that is the first table chosen, followed by **_VIEW**. This is a good convention to use. Simply accept this default.

10. **Review your choices in the Completing the Create View Wizard dialog box (see Figure 13-10). If you like what you see and it's exactly what you want, click Finish.**

    To complete the Create View Wizard, review the SQL that creates the view. This SQL is generated by answering the questions presented by the steps in the Create View Wizard.

    Notice that the first line of the SQL shown in Figure 13-10 shows the **USE** keyword. This keyword indicates which database the system is to "switch to" before continuing — thus ensuring that the tables specified will be those from the correct database. It also ensures that the view is created in the correct database.

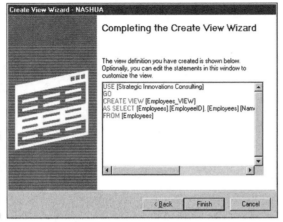

Figure13-10:
Review your
choices and
click away!

If you wish to change any of the criteria that you specified in an earlier step, you can do so by clicking the Back button until you reach the desired step to change.

Creating a view with the SQL Server Enterprise Manager

Using the Create View Wizard is a bit easier, but Microsoft also includes a more graphical way to create views. Besides the Create View Wizard, you can use the SQL Server Enterprise Manager to create views. You may want to use the Enterprise Manager instead of the Create View Wizard if you want to create all your database objects the same way. After all, the Enterprise Manage is supposed to give you a single point of entry to manage your enterprise. To use the SQL Server Enterprise Manager for creating a view, follow these steps.

1. **Choose Start⇨Programs⇨Microsoft SQL Server 7.0⇨Enterprise Manager to start the SQL Server Enterprise Manager.**

2. **Expand the tree so that you see the Databases folder, then the database in which you want to create the view, and finally the SQL Server Views folder.**

   For more information about expanding the tree, see Chapter 1.

3. **Highlight the SQL Server Views folder.**

   After highlighting the SQL Server Views folder, notice the list of views on the right-hand part of the screen (see Figure 13-11). Most (or all) of these views are created automatically when you install SQL Server 7.0.

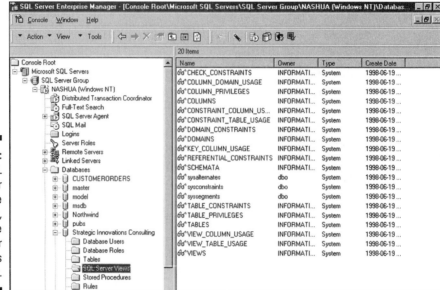

Figure 13-11:
The SQL
Server
Enterprise
Manager,
showing the
SQL Server
Views
folder.

4. **Select Action⇨New SQL Server View to bring up the New View screen within the Enterprise Manager.**

   Alternatively, you can use the mouse to right-click anywhere on the right-hand part of the screen and select the New SQL Server View menu. Also, you can right-click the SQL Server Views folder in the tree and select the New SQL Server View menu.

   Each method brings up a screen, enabling you to create your new view. (See Figure 13-12.) This screen is created within the context of the Microsoft Management Console (MMC), or more commonly known as the SQL Server Enterprise Manager.

   Because multiple windows are open in the Enterprise Manager, you can switch between the open windows by choosing the Window menu. The drop-down list presents the names of all open windows — take your pick! Choose the desired open window.

   Creating the view is done in a series of logical steps. These steps are not actually listed on the screen. I have broken the process into these logical steps because this is one of the few tools in SQL Server 7 that is not very intuitive to use.

5. **Indicate which table(s) to use in your view by entering a SQL statement.**

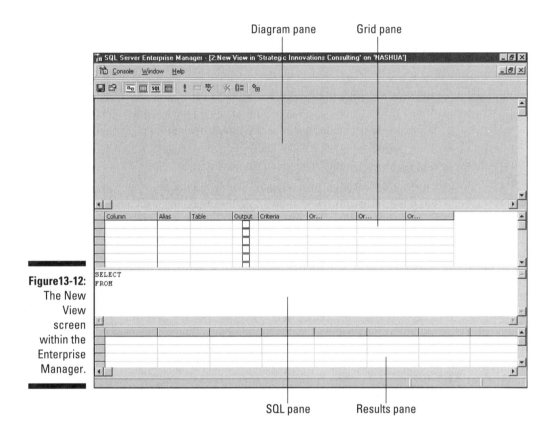

Diagram pane   Grid pane

Figure13-12:
The New
View
screen
within the
Enterprise
Manager.

SQL pane   Results pane

To determine which table(s) to use in your view is sometimes no easy task. I can't really tell you, either. All I can mention is that you need to logically decide which tables store the data to be included in the view. If the data resides in more than one table, you need to decide which columns in those tables are used to join the two tables together. For more information about joins, see Chapters 4 and 8.

It isn't very intuitive, but the SQL pane shown in the middle of the screen is used to generate a graphic in the Diagram Pane, showing all the tables enteredin the diagram pane. (Refer to Figure 13-12 for the location of these panes.) Type the table names into your SQL statement (in the SQL Pane) using this syntax:

```
SELECT *
FROM table1[,table2][,n…]
```

Substitute table1 and table2, and so on, for the name(s) of your tables. For example, I create a simple view and use the table **Employees**.

Therefore, I enter:

```
SELECT *
FROM Employees
```

6. **Execute the SQL statement by clicking the exclamation point icon on the toolbar.**

   A graphical representation of the tables appears, showing all columns in the diagram pane (see Figure 13-13).

   For more information about SQL, see Chapter 8.

7. **In the table shown in the diagram pane, check any columns that you want to expose in your view. Build your query by checking columns to expose.**

   Any columns that you want to expose in your view need to be chosen, or checked in the respective tables shown in the diagram pane. As you click a column, notice that the query is being built dynamically in the SQL pane as you make your choices.

   If you have followed my example earlier in this chapter and you wish to make only the EmployeeID, Name, Hire Date, and Terminate Date available (exposed) in the view, click these columns (see Figure 13-14).

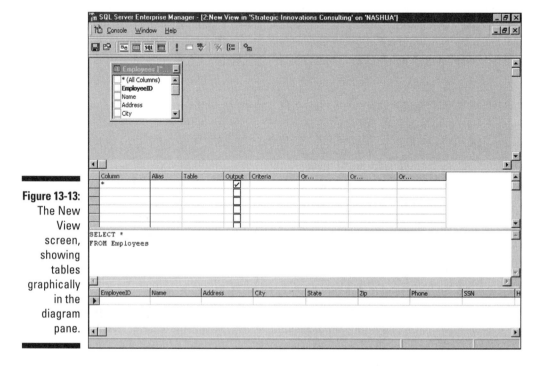

Figure 13-13:
The New View screen, showing tables graphically in the diagram pane.

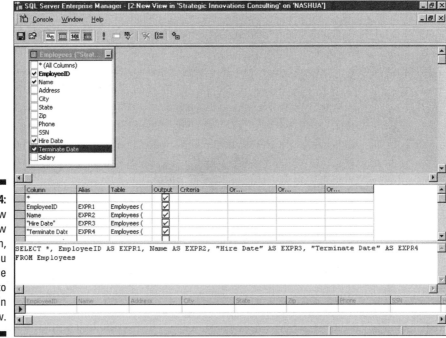

Figure 13-14:
The New
View
screen,
after you
choose
columns to
expose in
your view.

8. Review your view. (Sounds like a schoolhouse rock episode!)

Check the results pane to make sure that your view looks the way you expect. Also, check the names of your columns. When you check columns that you want to expose in your view in Step 7, the system automatically gives your columns alternate names — or an *alias* to your columns.

To "alias" your columns is to give your columns alternate names. Your SQL statements then refer to these alternate names. Therefore, it's important that your columns are not "aliased" if you don't want them to be.

If you want your columns to be named the same as the actual column names in the real underlying tables, simply click the grid in the **Alias** column for the desired row in the grid pane. Then clear out the alias text by pressing the backspace key until the line's completely clear. Notice that the query is being built dynamically in the SQL pane as you make your choices.

Also, by default, the wildcard * is shown in the first row in the grid pane. If you don't want to see every column, you need to either deselect this row or completely delete the row. To deselect the row, ensure that there is no check mark in the **Output** column of this row. If a check mark is there, click the check mark to deselect it. To remove the row, right-click the left-most column in the desired row, and then click the right mouse button and choose the <u>D</u>elete menu option.

If you have any errors to correct, make your changes and re-execute the query. After you are finished, your screen will look something like Figure 13-15.

9. Save your view by clicking the save icon.

You are prompted to enter a name for the view. Make the most of this creative opportunity — this is the name that you'll use when you create SQL statements, so go for a name that is something meaningful. For example, if you're creating a view for the Human Resources Department, consider a name such as **personnel**; for the technology group, think **techgroup**.

Creating a view with SQL

By using the SQL Server Query Analyzer, you can issue SQL statements directly to the server to create a new view. I've seen many people who like to do things the "old-fashioned" way — they code it. Therefore, this section is for those people.

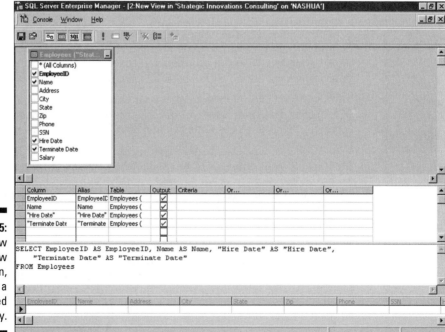

Figure 13-15: The New View screen, showing a finished query.

To issue the SQL statement to create a view, follow these steps:

1. **Choose Start⇨Programs⇨Microsoft SQL Server 7.0⇨Query Analyzer to start the SQL Server Query Analyzer.**

2. **Type the SQL needed to create a view.**

   You create a view with SQL by issuing the CREATE VIEW statement in the Query Analyzer (see Figure 13-16). For more information about the CREATE VIEW statement, see Chapter 8.

   Here's how you can create a view named **EMPLOYEE_VIEW**:

   ```
   CREATE VIEW EMPLOYEES_VIEW
   AS
   SELECT EmployeeID, Name, [Hire Date], [Terminate Date]
   FROM EMPLOYEES
   ```

In the sample CREATE VIEW statement, I show the use of square brackets on some of the column names, and not on others. Why? The answer is that because the two columns, Hire Date and Terminate Date, all contain spaces in the names. If the brackets were not used, SQL Server would have no idea what the column names are.

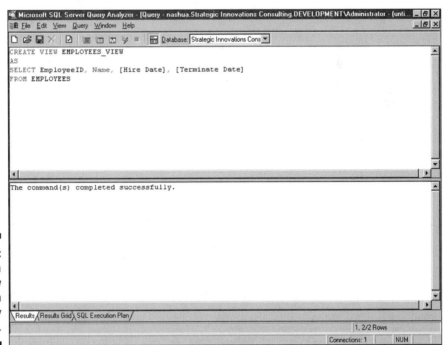

Figure 13-16:
Creating a new view with SQL in the Query Analyzer.

Everything in the CREATE VIEW statement after the AS clause is a regular SQL Statement that returns results when you execute the view. Therefore, I recommend that if you create your views by using the CREATE VIEW SQL statement, issue the statement after the AS clause by itself to see if you get the results you expect. If you don't, you certainly don't want to create a view using these results. For example, issue this statement:

```
SELECT EmployeeID, Name, [Hire Date], [Terminate Date]
FROM EMPLOYEES
```

If the results are what you expect, you can use it within the CREATE VIEW statement. If the results are not what you expect, alter the statement. Issuing SELECT queries by themselves in the Query Analyzer is easier than recreating your view object.

3. **Execute your query by choosing Query⇨Execute Query.**

    After executing your query containing the **CREATE VIEW** SQL statement, you will notice the statement **The command(s) completed successfully** in the results tab of the Query Analyzer.

4. **Test your view with the SELECT statement and execute the statement.**

    After your view is created, you can test it by using the Query Analyzer. Clear the text in the top part of the Query Analyzer and type this:

```
SELECT * FROM EMPLOYEES_VIEW
```

Then execute your query by choosing Query⇨Execute Query. You'll see a screen like the one in Figure 13-17. Notice that the columns returned are only the ones that you've defined when you created your view.

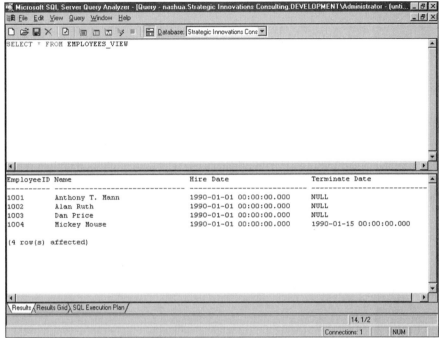

Figure 13-17:
Results of
querying
your view in
the Query
Analyzer.

Chapter 14

Preventing the Inevitable Disaster (Losing Data)!

*H*ave you ever lost data? If you have, you probably wish that you had backed up your data. I know I have. Backing up is the process of copying data to another location so that you have a way to recover if your original data is lost. Fortunately, Microsoft made backing up data in SQL Server 7 easy. You can back up your data either manually or automatically. I illustrate both ways of backing up data in this chapter.

Setting Up a Backup Device

Before you can backup your data, you need to set up your backup device. Otherwise, SQL Server doesn't know where to back up your data to. A backup device can be either a tape or disk. You notify SQL Server about the backup device when you give the device a name and assign it to either a tape drive or a disk drive. If you're using a tape, you specify which tape drive the device uses (even when you have only one tape drive). If you're using a disk, you specify the disk drive and directory that the device uses.

To set up a backup device, follow these steps:

1. **Choose Start⇨Programs⇨Microsoft SQL Server 7.0⇨Enterprise Manager to start the SQL Server Enterprise Manager.**

2. **Expand the tree so that you see the Backup Devices folder (see Figure 14-1).**

   For more information about expanding the tree, see Chapter 1.

3. **Choose Action⇨New Backup Device to bring up the Backup Device Properties dialog box.**

   Alternatively, you can right-click the Backup Devices folder in the tree. Any method you choose to create a new backup device brings up the Backup Device Properties dialog box, allowing you to configure the new device. (See Figure 14-2.)

4. **Type information about the new backup device in the following fields:**

   • **Name:** Give your backup device a name. If you intend to use a tape device, you may want to use a name such as **Tape Device**. If you intend to use a disk to back up your data, you may want to use a name such as **Drive C**. In either case, you will be using this name to identify the device later.

   • **Tape drive name:** If you are using a tape device for your backups, choose from the drop-down list of available devices. If you have more than one tape device, the devices all appear in the drop-down list. If you don't have a tape device, this field will be disabled. If you do have a device but this field is disabled, check the Tape Devices applet in the Windows Control Panel. For more information about configuring tape devices, refer to *Windows NT 4 For Dummies,* by Andy Rathbone and Sharon Crawford (IDG Books Worldwide, Inc.). This option is chosen by default if you have a tape device on your computer. For my examples shown in this section, I chose this option because I have a tape drive.

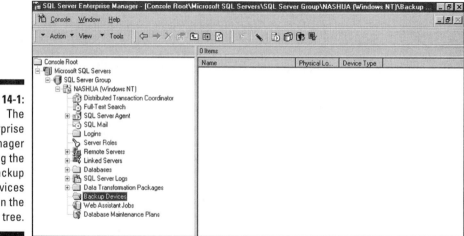

Figure 14-1: The Enterprise Manager showing the Backup Devices folder in the tree.

Figure 14-2:
The Backup
Device
Properties
dialog box
is where
you indicate
your
backup
device.

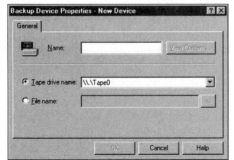

- **File name:** If you are using a disk drive for your backups, click the ellipsis button (...) to choose a drive and directory on your computer. This drive can be a networked drive. The drive and directory you choose is used to place the file containing the SQL Server backup. This option is chosen by default if you do not have a tape device on your computer.

  You need to indicate a file name along with a directory. To help you with this, SQL Server automatically appends the name you entered in the Name field with a .DAT extension to the directory you choose. For example, if you give a name of **Drive C**, and you choose a directory `C:\MSSQL7\BACKUP`, SQL Server presents the file name `C:\MSSQL7\BACKUP\Drive C.DAT`.

The **View Contents** button is enabled only if you bring up the Backup Device Properties dialog box for an existing backup device. Because you are creating a new device, the button is disabled. If the button is enabled, clicking it will read the medium and allow you to review the data contained within.

5. **Click OK to save the data.**

   Notice that your newly configured backup device appears on the right-hand pane of the SQL Server Enterprise Manager screen (see Figure 14-3).

Editing an Existing Backup Device

What if you already have a backup device and you want to edit it? The answer to this is quite simple. You edit a backup device by using the Backup Device Properties dialog box. This is the same dialog box you use when you create the backup device.

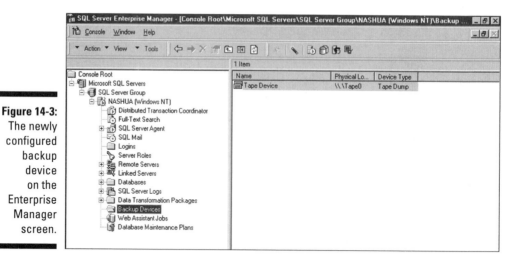

Figure 14-3:
The newly configured backup device on the Enterprise Manager screen.

To edit the backup device, follow these few steps:

1. **Choose Start⇨Programs⇨Microsoft SQL Server 7.0⇨Enterprise Manager to start the SQL Server Enterprise Manager.**

2. **Expand the tree so that you see the Backup Devices folder.**

   For more information about expanding the tree, see Chapter 1.

3. **Click the existing backup device that you want, listed in the right-hand pane in the Enterprise Manager.**

4. **Choose Action⇨Properties to edit the properties of the already configured backup device.**

5. **Edit the properties as you wish.**

   For example, for a disk drive backup, you may wish to change the drive and/or directory where the backup takes place.

6. **Click OK to save the data.**

Performing the Backup

Before you back up your data, you need to configure one or more backup devices. Refer to the section, "Setting Up a Backup Device," earlier in this chapter to see how to configure one or more backup devices. To start the backup, follow these steps:

1. **Select Start⇨Programs⇨Microsoft SQL Server 7.0⇨Enterprise Manager to start the SQL Server Enterprise Manager.**

2. **Expand the tree so that you see the Databases folder.**

   For more information about expanding the tree, see Chapter 1.

3. **Click the database you want to back up.**

4. **Choose Action⇨Task⇨Backup Database to bring up the SQL Server Backup dialog box.**

   Alternatively, you can right-click the database folder that you want in the tree and choose the Task⇨Backup Database.

   Each method brings up a dialog box, consisting of two tabs (General and Options), to allow you to enter the parameters and data relating to the backup (see Figure 14-4). The General tab appears by default.

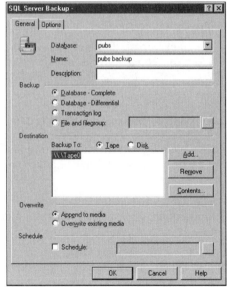

Figure 14-4:
The General
tab of the
SQL Server
Backup
dialog box.

Specifying general data about the backup

Use the General tab to specify general information about the backup — the minimum amount of data necessary — to begin the backup. (See "Specifying optional data about the backup," later in this section, to see the optional data you can specify about the backup.)

To specify general information about the data on the General tab, follow these steps:

1. **Type data in the fields.**

   - **Database:** Choose the database to back up. By default, the database that is selected when you bring up the SQL Server Backup dialog box is shown in the drop-down list. Because I chose the **pubs** database, pubs is listed in the Database field.

   - **Name:** Give your backup a name. By default, SQL Server enters the name of the database you choose, followed by the word **backup**. For example, if you choose the pubs database, SQL Server will enter **pubs backup**.

   - **Description:** This field is optional. You need to enter a description only if the value you typed in the Name field is not descriptive enough.

   - **Backup:** Choose the type of backup you want to perform. By default, **Database - Complete** is chosen. The available options are:

     Database - Complete: Backs up all database objects in the current database, such as indexes, tables, and data.

     Database - Differential: Backs up only the changes made since the last backup.

     Transaction Log: Backs up only the SQL Server transaction log. A *transaction log* is a log that SQL Server maintains automatically to know what operations have been performed on the SQL Server. This allows a user or a process to roll back changes to a prior state, if necessary.

     File and filegroups: Allows you to break up a large database into separate files or groups of files. Click the **...** button to choose the file or filegroup name.

   - **Destination:** Choose either the **Tape** or **Disk** option button. After you choose an option, click the **Add** button. This allows you to add any device that has been previously set up or to specify a device (for tapes) or location (for files). By default, the Tape option is chosen if you have a tape drive on your server.

   - **Overwrite:** Choose the type of action you want to perform. By default, **Append to Media** is chosen. The available options are:

     Append to media: Appends data onto the end of the data already existing on the tape or disk.

     Overwrite existing media: Overwrites the data that already exists on the tape or disk.

2. Specify a schedule by clicking the Schedule check box.

Make sure that the Schedule check box has a check mark in it (by clicking it) if you wish for the backup to run on a specified schedule. After you click this check box, you can click the **...** button to specify the scheduling options (see Figure 14-5).

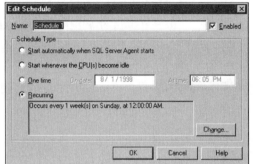

Figure 14-5:
The Edit Schedule dialog box of the SQL Server Backup dialog box.

If you create a schedule, SQL Server creates a job for you. For more information about jobs, see Chapter 10. You can specify from these options:

- **Name:** Give your schedule a name. By default, SQL Server enters **Schedule 1**.

- **Start automatically when SQL Server Agent starts:** Choose this option if you want your backup to begin every time you start the SQL Server Agent service. For more information about services, refer to *Windows NT 4 For Dummies* by Andy Rathbone and Sharon Crawford (from IDG Books Worldwide, Inc.).

- **Start whenever the CPU(s) become idle:** Starts the job whenever the system processor(s) is not busy. If a very calculation-intensive query is running, there is no time for the job to run. This option enables you to perform periodic system processing without sacrificing CPU cycles for a user's query.

- **One time:** Runs the job once, at a specified date and time. Choosing this option enables the **On date** and **At time** fields, allowing you to specify the date and time, respectively.

- **Recurring:** Runs the job on a recurring basis, at intervals that you specify. Because this is the most popular option for a job, it is selected by default. Also by default, the schedule runs once a week, on Sunday, at midnight. To change the Recurring option, click the **Change** button.

3. Click OK to save data and begin the backup.

You can close the dialog box and begin the backup by clicking OK, or you can choose additional options (refer to the next section, "Specifying optional data about the backup").

Specifying optional data about the backup

Use the Options tab to specify additional data about the backup that isn't mandatory to begin the backup (see Figure 14-6).

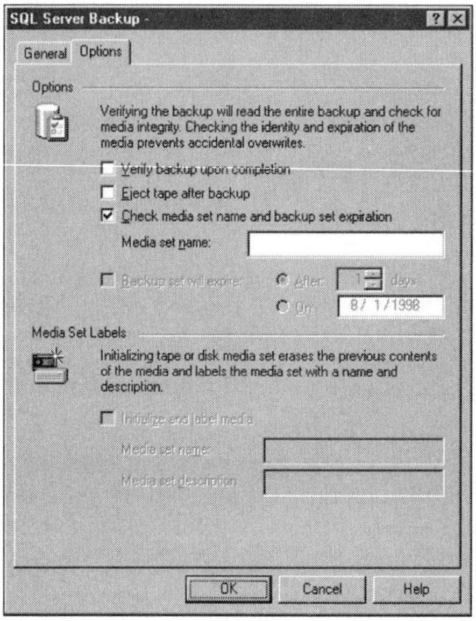

Figure 14-6:
The Options tab of the SQL Server Backup dialog box.

To specify optional data on the Options tab, type information in the following fields:

Options

Choose the options you want. Check boxes are next to each option — you can choose any or all of these options. The available options are:

- ✔ **Verify backup upon completion:** I always choose this option. This option ensures that the data copied to the tape or disk is an exact copy of the original data.

- ✔ **Eject tape after backup:** Ejects the tape when the backup completes. This option is only enabled if you choose **Tape Device** under the **Media** field on the General tab.

✔ **Check media set name and backup set expiration:** This option checks the **Media set name** and the expiration data listed in the **On** field to determine whether it can be overwritten.

✔ **Backup set will expire:** Designates when the backup will expire. After that time, it can be overwritten. This option is available only if you choose the **Overwrite existing media** option in the **Overwrite** section on the General tab. If you choose this option, you must select the number of days or a specific date the backup will expire. To do this, click the appropriate option button and type the data related to the number of days or a specific date you want the backup to expire on.

Media set labels

This section allows you to first initialize (delete) the media that you selected for backup. There are two fields that you must fill out if you choose this option. This option is not available unless you choose the **Overwrite existing media** option in the **Overwrite** section on the General tab.

✔ **Media set name:** Type the name of the media set. This will be used to check whether the data can be overwritten. The data typed in this field will be written to the tape or disk drive.

✔ **Media set description:** Type the description of the tape if the **Media set name** is not descriptive enough. The data typed in this field will be written to the tape or disk drive.

Click OK to save data and begin the backup.

Restoring Your Data

Backing up your data is an important safeguard against losing important data. But what if you need the data you have backed up (besides panicking)? Restoring data is the only way to use the backed up data. To restore data from a backup (also referred to as a restore), follow these steps:

1. **Select Start⇨Programs⇨Microsoft SQL Server 7.0⇨Enterprise Manager to start the SQL Server Enterprise Manager.**

2. **Expand the tree so that you see the Databases folder.**

   For more information about expanding the tree, see Chapter 1.

3. **Click the database you want to restore the data into.**

4. **Choose Action⇨Task⇨Restore Database to bring up the Restore Database dialog box.**

Alternatively, you can right-click the database folder that you want in the tree and choose the Task⇨Restore Database.

Each method brings up a dialog box consisting of two tabs (General and Options) to allow you to enter the parameters and data relating to restoring your data from backup (see Figure 14-7). The General tab appears by default.

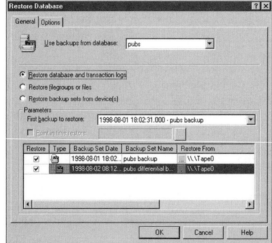

Figure 14-7:
The General tab of the Restore Database dialog box.

Specifying general data about the restore

Use the General tab to specify general information about the restore — the minimum amount of data necessary — to begin the backup. (See "Specifying optional data about the restore," later in this section, to see the optional data you can specify about the restore.)

To specify general information about the restore on the General tab, type data or select from these fields:

- **Use backups from database:** Choose the database to restore into. The database that you choose to restore into must be the same database that you backed up from. By default, the database that is selected when you bring up the Restore Database dialog box is shown in the drop-down list. Because I chose the **pubs** database, pubs is listed in the Use backups from database field.

- **Restore database and transaction logs:** Choose this option if you want your restore to be an exact image of the way your database looked when you performed the backup (refer to Figure 14-7). I recommend this option. It is also the default option.

If you choose this option, there are options that become enabled in the Parameters section. The first is **First backup to restore**. Choose from the drop-down list of prior backups that you wish to restore. The second option is **Point in time restore**. Check this option if you want to restore your database as it was at a specific point in time. For example, you can restore a database to look the way it did on January 15, 1998 at 3:00 p.m. (assuming you performed a backup at that point in time). After you check this option, the **...** button becomes enabled, allowing you to change the time for the restore. The third option is a grid that shows a list of available backups to restore. Ensure that there is a check mark in the first column for each backup you wish to restore.

✔ **Restore filegroups or files:** Choose this option if you wish to restore one or more specific filegroups or files (see Figure 14-8).

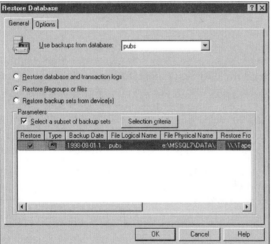

Figure 14-8:
The General tab of the Restore Database dialog box, but showing the **Restore filegroups or files** option checked.

If you choose this option, options in the Parameters section become enabled. The first is **Select a subset of backup sets**. Check this option if you want to restore only a *subset* of a prior backup. A *subset* of a backup is any part of the complete backup. If you check this option, the **Selection criteria** button becomes enabled, allowing you to select the criteria that defines the subset. The second option is a grid that shows a list of available backups to restore. Ensure that a check mark is in the first column for each backup you wish to restore.

✔ **Restore backup sets from device(s):** Choose this option if you wish to restore the data exactly as it is stored on a device that you have already configured (see Figure 14-9).

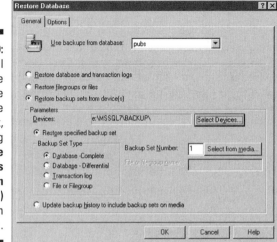

If you choose this option, two main options become enabled in the Parameters section. The first is **Restore specified backup set**. Choose this option if you want to restore a database from a specific backup set that you have stored on some medium (tape or disk). You can choose from a complete backup, differential, Transaction Log, or File or Filegroup. You then need to specify the backup set number to restore. If three backup sets are available, you can choose from 1, 2, or 3.

The second option is **Update backup history to include backup sets on media**. If you choose this option, every backup set stored on the backup will be restored. Therefore, you do not need to specify a specific backup set.

Specifying optional data about the restore

Use the Options tab to specify additional data about the restore that isn't mandatory to begin the backup (see Figure 14-10).

To specify optional data on the Options tab, type information in the following fields:

- ✔ **Eject tapes after restoring each backup:** Check this option if you want your tapes to be ejected after each backup. Your tape drive(s) must have the capability to eject a tape for this option to work.

- ✔ **Prompt before restoring each backup:** Check this option if you want to be prompted before restoring each backup in a backup set.

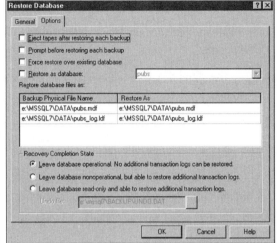

Figure 14-10:
The Options
tab of the
SQL Server
Backup
dialog box.

✓ **Force restore over existing database:** Check this option if you want to overwrite an existing database with the data that was backed up.

✓ **Restore as database:** Check this option if you want to restore to a different database, other than the database that was backed up. If you check this option, a drop-down list becomes enabled allowing you to choose the database to restore into.

✓ **Backup Physical File Name:** This is a column in the grid of available file names in the restore chosen on the General tab. You cannot change the data in this column because it is stored as part of the backup that you are going to restore.

✓ **Restore As:** This also is a column in the grid of available file names in the restore chosen on the General tab. However, you can change any row in this column. By default the name of the restored file is the same as the Backup Physical File Name file. This is because the intent is to restore a backup exactly as it was when it was backed up. If you want to change the name of the files as they will be restored, click the file name you wish to change and type in the desired file name.

✓ **Leave database operational. No additional transaction logs can be restored:** This option is chosen by default. While the restore is being completed, the database is left in an operational state, but the transaction logs cannot be restored because an action taking place by another user can update these logs while the restore is underway.

✓ **Leave database nonoperational, but able to restore additional transaction logs:** While the restore is being completed, the database is left in a nonoperational state. This allows for the transaction logs to be restored, but no other user can access the database.

✔ **Leave database read-only and able to restore additional transaction logs:** While the restore is being completed, the database is left in an operational state, but users cannot write any data to the database. It is read-only. This allows for the transaction logs to be restored and users to have limited access to the database. If you choose this option, you can choose an undo file. This file allows you to undo the restore, if you wish.

Chapter 15

So You Want to Be Published?

In This Chapter

▶ Publishing your data

▶ Using the Microsoft SQL Server 7 Web Assistant

▶ Accessing your published data

Data publishing may sound like a difficult, drawn-out undertaking. Actually, the process isn't that overwhelming. Publishing your data really refers to creating an HTML Web page that contains your data in an HTML table. To view the data, you need a browser that supports HTML tables, such as Microsoft Internet Explorer 4.0.

Are you an experienced creator of HTML? If you've been there and done that, hurrah! If you're just starting out, not to worry — the Microsoft SQL Server 7 Web Assistant does everything for you.

If you want to know even more about HTML, check out the *...For Dummies* array of titles on the topic, including *HTML For Dummies,* 3rd Edition, by Ed Tittel and Stephen N. James (IDG Books Worldwide, Inc.).

Harnessing the Power of the Microsoft SQL Server 7 Web Assistant

The Microsoft SQL Server 7 Web Assistant is a wizard that's designed to help you get published — that is, to publish your Web pages. Your Web pages are generated from HTML, but, with the generous help of the Assistant, you don't need to know anything about HTML. Just follow these steps.

1. **Choose Start⇨Programs⇨Microsoft SQL Server 7.0⇨Enterprise Manager to start the Enterprise Manager (shown in Figure 15-1).**

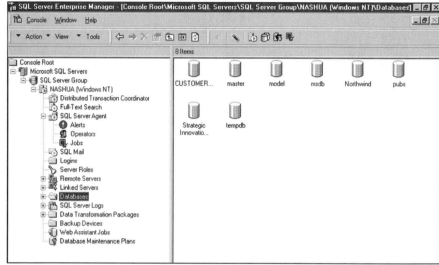

Figure 15-1:
The
Enterprise
Manager
screen.

2. **Expand the tree so that you see the name of your server and click either the name of the server or any tree item below the server name.**

   If you need more information about expanding the tree, see Chapter 1.

3. **Bring up the Select Wizard dialog box by choosing Tools⇨Wizards.**

4. **Click the Web Assistant Wizard (under the Management folder) and click OK to start the Wizard.**

   The Microsoft SQL Server Web Assistant welcome dialog box presents a synopsis of what the Wizard can do for you. Click Next when you're ready to move on. To help you understand the logic flow of this wizard, refer to the flowchart diagram in Appendix A. Because the way a dialog box is presented is based upon the options you choose in prior steps, you may want to refer to this flowchart as you go through the rest of this chapter.

5. **Click the name of the database that you want data published from in the Databases list box (see Figure 15-2); then click Next.**

6. **Specify job information (see Figure 15-3) and then click Next.**

   Publishing data is performed by creating a job. For more information about creating jobs, see Chapter 10. This step allows you to configure the job information.

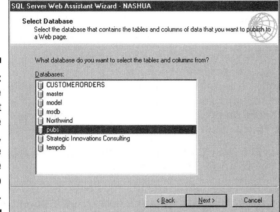

Figure 15-2:
From the
Select
Database
dialog box,
indicate the
database
you wish to
use.

Figure 15-3:
Fill in job
information
in this
dialog box.

You can enter data and choose from these fields:

- **What do you want to name this Web Assistant job?:** Type the name of your job. By default, SQL Server enters the name of your database, followed by **Web Page**. In my example, the name **pubs Web Page** is automatically entered.

- **Data from the tables and columns that I select:** Select this option if you want to specify the tables and columns for HTML Web publication. This option is chosen by default.

- **Result set(s) of a stored procedure I select:** Select this option if you want to indicate a specific stored procedure, the results of which will be contained in the HTML Web publication.

• **Data from the Transact-SQL statement I specify:** Select this option if you want to enter a SQL statement directly, the results of which will be contained in the HTML Web publication.

Because so many options are available in the Web Assistant Wizard, I have supplemented the numbered steps with the letters a, b, and c. The reason that I did this is not to confuse you, but actually to clarify. The letters indicate that different dialog boxes are presented at a specific step number, based on options that you choose. Please take a few minutes to see the diagram in Appendix A to see what I mean.

7a. In the Select a Table and Columns dialog box, specify a table and columns (see Figure 15-4). Then click Next.

You can publish from one table and multiple columns. This step is only available if you chose the **Data from the tables and columns that I select** option.

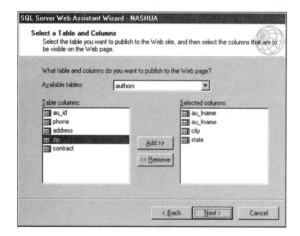

You can enter data and choose from these fields:

• **Available tables:** Choose the desired table from the drop-down list of available tables. These are all the tables in the database chosen earlier.

• **Table columns:** Choose the desired columns of data to publish to the Web. You must choose each column one at a time. To do so, click the desired table and click the Add button.

• **Selected columns:** This list shows all of the columns in the chosen table that are to be published to the Web. If you wish to remove any of the columns, click the desired table and click the Remove button.

8a. In the Select Rows dialog box (see Figure 15-5), specify how rows are to be limited. Then click Next.

You can opt to limit the number of rows to be published to the Web. This step is available only if you chose the **Data from the tables and columns that I select** option.

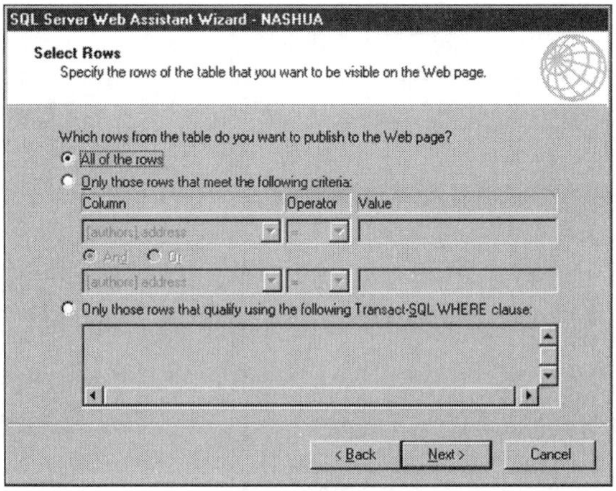

Figure 15-5:
In the Select Rows dialog box, indicate the rows to publish on the Web page.

You can enter data and choose from these fields:

- **All of the rows:** Choose this option if you do not want to limit the number of rows that are published to the Web. This option is selected by default.

- **Only those rows that meet the following criteria:** Choose this option if you want to limit the number of rows that are published to the Web, based on criteria that you specify. If you choose this option, the fields that allow you to specify that criteria become enabled. For example, you can choose to publish all authors with a last name beginning with letter **M**. (Where do you think I got that example from?)

- **Only those rows that qualify using the following SQL WHERE clause:** Choose this option if you want to limit the number of rows that are published to the Web, based on a SQL WHERE clause that you specify. If you choose this option, the text box that allows you to specify that SQL WHERE clause becomes enabled. For more information about SQL or a WHERE clause, see Chapter 8.

7b. In the Select Stored Procedure dialog box (see Figure 15-6), specify a stored procedure. Click the Next button when you are finished with this step.

Whatever columns of data have been specified in the stored procedure that you select will be published to the Web. This step is only available if you chose the **Result set(s) of a stored procedure I select** option.

To select a stored procedure, simply click the desired stored procedure from the **Stored Procedures** list box.

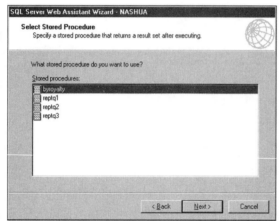

Figure 15-6:
In the
Select
Stored
Procedure
dialog box,
indicate the
stored
procedures
you want
to use.

8b. Specify Stored Procedure Parameters. Then click Next.

After you have chosen a stored procedure, you are prompted in this step to enter values for the parameters of that stored procedure. This step is only available if you chose the **Result set(s) of a stored procedure I select** option.

For each parameter defined in the stored procedure, you must specify a value if there is no default value indicated in the stored procedure itself. The parameters and data are shown in a grid. Simply click the cell in the grid for each **Value** you wish to enter. Then type in the **Value**. Continue doing this for every parameter.

7c. Enter your SQL statement; click Next when you are finished with this step.

Type the SQL necessary to return a result set that you wish to publish to the Web. This step is only available if you chose the **Data from the Transact-SQL statement I specify** option. After you enter a SQL statement, the Next button becomes enabled.

9. In the Schedule the Web Assistant Job dialog box, specify the updating and generating schedule; then click Next.

After you have defined the record set that is to be published (in steps 7a and 8a, 7b and 8b, or 7c), you must schedule the job for the Web Assistant to publish the data (see Figure 15-7).

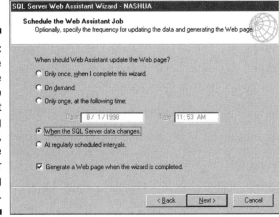

Figure 15-7:
In the
Schedule
the Web
Assistant
Job dialog
box,
indicate
your
scheduling
preferences.

You can enter data and choose from these fields:

- **Only once, when I complete this wizard:** Choose this option if you wish for the Web Assistant to create the HTML page when the wizard is finished. This option is chosen by default.

- **On demand:** Choose this option if you wish to create and update your HTML page only when you manually run the job named in Step 7.

- **Only once, at the following time:** Choose this option if you wish for the Web Assistant to schedule a date and time to create the HTML page. However, this job runs only once. If you click this option, text boxes are enabled that allow you to type the date and time desired to run the job.

- **When the SQL Server data changes:** Choose this option if you wish for the Web Assistant to regenerate the HTML page every time the data changes. This makes for a dynamic solution.

Just because I said this is a dynamic solution does not mean that you are using Dynamic HTML, or *DHTML*. DHTML is HTML that is dynamically determined at the time the Web page is viewed in a browser. The HTML generated here is static text. The data from the table is actually placed in the HTML file. The reason I mentioned this as being a dynamic solution is because the job can regularly run, thereby recreating the HTML with updated data.

- **At regularly scheduled intervals:** Choose this option if you wish for the Web Assistant to regenerate the HTML page at intervals that you specify in a later step. This makes for a dynamic solution. (See my earlier note about dynamic HTML!)

- **Do not generate an initial HTML page:** Choose this check box if you only want to schedule the job and not to create an initial HTML page. This check box is only enabled if you choose one of these options:

  On demand

  Only once, at the following time

  At regularly scheduled intervals

10a. In the Monitor a Table and Columns dialog box, specify a table and columns to monitor (see Figure 15-8). Click Next when you are finished with this step.

You can indicate to SQL Server which columns in a table should be monitored for changes. When these changes are detected, your HTML page is automatically regenerated. This step is available only if you chose the **When the SQL Server data changes** option.

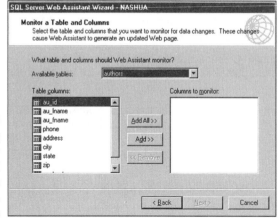

Figure 15-8:
The Monitor
a Table and
Columns
dialog box.

You can enter data and choose from these fields:

- **Available tables:** Choose the desired table from the drop-down list of available tables. These are all the tables in the database chosen earlier.

- **Table columns:** Choose the desired columns of data to publish to the Web. You must choose each column one at a time. To do so, click the desired table and click the Add button. Also, you can click the Add All button to select every column in the chosen table to be monitored.

- **Columns to monitor:** This list shows all the columns in the chosen table that are to be monitored for changes. If you wish to remove any of the columns, click the desired table and click the Remove button.

10b. In the Schedule the Update Interval dialog box, specify the update interval (see Figure 15-9). Click Next to continue.

Specify the conditions of the update interval. This step is only available if you chose the **When the At regularly scheduled intervals** option.

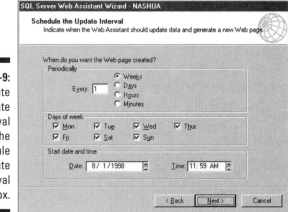

Figure 15-9:
Indicate
your update
interval
in the
Schedule
the Update
Interval
dialog box.

You can enter data and choose from these fields:

- **Every:** Type the value in the text box that represents the frequency of your desired update schedule. For example, if you want the schedule to run every other day, enter a **2** in this field. **1** is entered by default.

- **Weeks:** Choose this option if you want the schedule to run every *x* number of weeks, where *x* is the value in the **Every** text box. This option is chosen by default.

- **Days:** Choose this option if you want the schedule to run every *x* number of days, where *x* is the value in the **Every** text box.

- **Hours:** Choose this option if you want the schedule to run every *x* number of hours, where *x* is the value in the **Every** text box.

- **Minutes:** Choose this option if you want the schedule to run every *x* number of minutes, where *x* is the value in the **Every** text box.

- **Days of week:** Check the desired days of the week that you wish the schedule to run. You can check any or all of the check boxes to represent the desired days of the week.

- **Start date and time:** Enter into the **Date** and **Time** text boxes the desired date and time for the update interval to begin. For example, if you want the schedule to run every day, but not starting until midnight January 1, 1999, you enter that date and time here.

11. In the Publish the Web Page dialog box (see Figure 15-10), specify the file name of the HTML page to be generated and click Next.

The HTML page that you specify must be a path that can be written by SQL Server. For example, if the security on SQL Server does not allow access to **C:\HTML**, SQL Server can't write the file there. By default the file name is a sequential file name, named **WebPage*x*.htm** in the **HTML** subdirectory of wherever you installed SQL Server 7, where *x* is the sequential number.

Type the desired HTML file into the **File name** text box.

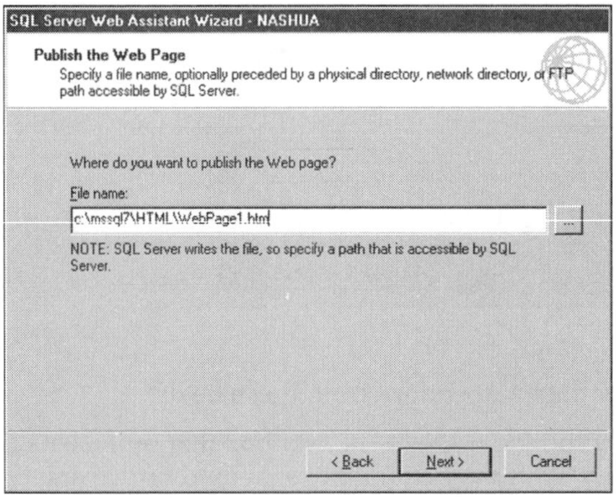

Figure 15-10: Indicate where you want to publish the Web page in the Publish the Web Page dialog box.

12. Specify the format of the Web page and click Next.

You can have the Web Assistant Wizard help you with the formatting of the Web page, or you can choose from an existing template. The format will be derived from this template. You can choose from these fields:

- **Yes, help me format the HTML page:** Choose this option if you want the Web Assistant Wizard to guide you through formatting the Web page.

- **No, use the template file from:** Choose this option if you are going to use a template HTML file that already contains formatting. After you choose this option, the text box becomes enabled, allowing you to select or type the HTML template file. To browse for the file, click the **...** button.

13. In the Specify Titles dialog box, specify title information used in the Web page (see Figure 15-11). Click Next to continue.

Specify the information used to generate the HTML title. This step is available only if you chose the **Yes, help me format the HTML page** option.

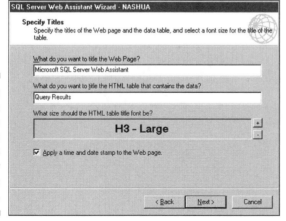

Figure 15-11:
Indicate the
titles of the
Web page
in the
Specify
Titles
dialog box.

You can enter data and choose from these fields:

- **What do you want to title the Web Page?:** Enter into the text box provided the title you wish to use for your Web page. You may want to enter something that is germane to the result set returned from the query. You can enter something like **All Authors with the Last Name Beginning with 'M'**. By default, SQL Server enters **Microsoft SQL Server Web Assistant**. Obviously, this does you no good! I suggest you rename the title.

- **What do you want to title the HTML table that contains the data?:** Within the HTML page, SQL Server generates an HTML table for the data itself. Enter into the text box provided the title you wish to use for this table. By default, SQL Server enters **Query Results**. This is an acceptable table title, although you can change it if you wish.

- **What size should the HTML table title font be?:** Click the plus (+) or minus (-) buttons to increase or decrease the size of the HTML table title font. By default, the HTML table title font size is H3.

- **Apply a time and date stamp to the Web page:** Choose this check box if you wish for the time and date of creation to be placed on the Web page. This check box is not selected by default.

14. **In the Format a Table dialog box, specify HTML Table formatting information (see Figure 15-12). Then click Next.**

    This step allows you to indicate how you want the HTML table to be formatted. This step is available only if you chose the **Yes, help me format the HTML page** option.

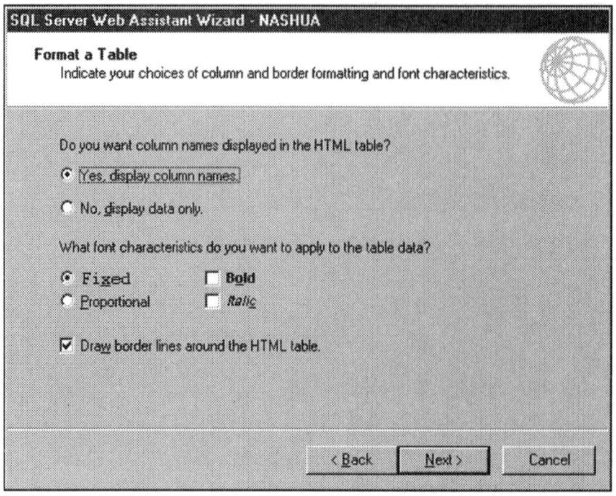

Figure 15-12:
In the
Format a
Table dialog
box,
indicate
your
formatting
preferences.

You can enter data and choose from these fields:

- **Yes, display column names:** Choose this option if you want your HTML table to include the names of the columns you chose. This option is chosen by default.

- **No, display data only:** Choose this option if you don't want your HTML table to include the names of the columns you chose.

- **Fixed:** Choose this option if you want the font displayed in the table to be a fixed size. This means that every character is the same width. For example, a **W** is the same width as an **I**. Fixed size can be easier to read for result sets because all the characters line up nicely. This option is chosen by default.

- **Proportional:** Choose this option if you want the font displayed in the table to be a proportional size. This means that every character is as wide as it needs to be. For example, a **W** is wider than an **I**.

- **Bold:** Choose this check box if you wish for all of the data in the HTML table to be bold. The data in the HTML table can also be italic at the same time.

- **Italic:** Choose this check box if you wish for all of the data in the HTML table to be italic. The data in the HTML table can also be bold at the same time.

- **Draw border lines around the HTML table:** Choose this check box if you wish for all of the data in the HTML table to be encompassed within a border. This formatting sometimes makes the data easier to read because it doesn't "float" in the middle of your Web page. This option is chosen by default.

15. **In the Add Hyperlinks to the Web Page dialog box, specify whether or not to add hyperlinks to your Web page (see Figure 15-13); click Next when you finish with this step.**

    This step allows you to indicate whether or not you wish to show hyperlinks to other Web pages in the newly created Web page. This step is available only if you chose the **Yes, help me format the HTML page** option.

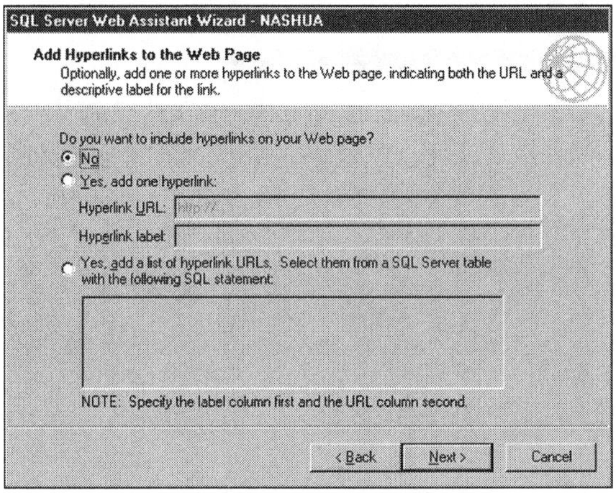

Figure 15-13: Add hyperlinks to the Web page, of course!

    You can enter data and choose from these fields:

    • **No:** Choose this option if you do not want additional hyperlinks to other Web pages added to your Web page. This option is chosen by default.

    • **Yes, add one hyperlink:** Choose this option if you want to add only one hyperlink to another Web page. After you choose this option, two text boxes become enabled, allowing for you to type the hyperlink data. These text boxes are **Hyperlink URL** and **Hyperlink label**. *URL* stands for Uniform Resource Locator. It is the standard Web address, such as my company's Web page, `www.strategic-innovations.com`. Additionally, you can specify a label for the URL, such as **SIC** (which stands for Strategic Innovations Consulting).

    • **Yes, add a list of hyperlink URLs. Select them from a SQL Server table with the following SQL statement:** Choose this option if you want to add more than one hyperlink to another Web page. After you choose this option, the text box to specify your SQL statement becomes enabled.

This option can also be used for one hyperlink that is retrieved from the database with your SQL statement. You don't have to choose the **Yes, add one hyperlink** option.

16. **In the Limit Rows dialog box, specify how to limit data rows (see Figure 15-14), and then click Next.**

This step allows you to not only limit the number of rows returned by SQL Server, but also to limit the number of rows displayed in the HTML table.

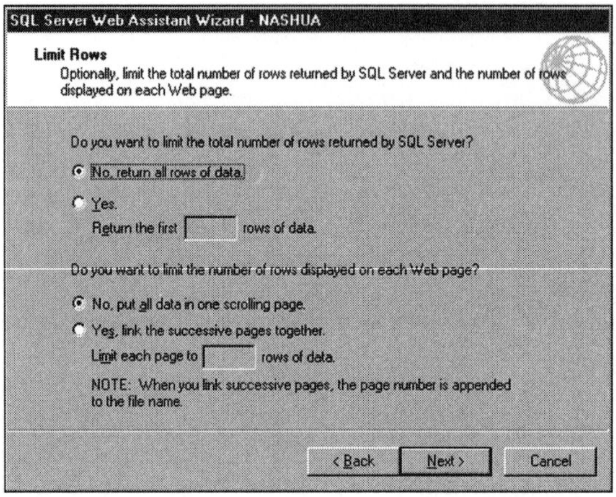

Figure 15-14:
Limit data
rows in the
Limit Rows
dialog box.

You can enter data and choose from these fields:

- **No, return all rows of data:** Choose this option if you do not want the number of rows returned by SQL Server to be limited. This option is chosen by default.

- **Yes:** Choose this option if you do want the number of rows returned by SQL Server to be limited. After you choose this option, a text box becomes enabled, allowing you to specify the maximum number of rows to be returned. For example, you might want to show only the first 100 rows.

- **No, put all data in one scrolling page:** Choose this option if you want the size of the HTML page to be as large as necessary to hold all the data in the HTML table.

- **Yes, link the successive pages together:** Choose this option if you want the size of the HTML page to be limited, based on the number of rows that you specify per page. After you choose this option, a text box becomes enabled, allowing you to specify the number of maximum rows to be included in the HTML table per page. For example, you may want to show only 50 rows in the HTML table per page.

17. **Complete the Microsoft SQL Server Web Assistant Wizard by reviewing your choices in the text box provided. Then click Finish.**

    Also, you can save the Transact-SQL statement generated by the Wizard to a file. To do so, click the Write Transact-SQL to File button and type the file name under which to save the generated SQL.

    If you wish to change any of the criteria that you specified in an earlier step, click the Back button until you reach the desired step to change.

Accessing Your Published Data

After you create your Web page using the Web Assistant Wizard, you can access two things. One is the job that you created while using the Wizard; the other is the actual HTML page. I show both in the following sections.

Accessing the Web Assistant Job

You can access through the Enterprise Manager all jobs created with the Web Assistant Wizard. To access the Web Assistant jobs, follow these steps.

1. **Choose the Start➪Programs➪Microsoft SQL Server 7.0➪Enterprise Manager to start the SQL Server Enterprise Manager.**

2. **Expand the tree so that you see the name of your server and then the Web Assistant Jobs entry; select it.**

    For more information about expanding the tree, see Chapter 1.

    Selecting the Web Assistant Jobs entry populates a list of Web Assistant Jobs already created on the right-hand part of the screen. The right-hand part of the screen shows the name of your job, the output HTML file name, and when the job was last run.

3. **View the Job Properties by right-clicking the desired job on the right-hand part of the screen and selecting the Properties menu option.**

Access the HTML page

Accessing the HTML page is quite simple. You do this with a Web browser that supports tables, such as the Microsoft Internet Explorer 4.0. To access the HTML page, follow these steps.

1. **Start the browser.**

   If you would like to use Microsoft Internet Explorer, choose Start➪Programs➪Internet Explorer➪Internet Explorer.

2. **Choose the File➪Open to open the HTML file.**

   This brings up a dialog box, allowing you to enter or specify your HTML file. You must know the name and location of the HTML file created by the Web Assistant Wizard. The default is the **HTML** subdirectory of wherever you installed SQL Server 7 (see Figure 15-15).

If you want to view the HTML that made up the Web page, choose the View➪Source menu option. This action brings up the HTML code in the editor registered on your system, such as Notepad.

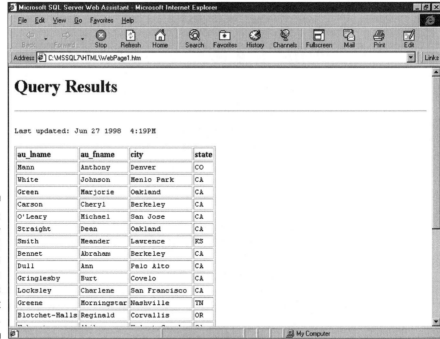

Figure 15-15:
The newly created HTML file shown in Microsoft's Internet Explorer 4.0.

Microsoft SQL Server Web Assistant - Microsoft Internet Explorer

File Edit View Go Favorites Help

Back Forward Stop Refresh Home Search Favorites History Channels Fullscreen Mail Print Edit

Address C:\MSSQL7\HTML\WebPage1.htm   Links

Query Results

Last updated: Jun 27 1998 4:19PM

au_lname	au_fname	city	state
Mann	Anthony	Denver	CO
White	Johnson	Menlo Park	CA
Green	Marjorie	Oakland	CA
Carson	Cheryl	Berkeley	CA
O'Leary	Michael	San Jose	CA
Straight	Dean	Oakland	CA
Smith	Meander	Lawrence	KS
Bennet	Abraham	Berkeley	CA
Dull	Ann	Palo Alto	CA
Gringlesby	Burt	Covelo	CA
Locksley	Charlene	San Francisco	CA
Greene	Morningstar	Nashville	TN
Blotchet-Halls	Reginald	Corvallis	OR

My Computer

Part V
The Part of Tens

The 5th Wave   By Rich Tennant

"We sort of have our own way of preparing
our people to become database administrators."

In this part . . .

*O*kay, say that you've read all my babble on Microsoft SQL Server 7.0. and (believe it or not), you're still having problems. This part shows you not only resources on the Web, but some of the best tools to help you get your job done. Some of these tools have demos on the CD (What a deal!).

Chapter 16

Ten Microsoft SQL Server Online Resources

In This Chapter

▶ Checking out cool Web pages

▶ Solving problems in discussion groups

The Internet is a great place to start for SQL Server resources. So get online and get going!

Web Pages

Every Microsoft SQL Server 7 user needs access to online Web pages to keep current in the latest technology, as well as with new products and resources. This section shows some useful Web pages.

I have found that the most useful resources on the subject of Microsoft SQL Server (and other Microsoft products) are produced by Microsoft itself. Therefore, I list more Microsoft Web pages than any other resource in this chapter.

The mother of all SQL sites: Microsoft SQL Server

```
http://www.microsoft.com/sql
```

This page is, of course, the SQL Server home page from Microsoft (shown in Figure 16-1), and it provides much in the way of resources for Microsoft SQL Server. Check this page often for news and information about SQL Server 7 and future releases.

Figure 16-1:
The
headquarters
for your
SQL Server
needs.

Microsoft's BackOffice products (of which SQL Server is one)

```
http://backoffice.microsoft.com
```

Because so many of the BackOffice products integrate with SQL Server, I consider this page to be one of the best online resources. You can get information about any of the Microsoft BackOffice products from this Microsoft Web page. (See Figure 16-2.)

Downloading Microsoft files

```
ftp://ftp.microsoft.com/Softlib/MSLFILES/
```

This Web page (shown in Figure 16-3) is a Microsoft FTP (File Transfer Protocol) page that allows you to browse and download free files from Microsoft. These files are not only SQL Server files, but all downloadable software files from Microsoft. For an index of the files available in this directory, view the **index.txt** file, which is located in the parent directory, **ftp://ftp.microsoft.com/Softlib/index.txt**.

Figure 16-2:
This is
where to
go for
BackOffice
products.

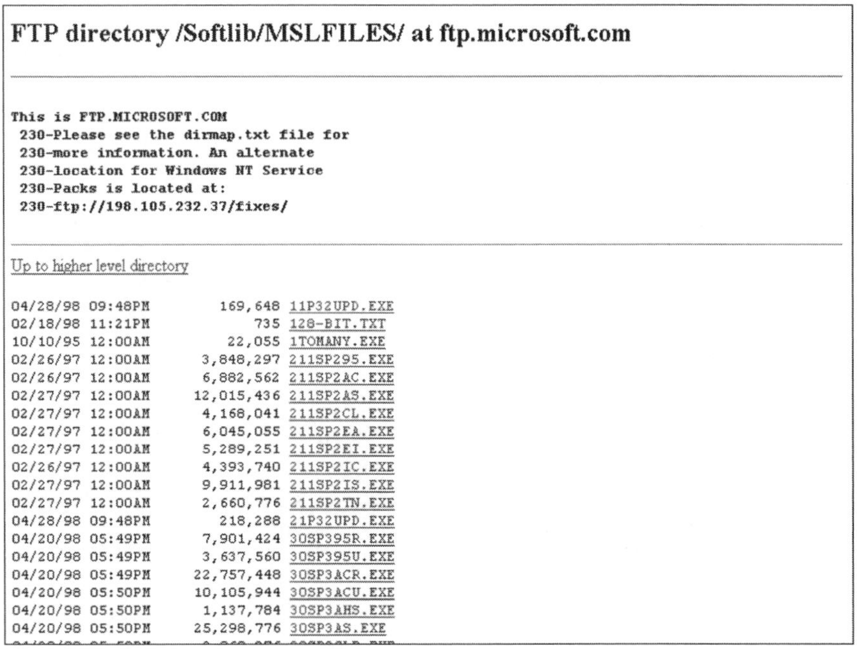

Figure 16-3:
What do
you want to
download
today?

Microsoft's Technet site

```
http://www.microsoft.com/technet/
```

The Microsoft TechNet Web page is a great resource to, as Microsoft says, "Evaluate, Implement, Support" solutions. This page includes Microsoft SQL Server and the BackOffice products (see Figure 16-4). Some features of this Web page are not free.

Microsoft Developer Network (MSDN)

```
http://www.microsoft.com/msdn/
```

The Microsoft Developer Network (MSDN) Web page is a great resource for finding out information about specific developer-related issues about SQL Server and other Microsoft technologies (see Figure 16-5). Some features of this Web page are not free.

Figure 16-4: The place to go for IT professionals.

Figure 16-5:
MSDN,
at your
service.

The Development Exchange

```
http://www.devx.com/home/devxhome.asp
```

The Development Exchange (DevX) Web site provides much useful information, not only on SQL Server, but development tools as well (see Figure 16-6). Some features of this Web page are not free.

Figure 16-6:
The DevX
home page.

Discussion Groups

Discussion groups, also known as *newsgroups,* have become quite a good resource for Microsoft SQL Server, all versions. A discussion group is useful mainly because you can get lots of people's opinions — and you don't even have to pay for it. You post a message regarding a problem you may be having. Hopefully, someone will respond who has experienced the very same problem.

The way that you access a news group is to use a news reader, such as Microsoft News, which is installed automatically with many programs, such as Internet Explorer 4.0. You need to configure your news reader to access a news server. Usually, your Internet Service Provider has a news server in the format of `news.domain.com|net`, which is a common format, but by no means a mandatory format. After you point your news reader to a news server, you can use it to download a list of newsgroups. The following section lists popular newsgroups.

What goes on in a newsgroup?

In these newsgroups, anybody can post anything. Groups can take on a particular character, or a distinguishing characteristic. Newsgroups can have several personalities even within them. You learn who knows something and who doesn't. Some people are helpful, while others seem to want to show off. Often you notice an atmosphere of kidding around and name calling, which can sometimes indicate some rifts in the newsgroup. At other times the kidding around is just people who are used to kidding around with each other. Newsgroups are great places to trade information and find useful techniques. The mood changes as different people participate at different times.

microsoft.public.sqlserver.programming

This Microsoft newsgroup specializes in programming issues with all versions of Microsoft SQL Server.

microsoft.public.sqlserver.connect

This Microsoft newsgroup specializes in connection issues with all versions of Microsoft SQL Server.

microsoft.public.sqlserver.misc

This Microsoft newsgroup specializes in miscellaneous or general issues with all versions of Microsoft SQL Server.

comp.databases.ms-sqlserver

This newsgroup specializes in general issues with all versions of Microsoft SQL Server.

Chapter 17

Ten Popular Ways to Give SQL Server More Pizzazz

* *

In This Chapter

▶ Tools that add on to the SQL Server product itself

▶ Tools that work in conjunction with SQL Server

* *

*M*icrosoft thought of many things with SQL Server 7. However, some vendors provide add-on tools that extend SQL Server 7's capabilities even further (hard to believe!). This chapter lists ten of the add-on tools and products that work in conjunction with SQL Server that I consider the most popular tools. I present these tools in no particular order.

Sylvain Faust — SQL Programmer

www.sfi-software.com/products.htm#sql_programmer

SQL Programmer is an award winning productivity tool from Sylvain Faust for making it easier to manipulate SQL Server objects, including Stored Procedures, Triggers, Functions, Views, and Indexes. (See Figure 17-1.) SQL Programmer was awarded a *Visual Basic Programmer's Journal* 1998 Reader's Choice Merit Award. Some of the exciting features include:

✔ Documentation generation

✔ Script generation

✔ Multiple database server connections

✔ Team programming

✔ Full version control

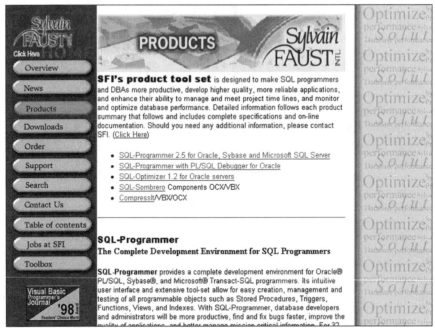

Figure 17-1:
The Sylvain
Faust home
page.

Sheridan Software — sp_Assist

www.shersoft.com/products/spassist/spagen.htm

What if you wanted some help creating and managing your stored procedures and other database objects? Well, Sheridan Software created such a
product, called sp_Assist (see Figure 17-2). However, it does much more
than those tasks. This software tool performs the following functions to
greatly help your daily SQL Server chores:

- Project source code management
- Coding and code generation
- SQL Server interaction
- Database administration

Figure 17-2:
Use
sp_Assist to
help you
with SQL
Server
chores.

Logic Works — ERwin/ERX

www.logicworks.com/products/erwin/erwinerx.htm

ERwin/ERX is an incredible tool from Logic Works that allows you to create and edit databases, as well as view and print Entity Relationship (ER) diagrams. I have found over the years that nothing substitutes for an ER diagram with small and large projects. ERwin/ERX is just such a product that produces these diagrams (see Figure 17-3).

ERwin/ERX performs these functions:

- ✔ Automatically generates your database
- ✔ Supports iterative design
- ✔ Supports data warehousing with dimensional modeling
- ✔ Speeds development of database applications

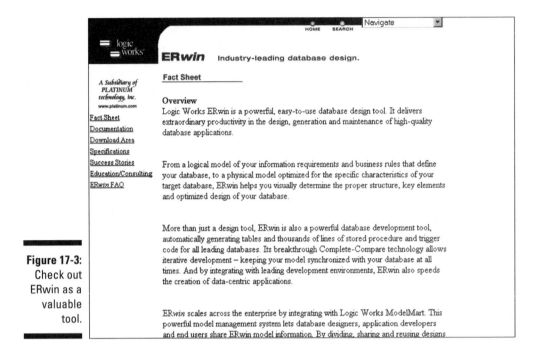

Figure 17-3:
Check out
ERwin as a
valuable
tool.

Soffront — Track for Windows

`www.soffront.com`

Track for Windows is a great tool from Soffront Software that integrates with SQL Server to allow you to track defects in your software (see Figure 17-4). Defect tracking is a must for any software product. Without defect tracking, you have no way to log the defects in your software and track fixes for those defects.

Figure 17-4:
Find out
what Track
can do for
you from
the Soffront
Web site.

Signature Systems — Great Plains Dynamics C/S+ for Microsoft SQL Server

`www.sigsysinc.com/gpdyn.htm`

Great Plains Dynamics C/S+ for Microsoft SQL Server is a tool from Signature Systems that provides Financial Management that runs on Microsoft SQL Server (see Figure 17-5). This product is targeted at mid-range businesses. Great Plains Dynamics C/S+ for Microsoft SQL Server is installed in more than 5,000 locations. The main features provided by Great Plains Dynamics C/S+ for Microsoft SQL Server are:

✔ Extensive lookup and drill-down capabilities

✔ Flexibility

✔ A complete macro system

✔ Multiple layers of data security

✔ Integration with many other products

Company Info

Accounting Systems

What Dynamics offers

Signature Add-On Products

Shareware

Download

Services

Training

Great Plains Dynamics C/S+ for Microsoft SQL is the current industry standard 32-bit Windows financial management solution for mid-range businesses. With more than 5,000 customer installations, Dynamics Release 4.0 is the most mature next generation financial system in the marketplace. In the most comprehensive review of multi-user Windows accounting software programs to date, Dynamics was awarded PC Magazine Editors' Choice. Signature Systems provides a unique expertise for our clients as one of a select number of developers permitted to access the Dynamics source code.

Dynamics offers a leading edge technology, specifically:

Graphical Interface

- Works the way you do by taking full advantage of the familiar ease of use and flexibility of the graphical interface you use (Windows, Mac, etc.)
- Quick, easy navigation allows multiple windows to be open at one time
- Modifiable navigation methods let you view only the tasks you need in the order you need them
- Open architecture allows programmers to create their own accounting modifications and applications

Extensive Lookup and Drill-Down Capabilities

- Immediate, intuitive, on-line access to original documents, master file records, and inquiry information
- Instant information for increased productivity

Association Management

Custom Programming

Case Studies

Figure 17-5:
The Web site tells you what you need to know.

Vision Software — Vision Builder

www.vision-soft.com/products/builder.htm

Vision Builder is a tool from Vision Software that provides developers the capability to model complex business logic using high-level rules (see Figure 17-6). This tool constructs business rules and objects using Microsoft SQL Server and Microsoft Transaction Server. The main features of Vision Builder are that it

✔ Provides Active Templates

✔ Allows you to specify business and data rules

✔ Allows for team development

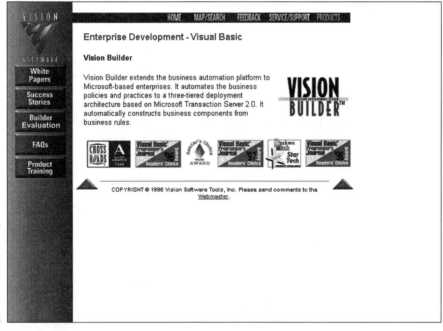

Figure 17-6:
Visit the
Web site for
all the
details.

Sequoia Softworks — Dbmail

www.sequoiasoft.com/products.asp

Dbmail is a tool from Sequoia Softworks that extends Microsoft SQL Server by adding system stored procedure(s) to perform mass e-mailings.

Seagate Software — Crystal Reports

www.seagatesoftware.com/crystalreports/

Crystal Reports is an industry standard tool from Seagate Software that allows you to report on data from Microsoft SQL Server by enabling you to manipulate data in many different ways. You can drill-down on data and provide multiple views. Crystal Reports even integrates with Microsoft Visual Basic. Crystal Reports supports:

- Visual Basic development environment
- Events and callbacks
- Most Microsoft technologies, such as RDO, DAO, and ADO

Platinum Technology

www.platinum.com/products/sqlservr.htm

Platinum Technology provides many different tools for Microsoft SQL Server. The easiest way to find out what these tools do is to visit their Web page (shown in Figure 17-7). As of this writing, Platinum Technology provides tools in these categories:

- Application development
- Backup and recovery
- Data access and analysis
- Data warehousing
- Database administration
- Fast utilities
- Performance management and analysis
- Systems management

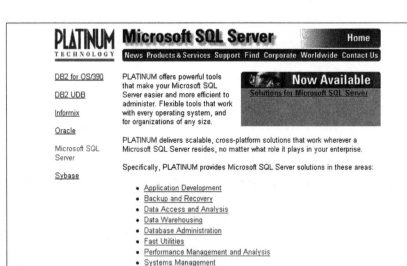

Figure 17-7: Find out about your SQL Server solutions here.

Visio Corporation — Visio Technical

`www.visio.com/products/technical`

Visio Technical is an excellent graphics tool from Visio Corporation that allows you to create drawings by using stencils and shapes (see Figure 17-8). In addition, Visio Technical allows you to link these shapes to Microsoft SQL Server. Visio Technical provides these major benefits:

✔ Many shapes and symbols

✔ Multiple wizards and add-ons

✔ Windows desktop integration

✔ Compatibility with IntelliCAD and AutoCAD

✔ Database connectivity

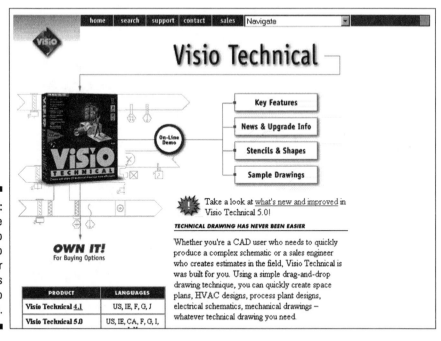

Figure 17-8:
Visit the Visio Web site to discover what this tool can do for you.

Part VI
Appendixes

The 5th Wave   By Rich Tennant

"Hey—who died to make you database administrator? I'm doing the best I can!"

In this part . . .

Not only because every technical book has one, I thought I'd provide you with some additional resources. Sometimes it's great to have everything you need in one place. You'd probably write me lots of hate e-mail if I put this stuff in the chapters themselves. In these appendixes, I include wizard flowcharts, a glossary of terms, and an explanation of what you can expect to find on this book's CD.

So, here you go.

Appendix A

Wizard Flowcharts

● ●

*T*his appendix contains flowcharts of several wizards that make Microsoft SQL Server 7.0 easier to use than ever before.

Create Database Wizard (Chapter 5)

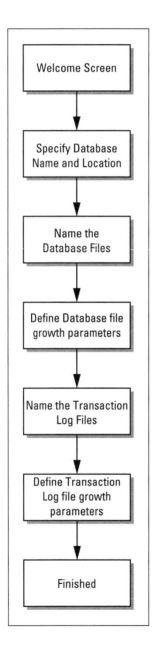

Create Index Wizard (Chapter 6)

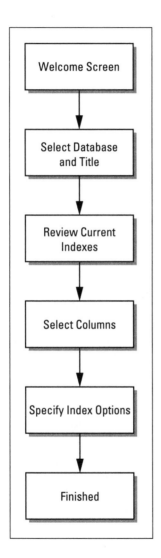

DTS Import and Export Wizards (Chapter 11)

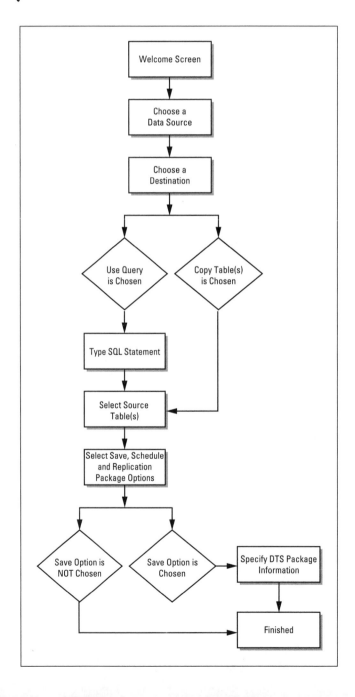

Configure Publishing and Distribution Wizard (Chapter 12)

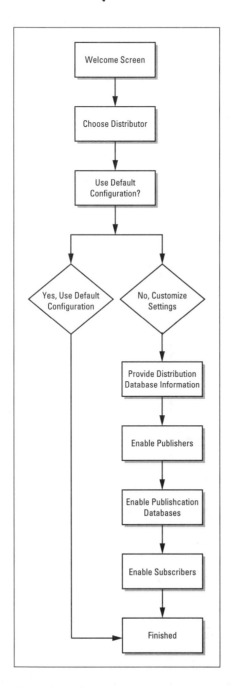

Create Publication Wizard (Chapter 12)

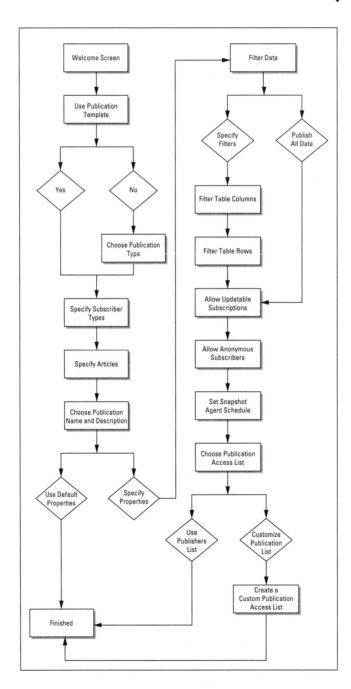

Pull Subscription Wizard (Chapter 12)

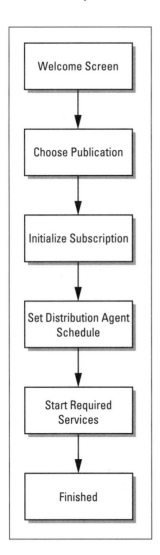

Push Subscription Wizard (Chapter 12)

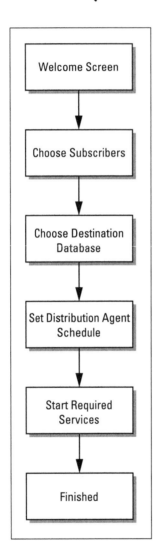

Uninstall Publishing and Distribution Wizard (Chapter 12)

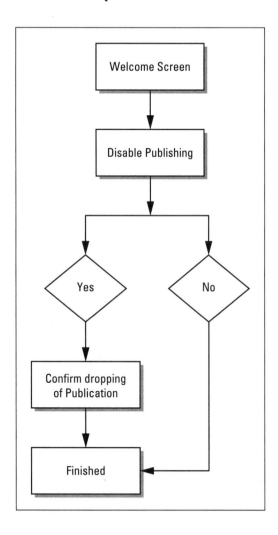

Create a View Wizard (Chapter 13)

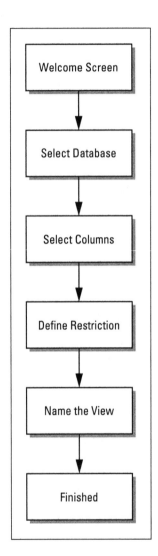

Web Assistant Wizard (Chapter 15)

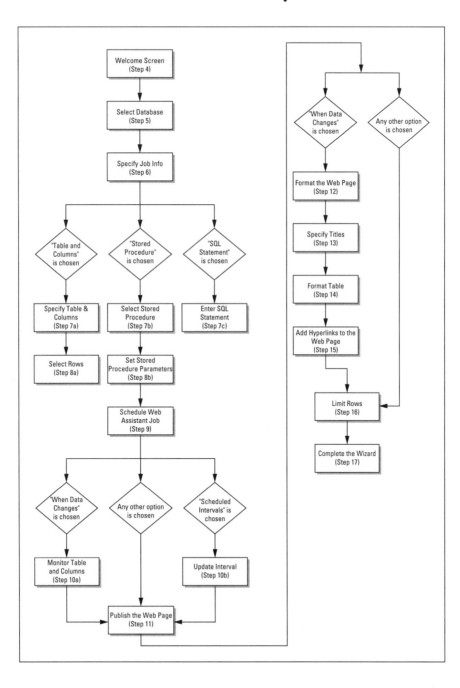

Appendix B
Glossary

ADO (active data objects)
A set of programmatic interfaces that Microsoft SQL Server talks to.

Alert
An *event* that responds to criteria that you specify.

Alias
An alternative name for a database object to make referring to said object easier.

Ambiguous join
A *join* between two tables that contain the same column name in each table but does not specify the table to which each column belongs.

Articles
Tables or stored procedures published in the course of *replication* or *data warehousing*.

Backup
The archiving of data in case of data loss.

Base Level Objects
Elemental SQL Server objects, such as databases and tables.

Batch
One or more processes designed to execute as a single unit.

Bind
To assign a rule or default to one or more columns in a table.

Bound
A *rule* or *default* assigned to a column in a table.

Clause

An identifiable part of a SQL statement that begins with a SQL-reserved keyword.

Client

The computer via which users connect to a server.

Clustered Index

An index that physically sorts records in order.

Column

Also known as a *field,* stores the individual attributes of a row of data.

Complete Backup

A backup of the entire set of data.

Complex select

A SELECT statement that consists of joining multiple tables.

Constraint

Any limitation placed on a table, such as an *index.*

Cursor

A virtual window that allows you to look at a specific number of rows in a *result set.*

DAO (data access objects)

A set of programmatic objects that manipulates SQL Server objects.

Data Warehouse

A method of storing data, normally in an external database, that allows for reporting without slowing down the main database.

Database

A container for objects that store data.

Database context

Term used to mean that a database must be selected prior to running a specific SQL Server wizard.

Datatype

Specification for the type of data a column is to represent.

DBA (database administrator)

An individual who designs and administers all components of a database.

DB-Library

A DLL that knows how to communicate with a specific type of database, such as Microsoft SQL Server.

DBO

Database owner, or, one who creates a database.

Deallocate

To free computer memory when releasing an object.

Default

The value for SQL Server 7 to use for a column in a table when a SQL statement lacks a specified value.

Delete

SQL statement that specifies data to delete from one or more tables.

Delimiter

A character that serves to separate columns of data in a text file.

Denormalize

To construct data in tables so that data repeats; opposite of **normalize.**

Derived Field

A field that does not actually exist in the database, but rather, consists of one or more fields that do exist in the database.

Destination

Indicates where the data is going.

Differential Backup

A backup (archiving) of only data that has changed since the last **backup.**

Disabled

A field in which users cannot enter data, and which appears grayed out on-screen.

Distributed Architecture

Many computers networked together, where each computer serves a specific purpose. All of the computers together serve the needs of the enterprise.

Distributor

A computer that acts as an intermediary between *publishers* and *subscribers*. Can be the same as the publishing computer.

DLL (dynamically linked library)

DLLs contain many procedures that achieve some functionality. DLLs can be called by *extended stored procedures*.

DRI (declared referential integrity)

A means of ensuring that a column of data in a table has a null or matching value in a corresponding table; normally enforced with *foreign keys*.

Drill-Down

A method of expanding folders in a hierarchical tree to find specific folders or leaves.

DTS (Data Transformation Services)

A way that Microsoft SQL Server allows you to import or export data.

Duty Schedule

Indicates hours during which you can notify an operator about a job *alert*.

Dynamic

A process, or data, that can change while it is being evaluated; the opposite of *static*.

E-Mail Operator

An individual who may initiate an e-mail message when scheduling a job.

Enabled

A field on-screen that allows the user to type data into it.

Enterprise Manager

A program (which comes with Microsoft SQL Server) that enables you to administer the server, databases, and objects within the databases.

Event

A process that occurs when specific conditions exist.

Extended Stored Procedure

A stored procedure that runs a function contained within a *DLL.*

Field

See *Column*.

Filegroup

A group of files treated as a single unit.

Fixed Field

Indicates that each value in a column is stored at the same size or length.

Folder

Item in a tree that indicates that there are more folders or leaves below it in the hierarchical format.

Foreign Key

A column in a table that relates to a primary key in another table; used to enforce referential integrity (see also *DRI*).

Hierarchical

A way to display data in an outline format in such a way that items are stored in layers of categories.

HTML (Hypertext Markup Language)

A text-based language that browsers use to display pages over the Internet.

Identity

A type of column in a table that increments automatically as new rows are added to the table.

Index
A database object that speeds up queries.

Inner join
Type of link between tables that does not guarantee every row of data that you expect will be returned.

Insert
SQL statement that specifies data to insert into one or more tables.

Job
Task that you can perform automatically.

Join
The link between two tables in a relational database.

Key
Fields in a table that normally indicate the primary key.

Leaf
Item in a tree that indicates the lowest level available.

Legacy data
Data stored in another, possibly obsolete, database system.

Logical Name
Name given to an object that you will use when you refer to that object after it is created. A logical name is different from a filename.

Login ID
Also known as a *logon ID,* indicates which specific user is logging in to the database.

Look-Up table
A table that contains data that serves only to validate and provide a list of valid values for a column in another table.

Many-to-many
A type of relationship in which many values in one table can have many corresponding values in another table.

MMC (Microsoft Management Console)

The familiar environment by which the SQL Server *Enterprise Manager,* and other tools, appears to the user.

Naming Convention

A method for naming database objects, making it easy for others to recognize the purpose and scope of those objects.

Net-Library

A *DLL* that knows how to communicate with a specific network protocol, such as Named Pipes or TCP/IP.

NetSend Operator

An individual who may initiate a message over the network when scheduling a job.

Non-clustered Index

An index that you place on a table to speed up queries, but which does not physically sort records in order.

Normalize

To construct data in tables so that data does not repeat. Typically requires more tables, resulting in slower queries, but less disk space. The opposite of *denormalize.*

Not null

Indicates that a column cannot be left blank, or null.

Null

Indicates that a column can be left blank.

ODBC (Open Database Connectivity)

A standard by which a program can communicate with *Microsoft SQL Server* and other *RDBMSs.*

One-to-many

Type of relationship in which a value in one table can have many corresponding values in another table.

One-to-one

Type of relationship in which a value in one table can have only one corresponding value in another table.

Operator

An individual who is notified of the status of a job. The operator receives a specific type of notification within the time period as defined by the *job.*

Outer Join

Type of link between tables that guarantees the return of every row of data, but which also can require more resources to execute.

Overhead

The amount of resources (in terms of memory or disk space) required for a procedure or operation.

Owner

One who creates the job or is responsible for maintaining the job.

Page Operator

An individual who may initiate a page when scheduling a job.

Parameters

Arguments used in stored procedures to accept and return variables.

Password

Security measure that prompts users individually for a means to identify the user (usually for a word that the user types). Only the user knows it and it typically is encoded so that a user cannot see the password typed on the screen.

Performance Hit

An adverse condition resulting in degraded performance in Microsoft SQL Server.

Physical Name

A physical location assigned to an object.

Primary Key

A column whose values uniquely identify a row in a table.

Publication

A series of one or more articles slated for publishing.

Publisher

A computer that publishes data to another computer.

Pull Subscription

A way of transferring published data from the server to the client at the client's request.

Push Subscription

A way of transferring published data from the server to the client at the server's request.

Query

A SQL statement that serves to retrieve data from one or more tables; typically includes the SELECT statement.

Query Plan

The method that Microsoft SQL Server uses to access data in the fastest way possible.

RDBMS (Relational Database Management System)

A database program that stores data in tables that relate to one another.

RDO (remote data objects)

Similar to *DAO,* but more efficient.

Read-Only

A mode in which a row or column in a table cannot be updated, only read.

Read-Write

A mode in which a row or column in a table can be updated or read.

Record

See *Row.*

Recursive

An operation that can actually call itself. If recursive operations are not handled carefully, your computer can lock up.

Referential Integrity

See *DRI*.

Relational Database

A database system that contains tables that relate to each other in some way defined by its creator.

Replication

A means of duplicating data from one or more tables or databases into another; typically used in a *data warehouse.*

Restore

Retrieving data from a backup.

Result set

The rows of data that a query returns.

Row

Also known as a *record,* represents the individual items of data that make up a table.

Rule

A *constraint* that indicates what values are valid for a column in a table.

Schema

The structure of a database.

Server

The computer that runs Microsoft SQL Server.

Server context

Term used to mean that a server must be selected prior to running a specific SQL Server wizard.

Service

A process or program that runs in the background.

Severity

A measure of how critical an error is.

Simple select

A SELECT statement that consists of only one table.

Source

Indicates where data is coming from.

SQL (Structured Query Language)

The standard language used by all relational databases, including Microsoft SQL Server.

Static

A process (or data) that does not change as it is being evaluated; opposite of *dynamic.*

Stored Procedure

A compiled set of SQL logic, stored within Microsoft SQL Server, that can be called from within any SQL statement.

String Literal

Series of characters that must be used exactly as entered; cannot be substituted the way a variable can.

Subscriber

A computer that receives published data from another computer.

Subset

A part of a result set or other mass of data.

Tab

A visual folder at the top of the screen that categorizes data entry fields into logical groups.

Table

A storage device that is contained within a database to allow for a two-dimensional array of data to be stored permanently.

Table Scan

A method by which Microsoft SQL Server does not use an index, but reads the entire table into memory.

Ticks

Single quote marks.

Tier

Layer of functionality that divides, or encapsulates, business rules into logical groups.

Transaction

Process by which every SQL statement contained within the transaction must succeed. If even one of the SQL statements fail, the transaction is rolled back to the state the database was in before the transaction began.

Transaction Log

A database file where temporary transaction data is stored so that the data can be rolled back if a transaction fails.

Transact-SQL

Version of SQL that Microsoft SQL Server uses. It contains some specific keywords and statements that only Microsoft SQL Server understands.

Tree

Visual hierarchical display of categorized items.

Trigger

Database object that executes (or, *fires*) SQL logic that you define, when data is inserted, updated, and/or deleted (depending on how you design the code).

Unicode

Specification for a character in Microsoft SQL Server so that it can be correctly translated in all languages. To store Unicode data, you must use a Unicode datatype.

Update

SQL statement that specifies data to update in one or more tables.

URL (Uniform Resource Locator)

The user-friendly address associated with a Web page.

USE

SQL keyword for switching to a specific database.

User

A person who accesses Microsoft SQL Server.

User-Defined Types

A way to define your own datatypes in Microsoft SQL Server. Also known as *UDT*s.

Variable

A placeholder in a SQL procedure that is substituted for an actual value when the procedure executes.

View

A database object that allows you to define the columns and rows that a specific user can see; also can serve as a tool for enforcing security within your database.

Visual Basic

A Microsoft product that enables you to write Windows applications that can access data in Microsoft SQL Server.

Appendix C
About the CD

*H*ere's a quick overview of what you get on this book's CD:

- ✔ Vision Builder, a great program for automatically building multitier applications by specifying rules. This is a great product for all you Microsoft product users out there.

- ✔ Vision JADE, another great program that allows you to build multitier Java-based applications by specifying business rules.

- ✔ sp_Assist, used to easily create Microsoft SQL Server objects and generate Visual Basic code (used in conjunction with Microsoft SQL Server).

- ✔ Microsoft Internet Explorer 4.01, for all your Web-browsing needs!

System Requirements

Make sure that your computer meets the minimum system requirements listed below. If your computer doesn't match up to most of these requirements, you may have problems using the contents of the CD.

- ✔ A PC with a 486 or faster processor.

- ✔ Microsoft Windows 95, Windows 98, or Windows NT.

- ✔ At least 8MB of total RAM installed on your computer. For best performance, we recommend at least 16MB of RAM installed.

- ✔ At least 110MB of hard drive space available to install all the software from this CD. (You need less space if you don't install every program.)

✔ A CD-ROM drive — double-speed (2x) or faster.

✔ A monitor capable of displaying at least 256 colors or grayscale.

✔ A modem with a speed of at least 14,400 bps.

If you need more information on the basics, check out *PCs For Dummies,* 6th Edition, by Dan Gookin; *Windows 95 For Dummies* or *Windows 98 For Dummies* by Andy Rathbone; or *Windows NT 4 For Dummies,* by Andy Rathbone and Sharon Crawford (all published by IDG Books Worldwide, Inc.).

Using the CD

1. **Insert the CD into your computer's CD-ROM drive.**

   Give your computer a moment to take a look at the CD.

2. **When the light on your CD-ROM drive goes out, double-click on the My Computer icon. (It's probably in the top-left corner of your desktop.)**

   This action opens the My Computer window, which shows you all the drives attached to your computer, the Control Panel, and a couple other handy things.

3. **Double-click on the icon for your CD-ROM drive.**

   Another window opens, showing you all the folders and files on the CD.

4. **Double-click the file called** License.txt.

   This file contains the end-user license that you agree to by using the CD. When you are done reading the license, close the program, most likely NotePad, that displayed the file.

5. **Double-click the file called** Readme.txt.

   This file contains instructions about installing the software from this CD. It might be helpful to leave this text file open while you are using the CD.

6. **Double-click the folder for the software you are interested in.**

   Be sure to read the descriptions of the programs in the next section of this appendix (much of this information also shows up in the Readme file). These descriptions will give you more precise information about the programs' folder names, and about finding and running the installer program.

7. **Find the file called Setup.exe, or Install.exe, or something similar, and double-click on that file.**

The program's installer will walk you through the process of setting up your new software.

What You'll Find

Here are some more detailed descriptions of what you'll find on the CD.

Build multitier applications

Vision Builder, from Vision Software, Inc.

Trial version. Do you use Microsoft products? If so, you can build multitier applications using Microsoft Transaction Server, Microsoft Visual Basic, and Microsoft SQL Server. With Vision Builder, you specify business rules, select a few options, hit a few buttons, and watch your multitier app be created.

Why not see the Vision Software Web site at www.vision-soft.com for more information?

If you have trouble accessing the files in the VISBUILD folder on the CD, you can install this program by running the self-extractor VISBUILD.EXE from the root of the CD.

Important Note: This software requires a registration key. To finish installing Vision Builder, enter Vb300ba103z9999 when you are asked. You must have Visual Basic 5, Enterprise Edition, with Service Pack 2 already installed on your computer before you install Vision Builder.

Vision JADE, from Vision Software, Inc.

Trial version. How would you like to easily build multitier applications with Java? Vision JADE lets you define your business rules and standards. Vision JADE does the rest by creating a multitier application that gets data from Microsoft SQL Server. This is a great way to get your apps on the Web!

Look up the Vision Software Web site at www.vision-soft.com for more information on Vision JADE. Or better yet, try it out! It's on the CD.

If you have trouble accessing the files in the VISIJADE folder on the CD, you can install this program by running the self-extractor VISIJADE.EXE from the root of the CD.

Important Note: This software requires a registration key. To finish installing Vision JADE, enter Vj300ba103z9999 when you are asked. This product requires Windows NT 4 with Service Pack 3.

Get programming help

sp_Assist, from Sheridan Software Systems, Inc.

For Microsoft SQL Server. Evaluation version. Do you want lots of flexibility in creating your SQL Server objects? sp_Assist not only allows you to easily create SQL Server objects, but generates code for Microsoft SQL Server and Visual Basic (if you happen to be using Visual Basic).

Further information can be obtained from Sheridan Software Systems at www.shersoft.com.

Important Note: This product does not officially support SQL Server 7, so you may get error messages. It seems to work well enough, though, that you can get an idea of whether it is a tool you might be interested in. Sequoia Software doesn't have any plans right now to release a new version for 7, but they do release update patches frequently, so keep an eye on the web site.

View Web documents

Internet Explorer 4.01, from Microsoft

Internet Explorer 4.01 is a powerful Web browser from Microsoft. It's also free, which makes it a true bargain. You can find a version for both Windows 95 and Windows NT 4.0 on the CD.

To learn more, visit the Web site at www.microsoft.com/ie.

If You've Got Problems (Of the CD Kind)

I tried my best to compile programs that work on most computers with the minimum system requirements. Alas, your computer may differ, and some programs may not work properly for some reason.

The two likeliest problems are that you don't have enough memory (RAM) for the programs you want to use, or you have other programs running that are affecting installation or running of a program. If you get error messages like Not enough memory or Setup cannot continue, try one or more of these methods and then try using the software again:

✔ **Turn off any anti-virus software that you have on your computer.**
Installers sometimes mimic virus activity and may make your computer
incorrectly believe that it is being infected by a virus.

✔ **Close all running programs.** The more programs you're running, the
less memory is available to other programs. Installers also typically
update files and programs; if you keep other programs running, installation may not work properly.

✔ **Add more RAM to your computer.** This is, admittedly, a drastic and
somewhat expensive step. However, more memory can really help the
speed of your computer and enable more programs to run at the same
time.

If you still have trouble installing the items from the CD, please call the IDG
Books Worldwide Customer Service phone number: 800-762-2974 (outside
the U.S.: 317-596-5430).

Index

Notes